BUDDHIST-CHRISTIAN DIALOGUE
Mutual Renewal and Transformation

Edited by
Paul O. Ingram
Frederick J. Streng

UNIVERSITY OF HAWAII PRESS
Honolulu

#12722915

Library of Congress Cataloging in Publication Data
Main entry under title:

Buddhist-Christian dialogue.

  Bibliography: p.
  1. Christianity and other religions—Buddhism.
2. Buddhism—Relations—Christianity. I. Ingram,
Paul O., 1939—   . II. Streng, Frederick J.
BR128.B8B818   1986   261.2'43   85-24528
ISBN 0-8248-0829-0

This book was set in Garamond on the Wang 5548Z by Sandra Chun and Janet Honda of the East-West Religions Project at the University of Hawaii, and made possible through the generous support of Sheri M. Cavallaro.

Cover illustration: Metal cross with a seated Buddha, 25 cm. From the private collection of Alfred Bloom, Honolulu.

Contents

Part IV. Christian Renewal in Japanese Culture

Religious Dialogue
in the Twentieth Century:
Issues, Approaches, and Possibilities

More than ever before, people throughout the world are experiencing threats to human community and meaningful survival. Traditional religious values are threatened by modern secularism in its various ideological and institutional forms. Often the insights which the great world religions offer for understanding the problematic of human life are bypassed when people make decisions for change in contemporary life. Even religious commitments themselves, seen in the context of the major worldwide developments during the past century, are deeply affected by two forces of modernity: (1) the influence of social and physical sciences for understanding human life, and (2) the sensitivity to a plurality of worldviews, ideologies, and value orientations.

People growing up in computer-marshalled and leisure-expanded societies are left with a bewildering multitude of important questions about the variety of rituals, creeds, saints, and symbols. Which bear truth corresponding to reality, "the way things really are," or, is truth a term for the coherence of an experienced environment? Do any of the religious visions which have grasped the human imagination possess any truth value, or are they simply expressions or symptoms of human anxiety and insecurity projected onto the universe? Is any religious tradition "truer" than another? Can any particular religious tradition justifiably claim an exclusively final vision of ultimate truth whether it is the command of the Lord God Almighty or that expressed by the Enlightened One, the teacher of gods and man? It seems in the modern world of competing secular ideologies and religious systems, we are left with the age-old questions of authority, relativity, and truth.

Perhaps the central issue for the modern world is, "Where are the sources of value for a rapidly changing world?" The discovery of new frontiers of knowledge and the awareness of competing significant ideals and hopes make it difficult to accept without question past models for quality living. Many people today feel the truth of the general description of modern consciousness as a bifurcated sense of living in a world of discovery with freedom to explore multiple options and an everwidening future, on the one hand, and a deep sense of losing control of one's life, of overwhelming complexity, and of worthlessness, on the other. They experience the challenge of making decisions without sufficient information, the terror of taking a step without quite knowing where it will lead, and the necessity of "betting one's life" on a personal view without sufficient positive reinforcement of experiences.

Members of the Christian and Buddhist communities also are aware of the relentless flow into modernity. While committed to self-transcendence as advocated in their respective traditions, some thoughtful Buddhists and Christians raise serious questions about the usefulness of traditional formulations and institutional practices for meeting today's needs. They are aware that they are affected by the historical-cultural situation, and that to engage modern life requires probing deeply into basic questions of life: How do we claim to know? What is the nature of selfhood? How are good and evil choices related to the nature of things? Are ultimate values constructed in practice, or are they part of an unconditioned dimension of life? While these questions have been raised from the time of earliest recorded thought, some members of both religious traditions are wrestling with them in recognition of a crisis of religious experience and effective behavior. As seen in some of the essays in this book, there is a readiness to reformulate the questions as well as the answers.

There are Buddhists and Christians who recognize that human life is at a new horizon of ethical, religious, and experiential possibilities, and that to make use of those possibilities the interchange between them must go beyond conflict, competition, or mere tolerance. The focus of the dialogue in these times of human crisis is to explore the traditional insights which can be implemented to enhance contemporary life. Such exchange is indeed "a witness," but at the same time this witness is made in the context of analytical and friendly critical assessment of traditional thought, practice, and life in society. Such a vision suggests that people committed to the ultimate ideal in one tradition may learn about that ideal from questions, analysis, and assessments from people of another tradition. It means that not only will one not disparage out of hand the particular teachings, practices, or symbols of religious traditions other than one's own, but that to learn to speak a "foreign religious language" may make possible a deeper comprehension of one's own religious experience. It is also important to note that interreligious dialogue is a corporate venture. In the engagement a person is participating in the humanity which transcends cultural and physical bounds. It is a humanity that not only speaks out of (i.e., from) specific historical forms, but it calls forth universal ideals of love, justice, insight, and truth and looks toward possibilities not yet achieved.

While evoking hopes for mutual enrichment and perhaps venturing into a new cooperative dynamic of spirituality, we should also recognize the limitations and difficulties in interreligious dialogue. Those who have participated in such efforts are quite aware of how noble intentions result in misunderstanding, misplaced judgments, and weariness. One of the recurring reflections of participants in dialogue is the necessity and limitation of language. In one way or another, the language we use structures our experience and the claims we make about experience. This is to recognize the truth of George Santayana's famous assertion that to try to be religious "in general" is like trying to speak language "in general." It simply cannot be done. For just as we can only speak one language at a time, so we can only be religious persons in a particular way, never "in general." However "the way things really are" might be named, its reality can only be experienced in this community or that, this specific symbol or that, this perception or that.

At the same time there is the affirmation by advocates from all religious traditions that words do not express adequately the reality known in faith or insight. There are, nevertheless, better or worse ways to use words. Several of the authors of the essays in this volume (e.g., Corless, Honda, Ichimura, King, and Yagi) suggest that there are ways of using symbols for the deepest awareness of life that are not mutually exclusive in their specificity. Throughout all the essays there is a clear sense that ideas and symbols are radically connected with experience, practice, and social structure as well as historically conditioned modes of behavior. A person's selfhood is perhaps best seen to have two dimensions: one part is made up of a dualistic sense, an either-or consciousness; the other paradoxically combines the particularity of experience and concepts with a transcendence of them. In both Buddhism and Christianity authorities express ultimate claims in concrete, culturally defined terms; and in both we find the affirmation that "ultimate reality" is not simply a conceptual abstraction, but a power and quality of personal experience that transforms life. In both traditions the deepest awareness of oneself is understood in an ultimate context, for example, God's will, or the Dharma-body of the Buddha. Likewise, what is known as ultimate is directly related to the way or manner one sees the world (e.g., in faith or wisdom). Thus, the deepest sense of one's reality is never only a private, isolated experience; it is an experience of relationships with the widest possible grasp of one's social, mental, and physical environment which goes beyond (or below) conventional perception and articulation.

The basic characteristics of the interreligious dialogue as represented in the essays of this volume might be summarized as (1) a sense of urgency to provide insights and a conceptual framework for authentic living today, (2) a conviction that exponents of Christianity and Buddhism can contribute to solving some basic ills in modern self-consciousness, and (3) a readiness to explore both the difficulties and the possibilities of religious renewal and creative transformation which arise from the serious engagement with another ultimate claim. Recognizing that there are different ways one can be influenced by dialogue—from a deepening clarity of the value found in one's own tradition to a re-forming of one's own approach to authentic living—this volume of essays partially expresses a process in which most of the authors have participated for decades: a deepening engagement with a life orientation other than that learned in the caress of one's mother's arms. While there is no naive and romantic idea of combining the different traditions into one world religion, or even the development of a new overall synthesis of Christianity and Buddhism, this volume grew out of the expectation that the Buddhist-Christian encounter is significant for wrestling with the questions of self-identity, evil, meaning, fulfillment, and communication as these relate to the spiritual dimension of life.

The essays have been grouped according to some basic issues in the dialogue. The first three, by Fritz Buri, Morris Augustine, and John Maraldo, deal with general methodological issues in the practice of dialogue through a consideration of specific content from the traditions. These essays focus on the possibility of understanding very different historical expressions which claim to have ultimate significance for all people in the past and the present. The issue is how can people from outside a tradition use ideas, reports of experiences (such as faith), and prescribed practices to understand and deepen their own religious life without assuming that one will convert to that religious community. Fritz Buri focuses on the impact that historical forms have on the human search for meaning. A contemporary participant in the dialogue cannot, he warns, overlook the differences in the original explication of the deepest spiritual problems and their solution or avoid the development and reformulation of the original message in different cultural contexts throughout the history of each tradition. The religious-cultural contexts in which the founders and subsequent advocates of these traditions defined salvation were so different that the claims are difficult to compare. Nevertheless, these differences are important because both claim to provide a solution to the problem of the meaning of existence in which all human beings participate. To complicate the problem, the reformulation of doctrines and the different emphases on practices and experiences that emerged in the historical development of each tradition has led to significant variations in that tradition. This demands that the contemporary participant in the dialogue must grant priority to some religious forms rather than others. The fact that there are differences within each tradition regarding the epistemological, ontological, and soteriological claims poses the first problem which directly confronts any person in the dialogue.

Morris Augustine takes an alternate tack to historical particularity and shows how a phenomenologically based sociology of knowledge interprets the relativism in religious pluralism in positive functional terms. He points out that religious faith (Jp., *shin*; Gk., *pistis*) in each tradition has common elements which provide a stabilizing form of consciousness in the daily lives of people. While he acknowledges that there are historically specific understandings of faith in each tradition, they all function to provide models that transform egocentric perceptions and emotions into a context of selfless awareness and behavior. While distinguishing faith from belief, Augustine holds that faith provides a symbolic system, which, at its best, does not limit ultimate truth to its formulation. In interreligious dialogue, he concludes, Christians and Buddhists share a common anthropology which makes possible an understanding of the dynamic of faith as a universal, necessary, and useful expression of social life.

John Maraldo's essay continues the discussion of the relation between different concrete religious expressions and the general human sensitivities by calling for a dialogue that requires a participant to practice the activities called for in a tradition. His paper takes the form of a comparison of the significance and content of the spiritual practice done by the Zen master Dōgen and St. Francis of Assisi. Practice for these spiritual guides was, says Maraldo, a hermeneutic whereby they understood deeply the words and admonitions of the masters in their respective traditions. The hermeneutic of practice incorporates the message passed from generation to generation into one's everyday life, where an existential meaning is discovered. To understand another's religious commitment requires knowledge of texts (and doctrinal formulations) plus practice, because the practice allows a direct personal grasp of the meaning of the words.

The second group of essays—those by Paul Ingram, Shohei Ichimura, and Roger Corless—again wrestles with the possibility and problems of dialogue; however, their discussion focuses on more programmatic formulations of the dynamic of interreligious dialogue, and each advocates a view of the world. Paul Ingram develops his view that interfaith dialogue is best understood as part of the natural dynamic process of existence. Written from the perspective of Whiteheadian process philosophy, this essay points to Process Theology as a contemporary Christian movement already demonstrating the need and possibility of "Christian creative transformation" through encounter with Buddhist faith and experience. The reformulation of one's religious images, he claims, results in a renewal within a tradition which is, at the same time, a creative transformation. The importance for both Christians and Buddhists to remain open to reformulation is emphasized as a way to meet the challenge of religious and secular pluralism in the contemporary world.

As an alternative, but in many ways parallel, approach to mutual understanding in a dialogic situation, Shohei Ichimura proposes the Buddhist concept of universal emptiness *(śūnyatā)*; it is useful for interfaith dialogue because of its integration of "teleological polarization" and "identity of
opposites." This notion places an emphasis on the multidimensional character
of a moment of consciousness such that various levels of action and qualities
of experience are going on simultaneously. Ichimura sees a redemptive character in universal emptiness in that it does not presume a metaphysically independent objective referent for concepts derived from empirical perception,
for instance, a person labeled a "Buddhist" or another a "Christian." Further,
it avoids an antagonistic view of alternative verbal claims (e.g., something *is*,
or *is not*) which result in a conscious expectation of mutually exclusive
opposites. Unfortunately the conventional mechanism of language tends to
petrify the dynamic flow of experience into mutually exclusive entities,
which structures unnecessary and false separation of experiences into one's
thinking. An awareness of universal emptiness, claims Ichimura, exposes the
manipulative character of conventional language; thus, sensitivity to *śūnyatā*
makes more fruitful dialogue possible.

In alternative answer to the question of the mechanism of dialogue is
given by Roger Corless. He claims that the point of religious contact in dialogue is not in the historical doctrinal or logical forms, but in a superconscious level of awareness. In order for interfaith dialogue to expose the religious reality it must be engaged in at the level of expressing revelation or enlightenment in each tradition. When one focuses on the conceptual and institutional forms of the traditions, the religious experience of each is perceived as a different mode of religion, but at a superconscious level they not
only co-exist, they co-inhere. Spiritual adepts in both Christianity and Buddhism recognize two levels of consciousness; in this superconscious awareness the transcendent reality co-inheres, while all diversities are experientially overcome. As Maraldo asserted in his essay, practice is itself a
hermeneutic; but it is important to note that Maraldo calls for practicing a
traditional discipline (like Zen) and letting it affect one's everyday life, while
Corless calls for the co-inherence of experience at an extraordinary level of
awareness. After practicing separate traditional disciplines, Corless advocates
using another *personal* discipline, and describes a *mandala* (mystical diagram)
for developing a consciousness of Buddhist-Christian co-inherence that was
useful for him. This proposal is an attempt to facilitate a dialogue, not to
begin a new religion. (It should be noted here that Corless took the Buddhist
bodhisattva vows after the original version of his paper had been given at the
East-West Religions Conference.)

In the third group of essays the authors wrestle with the possibilities and
implications of Buddhist-Christian dialogue through analyzing specific key

concepts found in each tradition. They suggest that a basic dialogue goes on within a person who is aware of alternate positions in formulating an understanding of central religious issues in life. Masao Abe analyzes the problem of evil; Winston King examines the plausibility of selfhood/no-self; and Frederick Streng compares contemporary Buddhist and Christian interpretations of the nature of religion. In each case the authors make some assessment of the notions examined in terms of their influence on the formulation of truth in each tradition. Speaking as a Buddhist, Masao Abe looks at some central notions of evil in Buddhism and Christianity in an attempt to show that the origin and nature of evil are best understood in the context of the Buddhist notion *śūnyatā* (emptiness). As Ichimura argued that the logic of *śūnyatā* prevents a dualism and substantialization of ideas in the Christian-Buddhist dialogue, Abe feels that an understanding of good and evil can best find a theoretical basis in the notion of emptiness. Such a notion is placed in contrast to an Augustinian understanding in Christianity which, Abe says, holds that the origin of evil is found in the mystery of (an evil) human will to disobey God, and asserts an ontological priority of good over evil. Abe finds the Buddhist views of dependent origination of existence and the sensitivity to the boundless solidarity of human beings with all other forms of life a better way to perceive both the relativity and the particularity of evil. If emptiness is recognized not only as a spiritual goal but, more fundamentally, as the point of departure for all moral action, the difference between good and evil will be seen with great clarity. If Buddhists misinterpret the perspective of emptiness and regard it only as the goal of human life, as has often happened in the history of Buddhism, it can be seen as an excuse for becoming indifferent to ethical questions and socio-political problems. The dialogical encounter with a Christian concern to remove sin in an authentic expression of reality can steer Buddhists away from the danger of ethical and social irrelevance by sharpening their social and moral consciousness. Thus the dialogue can renew the intention and transform the expression of Buddhism.

In the second essay of this section Winston King analyzes the Christian notion of selfhood and the Buddhist notion of no-soul in light of the effort found in both traditions to transcend a person's small (socio-psychologically determined) self. Critically assessing the stereotypes of thinking about personhood in each tradition, King speaks as a Christian who wants to expose and probe the fullness of the Christian understanding of personalism in dialogue with Buddhists. In his analysis of Buddhist ideas he recognizes a hidden, but very significant, functional self; and he calls on Buddhists to use their negative terms to express the experience of human freedom and flexibility. On the other hand, Christians should bracket their concern for ontology and assert the importance of personhood to show how human beings can transcend inanimateness, animality, time and space, and limited value. From such a dialogue new insight into the cultivation of self-transcendence may arise in which the Buddhist experience of no-self can inform the Christian experience of selfhood. At the same time, the Christian experience of selfhood can deepen the Buddhist insight of no-self.

Rather than probing a classical concept from the Buddhist and Christian traditions, Frederick Streng, in the final essay of this section, describes the understanding of the nature of religion by two contemporary philosophers of religion, one from each tradition. By examining the views of Paul Tillich and Keiji Nishitani on consciousness, ultimate reality, and evil as they apply to the effort to live an authentic existence, Streng shows that they have different representative perceptions of the nature of religious life. For Tillich authentic existence is found in the effort to construct meaning, while for Nishitani it is to be fully aware of the transient character of existence. Tillich views the highest authenticity as the courage to "be," while Nishitani holds that only in the deepest awareness of the "horizon of emptiness" can a person actualize the inherent fluidity and interrelatedness of life. As King suggested benefits for Christians and Buddhists in taking alternate views seriously, Streng indicates the value for Christians in recognizing the notion of the "field of emptiness" as a possible formulation for ultimate reality, and the advantage for Buddhists to articulate more clearly the positive activity of consciousness in attaining enlightenment.

The final three statements in this collection are the most directly focused on theological concerns. The last one, an epilogue by John Cobb, is a special case since it is a response to the eleven essays which precede it. The other two form a subsection which expresses how two Japanese Christian theologians who have lived in a culture permeated with Buddhist images and ideals respond to the presence of Buddhism in their lives. In their essays Seiichi Yagi and Masaaki Honda expose—through different forms—their Christian experience in relation to, and through, Asian lenses colored by Buddhism (much as Western theologians have been influenced by Greek and Latin categories). Both are expressions of committed Japanese Christians who wrestle with the articulation of the deepest level of faith in terms of Japanese concepts and orientation. Yagi's essay is based on an analysis of three different types of theology defined by different "axes of thinking" and different levels ("depths") of self-awareness. He uses the techniques of New Testament textual and literary criticism to compare the religious consciousness of Paul with that of Shinran, and of Jesus with that of Zen masters. By specifying three kinds of religious experience, the communal, individual, and interpersonal, he develops a conceptuality of the Christian vision of the transcendent whereby the levels and range of experience in Paul are correlated with those of Shinran, while Jesus' awareness and articulation of God parallels those Zen statements in which there is no longer a dualistic awareness of reality nor a focus on concerns pertaining to the usual self. In this restatement Yagi finds a foundation for Christian faith that transcends the usual categories of Western thought and philosophy, while at the same time being more relevant to the experience of Asian Christians living in a non-Christian sociality.

Whereas Yagi uses a comparative format to express his understanding of the depth of Christian consciousness, Masaaki Honda formulates a new Japanese theological understanding of such basic Christian doctrines as the Trinity, the two natures of Christ, and creation out of nothing. His essay, a revised statement of an earlier essay published in *Katorikku Kenkyū* (Catholic Studies), 1973, is an illustration of an actually transformed vision of Christian theology. Rejecting the epistemological assumptions of Greek philosophy, Honda rethinks key Christian notions using the thought of Japanese philosopher Kitarō Nishida as a base. The author focuses especially on Nishida's "topological logic," or "the Buddhist logic of *soku.*" He claims that the structures of the Buddhist and Christian "spiritual fact" of the irreversibility and the simultaneous reversibility of the relation of God to the world are the same. The ultimate claims expressing the deepest awareness of God, the origin of the world, the self, and knowledge should be expressed in the awareness of *soku* (not same, not different). The result is a transformed vision of Christian theology which attempts to remain true to the commitment to Christ, but yet in a form that critically appropriates the insights of Buddhist experience and doctrine.

In his epilogue, John Cobb comments on the contributions of the essays as they apply to Christian and Buddhist theological and philosophical reflection. He notes that, contrary to the belief of some Buddhists and Christians, Christian and Buddhist thought can no longer develop in isolation from each other. The essays in this volume, for example, attest to the dialogue that is now going on. At the same time he affirms Ingram's observation that Buddhist thought is not being influenced to the degree that Christian theology is being transformed. While Buddhism has adapted to diverse cultural settings and historical situations in the past — as has Christianity — there seems to be a reluctance to restate Buddhist thought in new forms. This, of course, is part of a larger question that affects all who are aware of the limitations of historical forms *and* the normative character of certain historical concepts and practices. Which, if any, forms expose best the "way things really are"?

The problem is complex and requires clarification both from the Christian and the Buddhist side of the encounter. For example, are there forms of transformation that are neither authentically Buddhist nor Christian? Are there differences between an authentic Christian response to Buddhism and an authentic Buddhist response to Christianity? As Buri's and Streng's analyses suggest, and as Cobb points out, the differences of the fundamental Buddhist and Christian historical and structural experiences may result in quite different dialogical responses to the other. Even if the dialogical encounter results in different kinds of renewal and transformation for each tradition, and in varying kinds within each tradition, could we say that several (if not all) might be authentic?

The question of possible authentic renewal and transformation has been at the heart of the reflection in each of the essays presented here. While the essays in Part 2 have dealt with this issue in the most programmatic way, the rest are attempts to wrestle with particular issues arising from a sensitivity to this question. The multiple approaches found in the papers suggest different dimensions of the future direction of continued Buddhist-Christian dialogue. What is an authentic Buddhist response to Christianity? Christians require instruction from their Buddhist colleagues in this regard. What is an authentic Christian response to Buddhism? Christian instruction regarding this question will be of interest to Buddhist colleagues. Likewise, we return to the situation of modernity as we contemplate the meaning of authenticity. Both Buddhists and Christians today will have to develop a vocabulary, as well as nonverbal skills of perception and sensitivity, to express the unconditional depth claimed in religious life in ways that enhance the quality of life in the present. Perhaps the most important contribution this particular collection of essays has to make is in partially forging a vocabulary and sensitivity for authentic dialogue. If this is the case, then it will have served an important purpose.

The occasion giving birth to these essays was an international Conference of East-West Religions in Encounter which took place at the University of Hawaii at Manoa, June 13-27, 1980. The focus of this gathering was "Buddhist-Christian Renewal and the Future of Humanity." Because eighty-one presentations were made, mostly in the form of papers and public addresses, a word must be said about why the specific essays of this volume were selected for publication. They were chosen primarily for their focus on the philosophical, theological, and structural issues of Buddhist-Christian dialogue. Indeed, interreligious dialogue occurs in ritual participation and ethical responsibility as well as in conceptual formulation; theory and practice are often joined in the actual experiences of religious persons. In spite of this interdependency, much dialogical discussion in religious matters is, in fact, analytical and theoretical. Consequently the editors along with some other conference participants thought it best to select those essays focused on theoretical issues emerging from the Hawaii Conference for one volume.

Gratitude must always be given to the numerous persons involved in any publication effort, and especially a publication of this nature. Perhaps the largest debt of gratitude is owed to David Chappell, Director of the East-West

Religions Project at the University of Hawaii at Manoa, along with his colleagues in the Department of Religion and their graduate assistants. It was this group of persons, under Professor Chappell's leadership, whose creative imaginations and organizational skill made it possible for Buddhist and Christian scholars to meet together for an exciting encounter and exchange of ideas. They and the other Conference leaders are also to be congratulated for making the Conference sessions open to the public so that our sharing of ideas and perspectives did not become merely another elitist academic exercise in abstract and irrelevant argumentation.

The editors also wish to thank each of the Conference participants for their communal sharing of ideas and experiences, as well as each of the contributors to this volume for their time and effort in working with us and in trusting us with the editorial processes necessary for publishing any collection of essays. A special acknowledgement is owed to John B. Cobb, Jr., for responding to the essays as an epilogue in this volume.

Marta Call, Debbie Florian, Kay Hirst, Susan Trainer, and Beverly Tschimperle, secretaries for the Division of Humanities at Pacific Lutheran University, typed and gave much needed editorial assistance in preparing the final drafts of each essay, whereas Janet Honda and Sandra Chun of the Department of Religion, University of Hawaii at Manoa, made final corrections and did the type-setting. Their hard work, careful attention to detail, and sense of humor are gratefully acknowledged and deeply appreciated.

Paul O. Ingram
Pacific Lutheran University

Frederick J. Streng
Southern Methodist University

PART I

METHODOLOGICAL PROBLEMS
IN THE ANALYSIS OF
SPECIFIC BUDDHIST AND CHRISTIAN FORMS

CHAPTER 1

A Comparison of Buddhism and Christianity According to a History of Problems

Fritz Buri

In all their divergency and opposition, Buddhism and Christianity have three common elements in their origins and histories: both are concerned with salvation, that is, with the problem of the meaning of existence in the world and with the solution to this problem; in the course of their histories, both have become something other than they originally were; and both have done so in quite different forms. Moreover in both, what has changed has directly to do with their answers to the problem of the meaning of existence. That is, these answers, too, have changed. Finally, this historical fate, this develop-ment into something other than what originally was, hangs together with a problematic contained in their original forms—a problematic which unfolds in their respective histories.

THE PROBLEMATIC IN THE ORIGINS OF BUDDHISM AND CHRISTIANITY

In spite of the historical differences in their origins, Buddhism and Christi-anity present a structurally similar, twofold problematic based on the under-standing of salvation as the solution to the problem of the meaning of human existence in the world.

The Buddha and Jesus see and answer the question about meaning from within the framework of a view of being given them by their respective traditions. These traditional views of being already contain a solution to the question of meaning, but to the Buddha and to Jesus the solution is insufficient, and each transforms it decisively.

For the Buddha the traditional presupposition consists of the idea of rebirth in samsara (the endless becoming and passing away according to karma, which is the web of entanglement woven in previous incarnations) and in the future prospect of being freed from this fate into nirvana. Within the traditional form, the Buddha sees the evils of growing old, of sickness, and death as confirmation that life is suffering under transience—suffering which, after innumerable rebirths, is extinguished in nirvana.

Jesus, on the other hand, sees human existence within the history of God and his creation, which has a beginning and an end and which is determined by the struggle of God against powers having fallen from and now in opposition to him. Under the hegemony of these powers, humans are bound not only in all kinds of evil, but also in guilt before God. Here, too, a final and definitive salvation is foreseen. Through his Messiah, God will bring the evil world to an end and establish his kingdom on earth or in a new world. Instead of a "karmic judgment" continuing in samsara and determining the level of rebirth, with Jesus, we have a judgment at the end of the world, when God or his Messiah will decide who does and who does not belong to the Kingdom of God.

These traditional views of human existence assumed by the Buddha and Jesus are basically transformed by both, specifically with regard to a possible fulfillment of meaning. In both, this transformation is rooted in a particular insight received at a particular moment: by the Buddha in his awakening beneath the Bodhi tree, by Jesus in his baptism in the Jordan, where it is revealed by the Spirit that he is destined by God to be the Messiah.

The Buddha's awakening contains two elements. First, it contains the insight that the cause of suffering lies in the thirst for life led astray by ignorance of the real nature of the world—and in the attachment to things arising from the thirst for life. Attachment to things is meaningless because there are finally no things to which one can cling. Rather, everything, even the "I" which holds to things, is only a momentary union of nonsubstantial essences, a union which constantly dissolves. Second, to free humans from this attachment to the illusion of things which actually are not is perceived by the Buddha as being a task of compassion—a compassion which is itself based on the interconnection of all things, in the "interdependent co-arising" (pratītya-samutpāda) in which all things stand. Out of mercifulness he wants to teach suffering humans his insight and its resulting nonattachment to things. Therefore, he adds to the first three "noble truths," which contain his basic insight, a fourth, which is the Eightfold Path. This path leads from the acceptance of the teaching to moral behavior and meditation and finally to the attainment of awakening.

In Jesus' proclamation, too, there is a similar appeal to a definite behavior based upon a change of heart. "Change yourselves [repent], for the Kingdom of God is at hand." That is the summary of his preaching in the synoptics. In both the Buddha and Jesus, a statement about the being of the world is the basis for an attitude that brings fulfillment of meaning. In the Buddha, it is the nothingness of the world; in Jesus it is the imminent end of the world. Jesus reveals this taste of the world in his miracles, in his forgiveness of sins, and in his condemnation of the unrepentent. In all of these actions he anticipates his messianic function at the last judgment. But in distinction to the Buddha, Jesus is not only teacher, but also an actor in the history of existence. His decisive intervention in this history consists in his sacrificial death, through which he intends to bring about the change of the aeons, just as he understands his messianic task as the "suffering servant of God" to be given up in atonement for others. In both cases, however, the corrections of the traditional idea of salvation are bound up with the problem of the understanding of being.

The Buddha finds liberation from samsara by his insight into the true nature of our entanglement in *pratītya-samutpāda* (the interdependent co-arising which creates unending karma) and by his teachings of a path of liberation through nonadherence to things. But does this mean that samsara is merely a product of imagination, an idea resulting from futile clinging to things, a mythological image for a human attitude and its consequences having nothing ultimately to do with reality outside or beyond the human? The Buddha seems to understand the whole chain of events in samsara—from rebirth and karma to nirvana—as independent of human thought, as a reality encompassing the human. But can there be rebirth if there is no individual to be reborn? If there is no individual, has karma not lost its object? Moreover, nirvana at the end of the chain of events is made superfluous if it can be attained through the Eightfold Path in awakening. Nevertheless, in his preaching the Buddha presupposes this whole idea-world as the condition of being, even as he, in the same teaching, explains it as unreal. Does he accept as valid the traditional statement of being, or does he expose it as mere fantasy for the sake of fulfillment of meaning by means of awakening and by behavior corresponding to it?

There is a corresponding equivocation in Jesus' teaching and actions when he radicalizes the expectation of the Kingdom of God into the nearness of the Kingdom, by understanding the end of the world as intruding into this world. The traditional expectation of the end did not presuppose that the end was already occurring. As Jesus radicalizes this tradition into an event which is taking place in the present, he places it in question. And yet, Jesus accepts the traditional teaching as reality, just as the Buddha accepts the idea of being of his own tradition. The difference consists merely in the fact that Jesus, unlike the Buddha, does not expose the tradition as illusion, but radicalizes it into the expectation of an immanent end of the world. He believes himself and his followers to be in a situation which is irreconcilable with the tradition because it does not foresee the nearness of the Kingdom nor, indeed, the presence of the Kingdom in he who knows himself to be the future Messiah. The traditional frame remains, but the picture that was once in the frame has been replaced by another.

There is a second problematic in the Buddha and Jesus which corresponds to the first. On the one hand, the Buddha establishes his instruction for behavior with reference to being in relation to *pratītya-samutpāda,* according to which there are neither individual things nor individual selves. On the other hand, he rejects as useless and harmful any discussion of metaphysical questions. He is silent about questions such as whether the world has a beginning or is eternal, or whether there is a life of the soul after death. Such discussions lead only to conflict and amount to adherence to things. The Buddha recommends instead the attempt to follow him on the Middle Path which lies between denial of world and being entangled with the world. This is the same as "to have as if one does not have," which is also advocated by Paul. Paul, however, arrives at the statement by different means.

Both the positive and the negative instructions contain problems. To what degree should one be ascetic? In striving to attain awakening through asceticism, can there not be as much thirst for life and egocentric adherence to things as in nonascetic life? On the other hand, in the moderation required by the Middle Way, how is world denial possible at all, if there is no individual being to be moderate with and no individual being which can strive for moderation? Is a person able to fulfill such requirements and in this way to attain salvation himself? Or is he in need of help — not only help from his nearest environment, but also from a higher world, as has always been taught by the religions? If one attempts, with his own salvation in mind and by his own power, to reach nirvana, one contradicts the "interdependent co-arising" which binds together all world events and the conduct of persons, and from which arises the Buddha's compassion for suffering humanity and for all life. Is the ideal of holiness enough? Can it be realized at all? Can one in such a way successfully separate oneself from the fate of the world? Are metaphysics and psychology required after all, or can one, as the Buddha apparently did, break off the questioning halfway and leave the rest in silence, unanswered?

These are the questions the Buddha was asked by his disciples and with which his disciples found themselves confronted after his death. Did they not see themselves forced to continue questioning, especially since the master himself had told them in his last speech, "Be your own light!"?

Even more radically than did the Buddha and his disciples, Jesus and his community saw themselves placed in question by the actual course of the world — Jesus on the cross and perhaps earlier, and his community after his death. The solution to the problem of meaning had been sought in the imminent end of the world which did not take place. He proclaimed the nearness of the Kingdom and thought to bring about the new aeon by his atoning death. In doing so he not only set aside an illusion, as did the Buddha, but he also proclaimed a state of the world and required conduct corresponding to this situation which would make one capable of participation in the Kingdom. By his own actions he tried to reach a goal which, like his message, proved to be illusionary in its eschatological expectation. It was possible, contrary to the factual course of history, to see a manifestation of the coming world in the resurrection of the crucified Jesus, in his appearances and in the reception of the spirit and its effects, and so to postpone the coming of the end of time, to continue to expect it in the future. But, on the one hand, these occurrences were only partial appearances of the promised and expected end, and, on the other, through the necessary postponement of the end one fell into contradiction with the message of its original imminence. In this way the faithful found themselves forced to make some sort of compromise with the existing world, to find some sort of place in it. This could only happen in a way which contradicted the requirements which Jesus had made for the attainment of fulfillment of meaning in the Kingdom of God.

This, in outline, is the twofold problematic with which Buddhism and Christianity in their origins found themselves similarly confronted. In their first emergence in history they speak of the realization of meaning within a framework of thinking which is actually canceled out by the intended realization of meaning. At the same time, this realization of meaning is found to be insufficient in the context of the given situation and placed in question by the reality of this new situation. The history of Buddhism and the history of Christianity are in great part the histories of attempts to solve their original problematic, and these attempts constituted problems of their own.

THE PROBLEMATIC OF THE ATTEMPTS TO SOLVE BUDDHISM'S
AND CHRISTIANITY'S ORIGINAL PROBLEMATIC

In both Buddhism and Christianity there are two main ways for attempting to overcome the original problematic. For the Buddhist community the point of departure consists in entering into the Middle Path which leads to nirvana. The Buddha had entered nirvana but his followers are still on this path in the world. Correspondingly Jesus' community also finds itself in the world expecting the return of its glorified Lord to establish the Kingdom of God, and preparing itself for that event. Standing in opposition to the striving toward and the hope to reach fulfillment is the world — in Buddhism the world in its form as samsara, in Christianity the world as ruled by demonic powers. In both, the world must be overcome in order for it to become what the Buddha or Jesus envisioned it to be.

In Buddhism this overcoming of the world has been attempted in ways which present a radicalization of the Buddha's instructions not to adhere to things. We have mentioned the problem involved in remaining detached from the world while still participating in the world by following the Middle Path. The first way tried to solve this problem by a discipline of detachment and renunciation. Being the more difficult, the way of renunciation and detachment promised more success for future incarnations, but in addition it was seen as more conducive to the meditation which leads to awakening than did involvement with the world. And so followers of this path, believing they were particularly true and avid disciples of the Buddha, became ascetics who strove to realize the ideal of holiness through the most rigorous renunciation. They refuted the objection that their asceticism violated the Buddha's instruction and example by collecting teachings and stories from the whole Buddhist tradition into the so-called Pali Canon. This tradition had, in three hundred years since the Buddha's death, become so copius that the arhat ideal, too, could be derived from it. Because it was possible for only a small circle, a community of monks, to follow this way the community came to be known as Hīnayāna, the Small Vehicle. The masses could gain participation in salvation only through the support of the monks.

The Hīnayāna Buddhists received their name from the representatives of the Great Vehicle, Mahāyāna Buddhism. For themselves the Hīnayāna Buddhists claimed to represent "the teaching of the oldest ones" *(theravāda)*. The Mahāyāna Buddhists distinguished themselves from them by emphasizing that the possibility to unite renunciation of the world with devotion to the world lies within the meaning of the Middle Path. In support of this position they could refer not only to the teaching of "mutual dependence" out of which arose the Buddha's compassion toward all things, but also to the Buddha's instruction not to adhere to things. They extended this explanation of the cause of suffering into the area of epistemology and saw in conceptual thinking as it distinguishes among objects and in the resulting conceptualizations, the source of the illusory world of samsara. If we compare this with Kant's phenomenalism, formulated two thousand years later, we can say that in both systems things are thought to be appearances. In Kant there stands behind the appearance the thing in itself. In Mahāyāna Buddhism there is no-thing. Nothingness stands behind the appearance as its cause. The unawakened has to do only with an imagined world of appearances. The awakened realizes that the void is the true essence of all that seems to be.

This teaching of no-thing-ness *(śūnyatā)* presents as enormous and complicated a picture of epistemological and metaphysical speculation as Kantian phenomenalism. It exposes the world standing in the way of nirvana as nothing. This philosophical concept of no-thing-ness is then equated with the mythological idea of nirvana; samsara as the totality of world coincides with nirvana. In the emptiness of nirvana things appear in their fullness, as they truly are in themselves. This *śūnyatā*-philosophy extends through the whole of Mahāyāna Buddhism from Nāgārjuna (A.D. 200) up to today's most representative Japanese Zen philosopher, Keiji Nishitani.

As one contemplates the intellectual achievements of the sutras and other texts which have grown from them, one asks about the Buddha's silence on metaphysical questions. What has become of that? Along with *śūnyatā* philosophy there are also in Hīnayāna, and particularly in Mahāyāna, numerous other metaphysical speculations in which the Buddha is equated with the whole of the world. He was to be found in all things. As well as this philosophy of being there is also an idealistic philosophy, for which everything is "merely consciousness." And at the other extreme there are the sayings of Zen masters which shock all logical thought and state, for example, "If you encounter the Buddha, then kill him!"

Besides Zen philosophy, or nonphilosophy, the other great achievement of Mahāyāna consists in the formation of a richly populated heaven of gods. These were taken over from divinities of those geographic areas into which Buddhism extended as well as from the world of bodhisattvas—those holy and awakened persons who, out of compassion for the unenlightened, renounce nirvana in order to assist lesser beings on their way to salvation. Through the cultic veneration of innumerable buddhas and bodhisattvas. Mahāyāna Buddhism has become a world religion—something that Buddhism in its origin, without doubt, was not.

In this connection we would like to focus on one figure among the multitude of buddhas and bodhisattvas. It is the one which comes from the myth of King Dharmākara, who as a bodhisattva vowed not to enter nirvana until he had brought all living things to the path of awakening and, therefore, into the "Pure Land." In exclusive trust in this vow, Amida believers hope to find salvation.

Higher, however, than all other buddhas stands the celestial Buddha which the historical Buddha has become in nirvana. After having lived as an incarnation of the Amida Buddha on earth, he is lifted into the series of those Buddhas who each rule over an entire world age. The relation in which his different ways of being stand to each other is regulated through the doctrine of the Trikāya, or the Three Bodies of the Buddha. Nirmānakāya is the Buddha's transformed earthly body; Sambhogakāya is the shining body of his glory which only the awakened one can see. Dharmakāya is the body of the teaching, presenting the embodiment of the one truth which illuminates the whole world and lets the world appear—again, only for the awakened—as the no-thing-ness in which samsara and nirvana coincide.

The transformations which the form of the Buddha has undergone in the course of time may be followed particularly clearly in the history of its presentation in the plastic arts. In the early period of Buddhism there were no pictures of the Buddha. In place of a picture there was the symbol of the wheel of the teaching the Buddha had set in motion. Or there were images of his feet and footsteps, especially to decorate the stupas in which his relics and those of other holy persons were kept. It was under Hellenistic influence in the Gandhara period that statues of the Buddha began to emerge. Later, according to the styles of the different countries into which Buddhism spread, these statues were given characteristic forms which present us with a history of the transformations of Buddhist teaching.

Beyond these ascertainable influences of the West on Buddhism in art, we may also suppose doctrinal influences — as, for instance, from the Nestorians in China, which possibly resulted in a bringing together of salvation figures (Christ and Amida, Mary and Kannon). Influences can also be traced from East to West, where, through the legends of Barlaam and Josaphat, the Buddha was unknowingly included among the saints of the Church. Other mutual fertilizations in the formation of legends may also have taken place, for instance in legends about the Buddha and Jesus, where formal and material priorities of origin cannot be easily determined.

What can be determined without any question, however, is the parallelism of problems in the historical development of Buddhism and Christianity. Despite differences in content and the time of emergence, the histories of both show a surprising similarity in basic structure. The sources for the origins of Christianity extend further back in time than those for the origins of Buddhism, and they have been researched more thoroughly. Furthermore, the content of these sources is more accessible to conceptual understanding than those of Buddhism, which, from a Western perspective, present many logical difficulties. One can, therefore, form a clearer picture of the history of Christianity, even if here, too, things did not always proceed logically. Even so, the structural parallelism is clear.

As we have seen, after an initial period of unity, the small and the Great Vehicle, the world-renouncing arhat ideal and the idea of the world-oriented bodhisattva, came to stand in opposition to one another. Looking at Christianity, we find a similar formation of devotional communities which await the return of the Lord on the one hand, and on the other, the formation of the large church out of many different syncretistic elements. Whereas in Buddhism it is the Hīnayāna school which compiles the canon, in Christianity it is the large church which does this. It establishes the rules for the canon's inspired interpretation in order to prohibit heretical use of the canon and individual prophetic witness, and it establishes a corresponding hierarchic organization. From the community of saints, of monks, the larger church derived the sacred form of organization supposedly established by Christ for the salvation of the believers. The first beginnings of this development lie already in the canonized tradition, and they are carried further to new spiritual horizons through time and by means of the new possibilities for understanding given by the course of history. Original Christianity had expected the end of the world to bring salvation. Because this expectation was not fulfilled in the course of time, the end of the world was pushed into a more and more distant future. In its place developed the Church, in whose possession of revelation and of means of salvation Christ is present and effects redemption in faith and through the use of the sacraments. In Buddhism, nirvana can be attained both in a future beyond death and presently in this life. In a similar manner the Church offers the prospect of a future salvation beyond death as well as the beginning, here and now, of a way of salvation that leads to paradise. In both Buddhism and Christianity there are manifold ideas of how all this comes about. They vary from immediate spiritual intervention to the regulation of the manifestation of spirit in strictly formalized cults and rites. Not without reason do Catholic theologians today find religious forms and expressions in Buddhism which appear similar to their own mysticism, cult, and practice of meditation. In the history of both, monasteries play an important role as places dedicated to achieving nirvana or the Kingdom of God, and as factors of culture within the world. Both have also repeatedly been torn by conflicts over doctrine; councils were called to solve the conflicts, and worldly powers intervened in some of the disputes.

In Mahāyāna Buddhism the original teachings underwent a long process of transformation regarding original Buddhism, which resulted in copious metaphysical speculations. In Christian theology a similar transformation of the original eschatological Christianity culminated in the institution of the Christian church. In both instances, a changed historical situation resulted in a new understanding of salvation, which in turn made a new understanding of the redeemer who brings about this salvation necessary. As a consequence of its turning toward the world, the Mahāyāna tradition evolved, out of the historical Buddha figure, the conceptions of the cosmic Buddha and the bodhisattvas. In Christianity the historical Jesus, destined to be the Messiah of the new aeon, no longer corresponded to the new idea of redemption in which immortality was mediated by means of sacraments. In view of the newly conceived idea of salvation, a new redeemer figure had to be put in his place. As the flesh of Christ was made divine, this could only result in the idea that the Redeemer himself was God—not just an incarnation of the divine Logos.

In Buddhism there was no problem at all for a buddha, appearing as God on earth, to find a place in the series of heavenly buddhas as one of their incarnations. The different earthly and heavenly manifestations of the Buddha could easily be related to one another. The problem was very great, however, in Christianity because of its monotheism and its concept of substance and person. Therefore, the doctrine of the Trinity and the doctrine of the two natures of Christ present a far more complex and, for orthodox belief, a far more essential statement than the Trikāya doctrine in Buddhology. But both speculations are far removed from the framework of ideas within which the historical Buddha and the historical Jesus apparently understood their mission. They can be viewed, however, as the consequences of the problematic which was bound up with the original self-understanding of both.

We could show in an analogous way how this historical connection of problems also applies to other parts of Buddhist and Christian doctrine, but that is not possible in the context of this presentation. Instead, we will consider one example of the parallels in the development of doctrine, namely, the reformations which occurred for somewhat similar reasons and with similar consequences in the thirteenth century in Japan and three hundred years later in the West. Before the reformation in Japan the dominant forms were the scholastic and magic traditions of Tendai and Shingon Buddhism. Monks emerged from these Chinese-inspired schools to found Japanese Amida Buddhism, Zen Buddhism, and Nichiren Buddhism. The first, with its emphasis on the grace of Amida, can be seen as a kind of Buddhist Protestantism. Zen corresponds to the mystics of the late Middle Ages and to the humanists and spiritualists of the age of the European reformation. Nichiren Buddhism, with its devotion to the *Lotus Sutra* as the only source of revelation, suggests the valuation of Biblical writings in the reformers and their descendants. In the West the orthodoxy of the Reformation was followed by pietism and the Enlightenment, resulting in what is called "new Protestantism." In Japan an enlightenment occurred under Western influence during the Meiji period. Japan also had its pietism in the Myōkōnin of Amida Buddhism, and in the so-called new religions it had a parallel to new Protestantism. Both the Japanese new religions and new Protestantism present a mixture of different forms of largely secularized tradition. Since the introduction of Western science and technology, Japan has become characterized by secularization in other areas as well. In the West, dialectical, theological, and existentialist philosophy arose in part as protests against secularization and in part as a continuation of it, and in their wake, attempts at demythologizing and existential interpretation of the Christian kerygma developed. In Japan today the so-called Kyoto school is impressed by Barthianism and attempts, influenced by Heidegger, to demythologize and to give an existential interpretation to Zen and Amida Buddhism.

These most recent developments show that the attempts of Buddhism and Christianity to overcome the problematic contained in their origins have hardly succeeded. They show, too, that Christians and Buddhists are just as perplexed by their original problematic as ever before. That is not intended as a negative judgment of the present situation or of the whole previous history of these religions. Rather, it is in this problematic that the truth of Buddhism and Christianity is contained. In order that this truth can really come into its own, however, the problematic of its container, the form in which it expresses itself, would have to be acknowledged and the necessary conclusions would have to be drawn. With this in mind, I shall summarize the problematic in Buddhist and Christian history in terms of a typological scheme to facilitate comparisons.

TYPOLOGY OF THE PROBLEMATIC OF REDEMPTION IN BUDDHISM AND IN CHRISTIANITY

The characterization and confrontation of typical Buddhist and Christian comprehensions of redemption may be summarized under four questions:

1. What is the nature of the insights on the basis of which Buddhists and Christians think they can speak of redemption?
2. What do they ultimately mean by reality and what significance does this interpretation have for redemption?
3. How does redemption come about?
4. How does the person stand in history with his expectation of redemption?

The first question has to do with epistemology. The second with the possibility and the nature of transcendence. The third question is of a soteriological-anthropological nature. The fourth has to do with the philosophy of history.

1. The Epistemological Question

Buddhism concerns itself with three characteristic aspects of the epistemological question. First, Buddhism sees in objectivizing conceptualization a reprehensible adherence to things; cognitive adherence thinks that there are "things" which one can comprehend and which can be incorporated into concepts. According to the understanding of being of *pratītya-samutpāda*, this is erroneous. According to the teaching of *pratītya-samutpāda*, there are no substances existing in themselves. Rather, all moments of being move constantly into one another in an unceasing becoming and passing away. That is as true of the course of events within the mind as it is of those outside the mind. Even the distinction between "within the mind" and "outside the mind" is an error. For in reality there is neither a perceiving subject nor a perceived object.

Secondly, the goal of meditation is to become free of this illusionary world of subject and object. On the steps of deepening meditation, the Maya-realm of objective reality dissolves increasingly, the self loses its self-adherence, the world loses its world-adherence, and subject and object become a no-thing.

Thirdly, however, this "no-thing is not simply nothing, not a non-object, but an emptiness, 'the place' in which the 'true self' appears, and the things show themselves as what they really are." For the Buddhist, the essence of awakening consists in this transformation of perception. In awakening true in-sight *(prajña)* occurs.

There is doubtlessly something to be said for this insight which leads to awakening in the emptiness of the nothing. One must only ask if one can still speak here at all of perception. Perception presupposes a subject which perceives and an object which is perceived. That is true even for the idea of two mirrors mirroring each other, which is used by Buddhists to illustrate *prajña*, a wisdom supposedly without subject or object. In the first place, the image of the mirrors presupposes a subject that makes use of the image as his object. In the second place, between the mirrors there must be something which can be mirrored, something different from the mirrors. If the subject himself is supposed to be this something as both subject and object, this image of the mirrors may be valid for his self-understanding. But it remains incomprehensible how the things are to show themselves as they are in it. Where are they supposed to come from? And even if they emerge like a wave from water, only to disappear again, what does the awakened have as a criterion by which to judge whether or not he has awakened to his true self and to things as they are? How does he know he is not dealing with a reflection of deceptions? Along with Hamlet, the Buddhist says here, "The rest is silence."

Let us look now at the epistemological problem in Christianity. It is no less problematic, at least in more or less traditional Christianity. As a consequence of the way Buddhism has encountered Christianity, it is just this traditional type which Buddhism generally regards as Christianity. In this "ordinary" traditional Christianity, the origin and presence of human beings in the world as well as the world of things itself present no problem. God created the world and human beings, and he preserves them after the fall of Adam. He wishes to remedy the consequences of the Fall in the present course of time through the saving work of his son and to complete this work in eternity. On the basis of his reason and his conscience, the human being can know about creation and preservation and about his sinfulness and its effects. The general natural revelation of God consists of such knowledge. This knowledge is not, however, sufficient for the perception of salvation. Such perception is, rather, the object of the special supernatural revelation of God, which God has, through the Holy Spirit, communicated to the prophets and the apostles, and finally through his son. This revelation of salvation is contained in the Holy Scripture, but—in connection with the Scripture—it can continue to occur through the witness of the Holy Spirit. However, this revelation is not a matter of reason but of faith, which is brought about through the Holy Spirit. Certainly this faith can use the powers of reason. These powers are themselves weakened by original sin and are, therefore, dependent on revelation.

In the framework of today's natural and historical science, this dogmatic system appears as the product of a past time and of long since outmoded mythologies and speculations. But it also contains unsolved difficulties, and first in connection with the epistemological question. How extensive is the damage incurred through Adam's fall which must be repaired by faith in revelation? The answers given to this critical question in Christian dogmatics are manifold and contradictory. At one extreme stands the position that God himself believes in the believer in a way which corresponds to the image of two mirrors mirroring each other. At the other extreme it is maintained that, before the light of reason, faith dissolves into an incomprehensible nothing. Between these extremes the connection between revelation and reason is seen and interpreted in a multitude of ways. There are, however, more often statements of the problem rather than of solutions, as is, for instance, the postulation of a so-called knowledge of faith, a concept which, to my way of thinking, is similar to "wooden iron."

This problematic of Buddhist and Christian epistemology has its consequences in the answers that are given to the question about the nature of reality. This leads us to the question about metaphysics.

2. The Metaphysical Question

Buddhism gives a threefold answer to the metaphysical question. First, the essence and the ground of reality is no-thing-ness, the void. Second, reality is the true self of the awakened. Third, the Buddha is the true, the only reality. He is the no-thing and the awakened self in one. Here two questions arise. Is there reality outside awakening? If the answer is yes, is this unawakened reality nothingness in the same way as the awakened reality? If this is the case, it would mean that the two cannot be distinguished from one another. Or is there only awakened reality? If so, why is awakening necessary, and in what way is the awakened actually different from the unawakened? Is nothing-ness an ontological statement about all reality independent of the way a person understands himself, or is it an existential statement, that is, a statement of human self-understanding about the meaning of existence in the world?

Just as Buddhism leaves the question about the relation of awakening and nonawakening undecided, so it also leaves the question about the difference between ontological and existential statements unanswered. Buddhism sees in the attitude which asks such questions an erroneous adherence to conceptualizations of reality and, therefore, in its either-or position, a false questioning from the start. With the principle of identity, we say that *a* is *a* (*a*=*a*). The Buddhist makes it a logical principle that *a* is *b* (*a*=*b*), precisely because *a* is *not b* (a b). To the principle of the excluded third, Buddhism opposes the principle of "non-twoness," that is, one is neither one nor two. Applied to the nothing, this means that no-thing-ness is beyond the opposition of being and non-being. Applied to awakening, it means that whoever claims to be awakened is not awakened. Buddhism can, of course, arrive at this point beyond all distinction only by means of the conceptual thinking it rejects. But this paradoxical situation does not trouble the Buddhist, because it represents conceptual thinking. He has no need to answer it and no interest in refuting it, because if he did, he would make himself guilty of conceptual differentiation, of adherence to things, of not being awakened.

The situation is completely different in Christianity, where strict distinctions are made between God the Creator on the one hand, and the world as God's creation on the other. The world is neither without beginning nor without end. God created it from nothing and preserves it in his omnipotence. This preservation is necessary, otherwise the world would fall back into chaos, and man would fall completely into evil. The chaos was obviously not fully overcome in creation. In the form of evil it enters God's first creation, so that God must save it with a second new creation.

Here, two critical questions also arise. God's existence has to be defined by human reason, and on the basis of his special revelation he must also be defined in his essence for faith. Even if the intention is quite the opposite, however, is God not through such definition made finite? Is he not "defined" as the word definition says? Not without reason have there always been attempts at a *theologia negativa*. Such theology is justified in its criticism of the all-too-human character of theology. Even where it does not concern itself with criticism but seeks the mystical experience of union with the Godhead, however, it negates the possibility of making statements about God. The second question has to do with the origin of chaos and evil. Where do they come from? Either God created and preserves these powers as well, or he is not omnipotent. This is the problem of teleology and of theodicy.

The mystery, the enigma of the meaning of being is solved neither by the no-thing-ness of Buddhism, which dissolves all distinctions, nor by Christian trust in God's rule over the world. This mystery is, however, the most urgent question of human existence, and neither Buddhism nor Christianity could rest content with its inability to solve the mystery. As religions of redemption, they need to answer the question about the possibility of a realization of meaning in the world. This common interest of Buddhism and

Christianity leads us to the third point of comparison of their problematic, the question of how they think redemption is possible.

3. The Question of Redemption

Since the origin of Mahāyāna, Buddhism has discussed the problem of self-redemption or redemption through something outside the self. Mahāyāna teaches, in distinction from the historical Buddha and from Hīnayāna, that the person cannot by his own power free himself from entanglement in samsara. Rather, he needs outside help, and in any case outside help is available. There are awakened holy ones who renounce entering nirvana in order to help the unenlightened in the world of samsara. These saints can be asked for their help and are revered because of it. According to the legend, the Buddha overcame the temptation to keep his awakening for himself alone and went out to preach his path of salvation to the world. But neither in this legend nor in Mahāyāna is redemption, in the strict sense, achieved through something outside the self from adherence to things. The Buddha's and the bodhisattva's will to help arises from the awakened insight into the universal connection of *pratītya-samutpāda*, "co-arising in mutual dependence," by virtue of which a receptivity for awakening and an attitude conforming to this receptivity is present in those who are in need of awakening.

The parallels to Christ and the saints of the Church is obvious, as is also the parallel to the capacity for redemption, not just the need for redemption of those entangled in the world. As the Buddha and the Mahāyānists refer to *pratītya-samutpāda* penetrating all existence, so the Church refers to the all-encompassing love of God with which the saints are filled and whose final revelation sinners await. As Buddhists speak of an awakened Buddha-nature in humans, so the doctrine of the Church speaks of an image of God in humans, which was not fully lost by Adam's fall, as the point of contact for divine revelation and grace, and as the presupposition for man's working together with divine revelation and grace. Here also one cannot speak of a redemption which comes exclusively from outside the person, but of a working together, a synergism of nature and grace.

In contrast to this relative salvation from outside, in Japan as in the West, and in both through a reformation, there has emerged a view of redemption which calls upon the historical origins of Buddhism and Christianity. Both emerged in the midst of a catastrophic world situation and a pessimistic mood of life. The monks Shinran Shōnin and Martin Luther despaired of their attempts to attain holiness. They found salvation in the unconditional assumption of the undeserved grace of Amida or Christ. Their message of redemption through grace without good works, *sola gratia*, found a powerful echo in the hearts of thousands. Both Shinran Shōnin and Martin Luther left the monastery and the priestly life, and both married. Both undertook the task of showing, in extensive writings, that they alone understood their tradition correctly. Through the composition of hymns both planted their piety in the hearts of their disciples. And both became the founders of new forms of Buddhism and Christianity.

Their denial of the necessity of good works for attaining salvation certainly made difficult any valuation of man's natural abilities as well as making a claim on and motivating these abilities in the ethical sphere. Therefore, we find in their descendants different attempts to tie together salvation from outside with elements of self-redemption. In old Protestant orthodoxy and its conflict with Catholicism, this can be seen in the arguments about justification and sanctification. The impossibility of solving this conflict led in new Protestantism to fresh formulations stressing the goodness of man in creation. In Japan today, some Zen Buddhist philosophers try to unite self-redemption and redemption from outside, by means of *nembutsu*, the formula for trust in the grace of Amida alone. In *nembutsu* they see a koan which suspends differentiating thought. The Shin Buddhists find in their devotion to Amida a dissolution into nothingness. In both East and West the inability to comprehend the nature of grace through conceptual thinking has led to the emergence of different kinds of mysticism: to God or nothing mysticism on the one hand, and to Christ or Amida mysticism on the other.

Here as there, theologians have been unable to be content merely with the discussion of individual redemption They have had to concern themselves with questions about the universal-historical aspect of salvation as well as questions which arise out of both traditions.

4. The Question of Redemption Under the Aspect of the Philosophy of History and Culture

Buddhism does have a universal-cosmic view of history. Universal-cosmic history is the eternal, unending succession of a series of descending stages or forms which begin in perfection but fall into greater and greater decay. This series of stages is the series of epochs of world time, a kalpa. Each kalpa has its own buddha who descends from the Tusita Heaven and then returns. As a whole, however, this endless series of kalpas belongs to samsara, which encompasses the series of kalpas and in which reincarnations follow each other according to the laws of karma. In the individual kalpas there is the possibility of redemption for the individual, but the world as a whole remains unredeemed. Therefore the Buddhist turns away from the world as a whole. He leaves it to its fate and concerns himself with the fate of sentient beings.

Since redemption is possible only through awakening, redemption consists in fleeing the world and entering nirvana. This can happen in a preliminary or in a final way insofar as one may attain nirvana while yet in this world. This is possible when nirvana is understood to coincide with samsara, and samsara with nirvana. This leads to the paradoxical combination of being-removed-from-the-world and being-involved-in-the-world at the same time. With this paradox the Buddhist knows himself in the world free from the world.

The impressive greatness of Buddhism consists in this freedom from the world within the world. But therein also lies Buddhism's problematic. Ultimate seriousness, engagement, and responsibility are difficult to realize in this attitude toward the world, in the idea Buddhists have about their own selves, and in their behaviour toward other beings. The Buddhist is in danger of withdrawing into ultimate noncommitment. He can as easily refer to the connection of all things in no-thing-ness as he can, by regarding them as nothing, negate that connection. The vow of the bodhisattva to redeem all living things sounds very moving. But what does he move when he carries out the vow, if the other is only his "shadow"? — to quote an expression used recently in conversation by a famous Buddhist philosopher. As the ethical commandments of the Buddhistic path of salvation serve merely for the attainment of awakening in meditation, so also the great achievements which Buddhism has brought about in the spiritual, cultural, artistic, and religious history of humanity have no intrinsic value for the Buddhist. They are seen as mere shadows destined to dissolve themselves for awakening into nothingness. The ascending ways of Java's crumbling Borobudur lead past innumerable representations of buddhas and bodhisattvas, but they end in the nothingness which is the Buddha, and the Buddha sinks into the silence of the void.

Christianity's understanding of history is no less problematic. In view of "to have as if not," its understanding of history is similar to Buddhism's, but its basis is entirely different. No less problematic, as well, is the course of spiritual and cultural history which has developed on Christian ground. Here we encounter not an eternal circular repetition of beings and events, of kalpa following kalpa, but a scheme of history beginning with the creation and moving under divine guidance toward its goal in the Kingdom of God. As there is only history, so there is only one messiah, whose *parousia* brings about the completion of history. However, contrary to the original expectation, this did not occur and thus the provisional time before the end had to be prolonged indefinitely. The expected completion of history at the end of time still cast its shadow, but at the same time an increasingly positive attitude began to develop toward this provisionally existing world. Consequently the idea of God's continuing creation achieves greater and greater significance for the understanding of history. Out of a history moving toward destruction there arose a history of progress. However, the grave new problems created by this process led again and again into a world situation, as well as a personal situation, in which a simple trust in God's providence within the world no longer seemed sufficient for many people. Thus theologies of individual salvation by supernatural means came again to the fore as well as more or less realistic ideas about an end of the world brought about by the return of Christ to establish his lordship on a new earth. Whether natural or supernatural, whether conceived as a completion in this life or beyond the grave, the cross of Christ stands victorious over this whole Christian understanding of history. And it does so in such a way that, in all its different interpretations, the cross appears to the Buddhist as a sign of the will to dominate and rule, which, in the eyes of the Buddhist, is the precise opposite of the Buddha's sinking silence.

The contrast between the Buddhist and Christian understanding of salvation can hardly be more sharply drawn than in the representations, on the one hand, of the Buddha dying in sublime peace while reclining near to the earth and surrounded by animals, and on the other hand, the image of the tortured blood-dripping Christ hanging from the cross. Buddhists have often referred to this contrast. As no other scholar, D.T. Suzuki succeeded in opening an access for Westerners to the essence of Buddhism. He thought that already in the elevated position of Christ on the cross one has to see a sign of the Christian will to rule. He repeatedly expressed his abhorrence of the idea of a salvation through blood. Most Buddhists can understand his attitude, and not a few Christians actually feel the same way. On the other hand, however, Christians exihibit a similar attitude of rejection toward the Buddhist teaching on redemption. True, the Catholic church acknowledges that elements of truth are also contained in Buddhism. But it does so only with the explicit faith of the Catholic church. And Protestants, astounded by the Buddhism of grace espoused by Shinran, can say—in accordance with a known model—that Shinran merely used the wrong name for his redeemer. He should have called him Christ instead of Amida. Suzuki concedes immediately that Amida with his vow is "not a historical person, but a manifestation of religious mind." Christians often think that the strength of Christianity as opposed to Buddhism lies in the fact that a historical person stands in the center of Christianity. These Christians do not notice that an essential reason for their problematic lies precisely in this fact, a problematic which, as Suzuki's concession shows, presents no difficulties to the Buddhist.

We have now to ask whether there is any truth at all to be found in the Buddhist and Christian teaching of redemption. The question about truth becomes urgent in view of both the obvious problematic and the mutual misunderstandings, and in view of the fact that innumerable persons in the more than two thousand year histories of these religions have believed they have found in their solutions an answer to the question about the meaning of existence and the way to its realization.

For us today the answer has probably become more difficult, and yet easier. More difficult, because we cannot solve the problematic in such a way as to rid ourselves of it. Easier, because we do not think we need to rid ourselves of it. We see its solution in the acknowledgment of its reality. And we are able to find in the history of problems we have presented, the appropriate symbols, by means of which we can understand both ourselves and one another in our differing traditions.

CHAPTER 2

The Sociology of Knowledge
and
Buddhist-Christian Forms of
Faith, Practice, and Knowledge

Morris J. Augustine

INTRODUCTION

When we Christians and Buddhists meet to discuss our own and humanity's future, it is imperative that we be honest with ourselves. Today this is more than a little painful because, in my opinion at least, it involves the honest admission that both religions are in a state of deep crisis. In the past twenty years especially, a deep malaise has settled over even the leaders of both groups, robbing them of the robust confidence of their predecessors.

The first step toward resolving a crisis is an honest admission that it exists, and the second step is always to determine the nature of the crisis. Only then is there any reasonable likelihood of finding effective solutions. There is little doubt as to the nature of this present religious crisis. It is basically a crisis of confidence in religious faith, religious truth, and religious knowledge itself. It is an epistemological crisis of doubt and uncertainty that our religious manner of knowing ourselves and the world and of solving our problems is really valid.

Let us then be brutally honest with ourselves. The objection raised by Marx—that religion is a purely human contrivance and that religious consciousness is a false consciousness, not resting on the solid foundations of man's everyday life—is in fact a very powerful argument. It has been bolstered with much impressive evidence. Further, Freud's argument that religion arises out of neurotic projections of our need for security in the face of pain, calamity, and death unquestionably contains far more than a grain of truth.

Such arguments have been mustered during the same period of impressive technological achievements in mathematics and the exact sciences, which

have brought relative abundance and at least physical well-being to a large
portion of today's world. Even more importantly perhaps, this ubiquitous
technology and its accompanying machine-oriented ways of thinking have
changed our apperception of reality itself, greatly eroding the truth-value accorded to religious realities. Such factors have in fact convinced the greater
portion of every nation's most educated, sincere, and sensitive people that
religious truth and knowledge are not a dependable foundation on which to
build a life, a society, or a world.

On this occasion of an international encounter between Buddhists and
Christians it seems a tragedy to allow a host of lesser problems to obscure our
vision of the much greater danger which is overwhelming both parties of our
encounter. The following presentation will therefore attempt two rather am-
bitious but necessary tasks. First, it will study the notion of faith (Skt.,
śraddhā; Gk., *pistis*) in Buddhism and Christianity, and by a phenomenologically oriented social scientific analysis elaborate an understanding of the
human dynamic of religious faith, which dynamic, it seems, Buddhists and
Christians already share. Secondly, it will offer a plausible interpretation of
the sociology of religious faith and knowledge according to which the different traditional and orthodox expressions of religious truth in Buddhism
and Christianity can be seen to be valid and extremely important forms of
human knowledge.

It is patently impossible to offer in the space of twenty-odd pages even an
adequate summary of the data necessary to build a solid case for both the
human and the "theological" solidity of these two contentions. We will have
to be satisfied with the briefest of sketches. We shall begin then by tracing
the outlines of an important emergent school in the sociology of religion
whose major principles and orientations hold out genuine hope for a
renewed legitimation of religious traditions such as Christianity and
Buddhism.

The conference of social scientists and theologians held in Rome in 1969
entitled "The Culture of Unbelief " seems to have been the catalyst which
crystalized concepts, orientations, and practical modes of investigation which
in effect created this new school and is still the guiding light of important
ongoing investigations. Flowing into and out of this meeting were such semi-
nal works as Thomas Luckmann's *Invisible Religion*,[1] Robert Bellah's publications on the phenomenon of "civil religion,"[2] Peter Berger's and Luckmann's
works on the sociology of religious knowledge,[3] and a series of sustained empirical investigations into contemporary patterns of religious expressions of
great scope and significance.

This movement, which for want of a better term we will call the Schutzian
school after the chief of its many mentors, might be described in briefest
terms as possessing five main characteristics: (1) It flows out of the sociologi-

cal thought of Durkheim and Weber, as creatively brought forward by the synthetic efforts of social scientists like Talcott Parsons and especially Alfred Schutz. (2) It rejects the positivistic and reductionistic bias against religion found in other schools of thought, affirming religion to be an irreducible *sui generis* and authentic social mode of human awareness. (3) In the place of a reductionistic approach, it bases itself on the phenomenological analysis of social reality and knowledge which Schutz amalgamated from the thoughts of Husserl, Weber, and Scheler.[4] (4) In spite of this rejection of earlier attempts to reduce religion to something "more authentic"—such as neurotic projections or economic oppression—it affirms the importance of traditional empirical methods of data gathering and interpretation. (5) The basis for its unique approach is the understanding of the sociology of knowledge—including a basic notion of religion and the type of knowledge it produces—worked out by Husserl and Schutz and applied by men like Luckmann and Berger.

To summarize in the briefest possible fashion the pertinent notions of this sociology of knowledge it is sufficient to state and briefly explain but a single proposition: primordially and always, all human knowledge, including the scientific, mathematical, and religious varieties, arises out of a person's day-to-day life-world. This life-world, the womb of all knowledge, is composed of a community of persons going about their most ordinary tasks of working, playing, eating, loving, reproducing, and dying. Whatever intimations of genuine transcendence there are, arise out of, depend utterly upon, and take their specific symbolic forms from what Husserl has termed this everyday "life-world," or "world of daily life."[5]

Using the categories of Berger and Luckmann, we can describe the process of coming to know anything and everything as accomplished in a three-stroke piston cycle, first involving routinization of labor and action in the outer world, then the objectification of these habitual ways of doing things into social institutions, and finally, an interiorization of these de facto structures, types, schemes, and procedures, so that they come to be perceived by persons as the real structure of the world, symbolized in their language and mobilizable by their thought.

It is not difficult to comprehend what is perhaps the most important inference from this understanding of human knowledge: the specific geographical and meteorological environmental factors of any particular life-world—together with this particular life-world's specific modes of providing itself with food, shelter, and means of production—will exercise the crucial, decisive influences on the basic tenor of that society's whole knowledge system, from its commonsense notions to its politics, to its ideological and religious viewpoints. It is by now a truism that as human communities moved through hunter-gatherer, agricultural, and into technological modes

of providing themselves with their basic needs—as these communities meta-
morphosed from isolated hunting bands, to agricultural villages, to the
medieval cities, and from thence to the contemporary urban
technopolis—every facet of their knowledge was necessarily transformed.

However, in each of the earlier stages it was religion which drew the many
facets of man's world view together into a meaningful, legitimate whole.
Today, however, religion has, temporarily at least, lost the ability to do this.
The most educated and knowledgeable find their world turned into a maze of
unrelatable corridors and feel the alienation of what Berger aptly calls "the
homeless mind." These people have not been able to find religious systems
capable of comprehending, ordering, and giving integral meaning to this
complex world. It was the general consensus of the conference in Rome that,
as a result of this exploding, fragmented world, much of the modern religious
consciousness has come to be expressed outside of traditional religious structures and systems. Whatever unity and meaning is achieved is the result of a
private synthesis by the individual. But as often as not, it remains diffused in
the form of "invisible" or "civil" religion.

Luckmann, Berger, Bellah, and Parsons agreed, in a general way at least,
that "belief " and "unbelief " in the traditional doctrines of churches and
similar religious institutions were not adequate concepts on which to base
solid investigations into the current status of religion in modern societies.
Rather, since religion serves to synthesize and express experiences of moral
and metaphysical ultimates, these social scientists thought—and still
think—that essentially religious symbolism can be and indeed is found scat-
tered throughout a culture's social, political, and cultural institutions.

As a result of this dual realization—that rational doctrinal "belief " in
traditional religious systems could not be a fitting object whereby to study
modern religiosity and that modern religiosity expresses itself in a broader
and more diffuse manner—these thinkers have focused their investigative attention on this broader phenomenon, giving relatively little attention to the
phenomenon of "belief " or "faith " in religions such as Christianity and
Buddhism.

For the purpose at hand, it is important to note that none of the major
thinkers mentioned above denied the validity and usefulness of belief in the
doctrines of traditional religions. On the contrary, they were emphatic in
their high evaluations of such traditional belief systems as valid and of great
social and personal value. They insisted that such religious
knowledge—whether only loosely connected or tightly knit into separate systems of religious doctrine—was indigenous to the very nature of human
thought and equal in epistemological validity to other symbolic systems of
knowledge, for example, legal and philosophical systems or the great traditions of art and literature. They further agreed that additional cross-cultural

research into the nature of belief or faith, and the human dynamic which underlies it, would be of great importance. Talcott Parsons went so far as to say
that "belief systems prominently involving cognitive components are essential
ingredients in all religious systems which have a prospect of stabilization."[6]
Caporale called for a cross-cultural study to determine the nature of belief or
faith in religious systems.[7]

Another more recent and more philosophic study of the notion of belief
helps furnish the missing link between the narrowly defined notion of cognitive religious belief and the deeper and broader phenomenon on which such
rationalized religious belief is based. It so happens that these social scientists'
dissatisfaction with the concept of religious belief corresponds to a similar
dissatisfaction among theologians and other religious thinkers. Paul Tillich
had already drawn a sharp distinction between such doctrinal belief and the
deeper trust and loyalty to symbolic presentations of the Ultimate itself.[8]
Wilfred Cantwell Smith has brought such thinking into maturity with his
recent work, *Faith and Belief*,[9] in which he shows clearly that Christian,
Buddhist, and Islamic thinkers have long recognized the same dichotomy between subscription to certain official doctrines and a deeper commitment to
and reliance on basic symbolic expressions of ultimate reality. Whereas
Smith himself does not allude to it, this distinction corresponds exactly to
the dichotomy noticed by the above social scientists between commitment to
certain traditions' religious doctrinal systems and the deeper and broader
commitment to symbolic presentations of transcending religious ultimates.

Neither theologians like Tillich, nor historians of religion like Smith, nor
social scientists like Luckmann, Berger, and Bellah are, in their
presentations, arguing against the wisdom or even the human necessity of
some manner of cognitive belief systems. Rather, each in his own way is con-
tending that such doctrinal commitment alone does not begin to adequately
reveal the rich human dynamic by which persons symbolize and bind themselves to their transcending religious experiences and bring them into full development as religious knowledge.

The following brief resume of an extensive comparative study of Buddhist
and Christian notions of faith proceeds out of the same presuppositions. It applies Tillich's and Smith's distinctions between faith and belief to the social
scientific distinction between broad religious commitment to symbols of
transcendence on the one hand, and belief in circumscribed rationalizations
of doctrinal propositions on the other.

The notion and practices of faith *(sraddhā, pistis)* are central in both Buddhism and Christianity. In neither is it seen as mere intellectual belief in certain conceptual formulas about the Ultimate—though in some periods of
their long histories, both systems overemphasized this aspect. In both, "faith"
is a far richer idea than "belief in"; it connotes "faith in," "trust in," "reliance

on," and "loyalty to" or "taking refuge in," not just with reference to religious symbols but to a religious community and the primordial Ultimate itself which is recognized as lying beyond all mere symbols.

I will look carefully at the notion in the two systems and then carefully compare them to see if beneath the two very different systems of symbols one might not discern a common human dynamic. If such a common anthropology can be shown to exist, then religious knowledge can be seen to develop according to the same sociological dynamic which produces other important symbolic forms of knowledge, even though the referent—a transcendent ultimate—is different. Such a realization, if authentic, should not only have revolutionary implications concerning the human credibility and authenticity of differing religious systems such as Buddhism and Christianity; it could also reveal the solid basis for mutual respect and deepening encounter between these two ancient and world-encircling fonts of religious wisdom.

BUDDHIST AND CHRISTIAN NOTIONS OF FAITH

Buddhist Faith

The Buddhist notion of faith (*śraddhā, hsin, shin*) received its first systematic formulation in the great scholastic synthesis of the *abhidharma*. The notion of faith expressed in the system is very similar in three works which form a bridge between the Pali and Sanskrit texts and between the Theravāda and Mahāyāna. They are the *Visuddhimagga*, the *Abhidharmakośa* of Vasubandhu, and the *Vijñptimātratāsiddhi*. In each of these, faith is seen as one of the good "faculties," powers, or "roots" of the mind. As such, it can be awakened and brought into vigorous action or allowed to remain dormant and unused. In a similar way, it is seen as the first of the five perfections or *pāramitās*: faith, vigor, mindfulness, concentration, and wisdom.

The definitive development of these notions of the Mahāyāna occurred in the *Awakening of Faith*, in Japanese, the *Daijo Kishinron*. Here, as in all the previous sources, faith is seen as a wonderful power of the mind. However, the notion is now seen in the framework of one of the branches of the profound philosophy of the "Mind only" (Skt., *Vijñaptimātra*; Jp., *Yuishiki*) school. What appears as a "power" (literally, "root"; Jp., *kon*) in the illusory ego-centered consciousness of the individual is actually the "perfume" or the "permeation" of the eternal Mind, of *tathatā* (Jp., *shinyo*, "suchness") or of the Tathāgata (Jp., *Nyōrai*) or ultimate Buddha himself, whose heavenly light penetrates into the darkness and ignorance of the ego. Since the Mind is really the only real mind, the power called faith is really the Mind itself or enlightenment itself as dimly perceived by the ignorant and illusory ego. It is this power or "root" which, when awakened by a Buddha's or a bodhisattva's preaching, causes the individual sentient being to begin to despise the worldly attractions of pleasure, wealth, and power, to love the Buddha's teaching and to firmly commit himself to the Way by "taking refuge in the Three Jewels" (Jp., *kie sambō*): the Buddha, the Dharma and the Sangha.

According to the *Awakening of Faith*, this Way is incredibly long and difficult. Only after countless lifetimes of laborious practice of the six *pāramitās* can those who are especially blessed with the proper karmic conditioning finally attain to the *hosshin* or *hotsubodaishin*—the "aspiration for enlightenment based on the perfection of faith." This aspiration, however, is itself but the absolutely resolute determination to attain enlightenment which marks the first of the Ten Stages of the bodhisattva. Thus, firm faith is seen as the first and indispensable step in the Way of the Tathāgata.

The whole aim of the Awakening of Faith is to encourage devotees to work hard at the long and rigorous practice of the precepts and the *pāramitās* in order to attain to this "perfection of faith" which marks the true bodhisattva. Faith then, in this most basic and influential interpretation of the Mahāyāna understanding, is the awakening and nurturing of that deep and good power or "root" in our minds, whereby we loathe ignorance, love true wisdom, and resolutely set ourselves to practice in consolidarity with the Sangha, the Buddhist precepts and Buddhism's six perfections or *pāramitās*.

This fundamental understanding was taken up and developed in all of the Mahāyāna sects in both China and Japan, each in accordance with its own particular insights and viewpoints. I wish to very briefly indicate how the two greatest Japanese patriarchs of the Kamakura era, Dōgen Zenji and Shinran Shōnin, applied and gave their own development to this central notion of Buddhist faith.

Dōgen took faith as one of the fundamental pivots of his Dharma. Time and again in the *Shōbōgenzō* he insists on faith as a primary requirement for the true Zen Way. The most striking of his own peculiar modes of teaching in this regard is his, at first sight, apparently absurd equation of faith with *zazen* (seated meditation), the practice of the precepts, and even enlightenment itself.

> Faith is properly so-called only when one's entire body becomes faith itself in the *samādhi* of *zazen*. Faith is one with the fruit of enlightenment; the fruit of enlightenment is one with faith. If it is not the fruit of enlightenment, then faith is not fully realized.[10]

Thus, Dōgen insists that sincere faith is already enlightenment, but that faith is not sincere faith unless it motivates one to the determined practice which produces *samādhi*—and, as he says elsewhere, such faith produces obedience to the precepts and scrupulous observance of all Buddhist and monastic traditions, of whatever kind.

The mystery of the equivalency of faith-practice and enlightenment itself becomes no less impenetrable when we note in the *Awakening of Faith* the same basic notion: "Beginning Enlightenment" *(shigaku)*, which commences with faith and is faith, is "none other than identical to 'Original Enlightenment' *(honkaku)*." For Dōgen, as in the *Awakening of Faith*, Buddhist faith is a seeing, albeit an indirect or extremely dim and distorted seeing, of the Ultimate Transcendent itself. For Dōgen emphasized the immediate oneness of faith and enlightenment, whereas the previous text emphasized the opposite aspect: the extremely long and laborious road from the beginning of faith to the end of full and unsurpassed enlightenment. In both cases, however, faith entailed total submission to the precepts, absolutely resolute practice in the *pāramitās* and "taking refuge" in the Buddha, his teachings, and the community of believers. That is to say, in both the *Kishinron* and Dōgen, faith involves becoming totally at one with the almost self-enclosed society wherein the Buddha's teachings were commonly espoused and practiced.

Shinran taught basically the same notion of faith. In his teachings, too, faith is the deepest and best power of the mind which is really none other than the Buddha himself. He explicitly refers to the *Awakening of Faith* in his *Kyōgyoshinshō*. However, he stressed an aspect of this faith which was at the opposite pole from that of Dōgen. Whereas Dōgen was fierce and adamant in his demand for absolutely unreserved striving in the practice of all Buddhist prescriptions, especially *zazen*, Shinran was equally fierce in his demand that one abandon all practice and simply cast oneself via the *nembutsu* ("I take refuge in Amida Buddha!") in utter faith in the compassion of Amida and his Vow to save all sinful beings. Faith was the one and only "practice" *(gyō)* required by Shinran, and even this faith did not arise from human power and good intentions in this utterly corrupt "age of the Dharma's dissolution." Faith itself, if it is pure, is Amida's all-pervasive Vow permeating through human ignorance and passion, for this Vow is in fact one with the Tathāgata himself. Thus faith for Shinran was, as in the *Awakening of Faith*, a deep movement within the deepest self which, though like a power of the mind, is actually the stirrings of the transcendent Tathāgata himself.

Shinran summarized and developed the teachings of a long line of previous Pure Land patriarchs stretching from India to China and Japan. For him as for the Pure Land patriarchs and the sutras of India and China, the One Mind of the enlightened Tathāgata was identical to the "one mind" whereby the Pure Land believer abandons himself to utter faith in Amida. This was the Way to rebirth in the Pure Land and to certain enlightenment. Any kind of ascetical practice was, for weak beings in this "age of the degeneration of the Dharma," corrupted by self-love, weak, and ultimately a hindrance to the complete faith by which one spontaneously uttered *"Namu Amida Butsu."* Perhaps the best way to see how this faith encompassed all of the traditional

Mahāyāna notions of Buddhist faith and gave them a new interpretation is to listen to the beginning words of the chapter on faith in the *Kyōgyōshinshō*:

> As I reverently consider the nature of the outgoing movement of Amida's merits, I find that there is a great faith, and as to this great believing mind I make this declaration . . . it is the miraculous act of longing for the pure and loathing the defiled . . . it is the true mind as indestructible as a diamond; it is the absolute faith cause leading to the realization of great Nirvana . . . It is the ocean of faith of Suchness and One Reality. This mind indeed is no other than the one that is born of Amida's Vow.[11]

Before turning to Christian faith, we can summarize the Buddhist experience and interpretation of faith as follows. For the Buddhist, faith is an interior power—ultimately the Mind of the Tathāgata himself—which, when awakened by hearing the Dharma, impels us to turn away from our ignorance and selfish passions and resolutely seek after and practice the truth by joining ourselves to the Buddha, his Dharma, and the community of the faithful.

Christian Faith

The outlines of the Christian notion of faith are much more easily drawn, though no less complicated than their Buddhist equivalents, since they have been the object of much more scholarly research during the past one hundred-odd years.

We are all aware than the whole Protestant reformation arose to a very large degree out of an apparently irreconcilably different understanding of faith on the part of the traditional Latin church on the one hand, and reformers such as Luther and Calvin on the other. This fact can serve as the first good, solid piece of evidence for our empirically oriented research into faith. The similarity between this clash and that between Shinran and traditionalists on Mt. Hiei is striking. Luther and his followers held that faith is an act of the believer whose weak and sinful will is seized by God's grace and borne to firm commitment to the revelation of a totally transcendent God. According to this general Protestant understanding (here it is impossible to do justice to the almost innumerable shades of meaning within the various branches of the Protestant tradition), the faith act alone is necessary and sufficient for being reborn to the divine by opening the floodgates of the infinite merit of Christ's redemptive death. Meritorious work and ascetical practice on the part of the individual were considered both unnecessary and impossible for corrupted human nature. To even attempt them was a misunderstanding of and a lack of real faith in God's forgiveness and the efficacy of Jesus' redemptive death on the cross.

On the other hand, the Roman Catholic tradition as epitomized in the thought of Thomas Aquinas takes quite a different view. For this tradition, faith is not merely a strong act of the will, but is an act of both intellect and the will in such a way that our natural reason can and must lead us to see the reasonableness of believing in Christ's teachings and even, with the help of grace, to see "at least darkly as in a mirror" (1 Cor. 13.12) the truth of the divine mysteries themselves. After we have, with the help of God's grace, believed, reason, supported by the grace of the Holy Spirits' life in the soul, continues to grow in the insight which strengthens and upholds our faith at every turn. Further, faith alone is not enough for salvation. A person must himself strive with all his might in cooperation with God's help. This combination of faith, grace-supported reason, and earnest striving can and normally will enable a person to grow toward perfect imitation of Christ's own life and thus attain even deeper insight into the divine life of God's son which he now shares.

This differing notion of the role of faith gives the whole of Catholic practice an orientation varying from that of the major Protestant understanding. Like the Zen Buddhist, the Catholic is urged to struggle with all his powers in prayer, meditation, and acts of self-sacrifice. Faith without practice is, in this view, not true faith at all. The Catholic may say with Dōgen, then, that "faith is practice, and practice is faith."

It is necessary to go back to the main source of Christian faith, the Bible, however, if we are to get a solid grasp on the overall common unmderstanding of what Christian faith is and how it operates. Protestant and Catholic scholars today are agreed on the major outlines of the biblical notion of faith.

In the Old Testament, faith generally had the notion of human faithfulness to God and to his covenant with God in response to God's faithfulness to human beings. When Jesus preached his "good news" (gospel, *euangelion*), those who believed his teachings were required first to *metanoien*, "to turn completely around" in their lifestyle and to enter into a completely new way of life in accord with Christ's teachings of love, selflessness, and forgiveness. This *metanoia*, usually translated insufficiently as "repentance," is closer in its fundamental meaning to conversion. Surely all Christians agree that Christian faith is first and foremost a conversion or turning around to harken to and obey the wonderful "good news" of Jesus about the new Kingdom of God that was finally being inaugurated through his teaching. In the words of John the Baptist, "Repent, for the Kingdom of Heaven is at hand" (Matt. 4.17). Jesus, as the Christ (the Messiah, the annointed king and savior), conceived of his mission specifically as one of calling people to faith in himself as the Messiah and in his message of the Kingdom and his Church. The central notion of Christian faith is made clear in Matthew's account of the conversion of Peter, Andrew, James, and John. Jesus said to the former two, "Follow me, and I will make you fishers of men" (Matt. 4.18-23). They, as well as the latter, completely abandoned their former fishermen's lives and gave themselves completely over to Jesus, following after him in utter trust, or faith. This first faith clearly involved above all trust in and loyalty to the person of Christ. But this included taking upon themselves the complete renunciation of worldly ambitions and pleasures for the sake of actually living the Kingdom of Heaven which Jesus announced and which became his Church.

Already from the beginning, then, Christian faith required both absolute trust in Jesus and the kind of belief in his message that involved and motivated a complete change of lifestyle and becoming a member of the group of Jesus' followers. Even those who doubted enough to be afraid of drowning in a storm on the sea of Galilee, Jesus declared to be men of "little faith" (Matt. 8.26). Jesus demanded absolute and unwavering faith and commitment.

Later, Paul developed the beginnings of a systematic understanding of this faith. He declared that if one's faith was genuine, it was itself the very grace-enlivened act by which the believer was reborn, shared God's own divine life, and was "justified" (Rom. 5). It was this divine sonship and divine life within the new creature which transformed him into a living branch on the vine which was Christ, or members of the divine body of which Christ was the head. Thus, St. Paul gave new clarity and meaning to the analogies which Jesus himself used. Therefore, the believer, via the transforming power of God, becomes immediately *already* a member of the Kingdom, *already* saved in that, in and by faith, we become united to God in Christ. As such, the believer differs only accidentally from the saints in heaven, who are already enjoying the full fruits of the rebirth which was accomplished by faith.

In addition to this—according to the common Catholic interpretation—it is this divine life itself which enlightens our natural mind and enables us to understand the divine truth and have faith in it. Thus, faith—while a person is in this life—is an actual direct contact with the object or the source of faith, God.

Thus, the Christian view of faith sees it not as a mere blind belief in doctrines incapable of being understood. Faith is not only the door to membership in the Church, but also and especially the critical act of trusting commitment to Jesus and his words. This faith by God's power makes one already saved while still in this life, even though one remains *in statu vitae,* "on the way." The Christian sees faith as a commitment which does not originate entirely within his or her own mind and heart. It is rather the result of the movement and presence of a transcendent God which suffuses his own powers of mind and heart and lifts the faithful to a level which they are incapable of reaching themselves. Faith involves both an act of knowing (the truth revealed by God) and an act of the will (firm and utter commitment). Through faith, the believer "sees darkly as in a mirror," whereas then (in heaven) he will "see face to face" (1 Cor. 13.12).

Yet this utter faith does not imply, even in the general Protestant exegesis which emphasizes God's transcendence and the human inability to know God, a trust which contradicts sane rationality and logic. This presumes the obvious fact that the believer realizes faith from these beginnings onward and always implies trust in a Transcendent whose wisdom goes far beyond the reach of ordinary human reason. Nevertheless, it never implies, as Buddhist thinkers have sometimes presumed, that faith involves a belief or trust which is actually in contradiction to reason. Various controversies and various individual thinkers—especially Kierkegaard—have at one time or another stressed the transcendence of God and hence the relatively blind quality of faith, and at other times its rationality and reasonableness. However, very seldom have Christian thinkers implied that there is no solid connection whatsoever between faith and human reason. Such a contention would be absurd, arguing rationally that reason is not involved in faith while teaching and explaining faith in rational categories.

St. Paul was the first to use reason to develop Jesus' teachings on faith; for it is especially in his Epistles that we encounter a highly developed rational theology of faith. Here faith is seen as taking the place of circumcision and works of the old Law of Moses in order to bring the whole world within the reach of the Jewish privilege of being God's sons and chosen people (Rom. 2.6 and Gal. 2.6).

During the great doctrinal controversies of the fourth and fifth centuries, the notion of Christian faith underwent a good deal of development. In the ecumenical councils such as Ephesus and Calcedon, crucial issues of dogma were resolved and the result was that Christian faith began slowly to take on a more doctrinal bent. For the Roman Catholic church, this tendency became more extreme in the Counter-Reformation, which in the sixteenth and subsequent centuries attempted to combat what it saw as the doctrinal errors of the Protestants. Only in the Second Vatican Council was a certain balance restored. The nature of faith as primarily assent to doctrinal propositions was finally played down and a more biblical interpretation restored.

The extent of the variation in the interpretations of Christian faith is almost limitless, and anything one says about the subject should be balanced with nuances to the contrary if one tries to be fair to all its historical ramifications. Still, even the brief outline of the uncontroverted central notions of Christian faith which we have stated here is quite enough to form the basis of a comparison with Buddhist faith and to see the framework of a common human dynamic.

TOWARD AN ANTHROPOLOGY OF FAITH
AND AN UNDERSTANDING OF THE
SOCIOLOGY OF RELIGIOUS KNOWLEDGE

This discussion by its nature will concentrate on the common elements evident in Christian and Buddhist understandings of their respective experiences. In doing so, however, we are not unaware of the great differences. A personal versus an impersonal notion of the Ultimate, central stress on love in one and on insight in the other, very divergent notions of the inerrancy of their scriptures, and totally different salvation histories are the chief among many discrepancies. These different symbolic structures and cultural influences, however, have for too long been emphasized by both traditions to the point of obscuring very striking similarities which point to a common human religious dynamic at least on the level of anthropology.

Space permits only the briefest listing of the similarities which link Buddhism and Christian faith in what, I submit, is a common human dynamic. These similarities are of utmost importance, for they furnish us with solid, verifiable material out of which it is possible to disclose the outlines of the cross-cultural dynamic of religious faith. Note carefully that they converge precisely at those social and psychological points which are crucial for all types of human knowledge: communitarian, intersubjective affirmation of an apperception of the Ultimate, of the meaning of everything in the light of that Ultimate, and a resulting Way which should guide all human action.

1. Faith is a firm commitment to a symbolically presented notion of the ultimate nature of reality (that *tathatā-Tathāgata* or God-creation) which gives a unified hierarchy of meaning to literally every aspect of one's everyday life.

2. This firm commitment of faith rests upon a special, though initially very dim, insight into the normally transcendent, ultimate ground or source of all that is. This insight is seen as dependent on the presence and aid ("permeation" of the One Mind or Amida's Vow, or the presence and inspiration of the Holy Spirit within the mind and soul) of the transcendent ground itself.

3. Faith is by its very nature an intersubjective or communitarian act, necessarily involving resolute consolidarity with a community (church or *sangha*) of fellow believer-practicers.

4. Authentic faith goes beyond mere affirmation of theoretical doctrines. It engages all of the believer's feelings, emotions, and actions in an existential religious manner of living.

5. Faith's total existential engagement includes submission — to the degree that human weakness permits — to a body of rules of precepts (the Ten

48   MORRIS J. AUGUSTINE

Commandments and the "law" of Christ's love, or the ten precepts and
guidance by *prajña* and *bodhi*) which guide human conduct into con-
formity with the ultimate nature of all things.

6. Authentic faith—involving as it does both commitment to a symbolic
and systematic notion of the Ultimate and an existential involvement
in the believing community and its precepts, way of life, and religious
practice—is a world-building act which gives meaning and motivation
to every facet of one's everyday life.

7. Authentic faith—permeating all of one's actions and
thoughts—provides an experiential spiral toward joy, freedom,
compassion, and wisdom. Faith is a process involving ideas, acts, and
experiences.

8. Faith involves, inchoatively at first and more clearly as its spiral grows
wider and stronger, the experience of special, nonordinary awareness
which may generally be characterized as "non-egocentric levels of
consciousness": love or compassion, humility or selflessness, wisdom
or *bodhi*, obedience or submission, poverty or simplicity, thanksgiving
or gratitude, ecstatic communion or enlightenment, and the like.

Space does not permit us to give proper nuance to these elements of an anthropology of religious faith. Neither does it permit a full and revealing docu-
mentation of the abundant material within Christian and Buddhist teaching
which corroborates and substantiates the presence of such a common dynamic
operating in both systems. In the space remaining it is possible only to show
briefly that these cross-cultural elements correspond to the notions concerning belief-faith which the principles of sociology of knowledge and culture
would demand.

First of all, faith is seen to have always and universally been conceived of
as extending beyond and beneath mere cognitive belief in rational doctrinal
formulas. Secondly, it is an essentially communitarian, intersubjective, or
social phenomenon. No one can claim to be Christian or Buddhist—or a real
number of any other religion it would seem—except in consolidarity with a
living social entity. Thirdly, faith as experienced in Buddhism and Christianity begins with, develops under, and finds its fulfillment in world views,
emotions, moods, norms, hopes, and existential modes of consciousness
which are characterized throughout as non-egocentric. Whereas this element
has not been noted by the social scientists, it seems not only compatible but
is a valuable aid in working out a full social scientific notion of faith which
is consistent with believers' understanding of their own faith.

Buddhist *samādhi*, the Bodhi-mind, and nirvana, as well as Christian love
of God and persons—along with such commonly held virtues as humility,
self-abnegation, obedience, simplicity of lifestyle, rejection of killing,

stealing, lying, sexual excess, pride, and the like—all have one thing in common: they are strikingly non-egocentered. It is by means of these virtues, seen as inspired by the Ultimate, that boundaries of self-centered reality are broken through and the eternal, unchanging source of self is approached.

This notion in turn can be seen to be a prime requirement for the very existence and survival of any society. However true may be the insistence of thinkers—from Hobbes and Hume to Freud and the socio-biologists—that all human actions are essentially egocentered and ego-preserving, it nevertheless remains true—as Freud, the socio-biologists, and social scientists from whatever school all, in their respective ways, teach—that sublimation of ego-centered drives, postponement of gratification, and the development of dependable, socially oriented modes of behavior are an absolutely necessary part of the healthy socialization of any individual and the healthy integration of any society. Recent thinkers like Eric Erikson and Lawrence Kohlberg have shown the intimate correlation between these patterns and religious modes of symbolic expression, belief, and action.[12] This is not to say that religion and faith are mere functions of society's need for social integration. A different integration is equally logical: society and human nature are a function of the transcendent, completely non-egocentric source-of-reality which our own actions and knowledge inevitably incorporate.

If, as was done above, we rely on Buddhist and Christian forms of faith to give us insight into the human cognitive dynamic which produced particularly profound and stable systematizations of such appresentations of or transcendent insights into the Ultimate, then we have good grounds to believe that such appresentations of the Ultimate rest on epistemologically solid grounds. I believe that this epistemological validity of Christian and Buddhist symbolic appresentations of the Ultimate can best be disclosed by briefly developing two of the above eight elements of our anthropology of religious faith.

First, it is clear to everyone that relatively non-egocentered types of emotions, moods, experiences, and modes of consciousness are daily experienced from infancy to adulthood: mother love, love between the sexes, patriotism, aesthetic wonder, the ecstasy of many kinds of transcendent insights, and benevolence of a hundred varieties. It is interesting to note that all of these have been treated as sacred and hierophantic by most traditional societies. Genuine human maturity is defined by both psychologists and philosophers in terms of developing a firm, responsible, and dependable ability to see beyond one's egocentered drives and spheres of interest to take into account the other as well as the abidingly non-egocentered cosmos.

Secondly, things such as the Buddha's enlightenment and Jesus' selfless love are central symbols of religious systems which synthesize strikingly clear and stable world views grounded in a transcendent Ultimate. This Ultimate is indeed beyond the normal egocentered realities which are appresented in the necessarily egocentered work by which we gain our food, shelter, and protection. Nevertheless, these stable non-egocentric visions of an ego-transcending Ultimate are still authenticated by frequent non-egocentered experiences in the everyday life-world. Common sense estimation has always placed mature and responsible selfless awareness and concern in a special, honored category. They are not thereby declared inauthentic or illusory, but rather belonging to a superior level of development. Every culture has its own way of affirming that beyond the world of narrow self-concern lies a realm of relatively free and joyful selflessness wherein even death can be met with some degree of equanimity.

The believer's notions of God or the Buddha, while clearly symbolic appresentations of a transcendent Ultimate, are not, therefore, mere neurotic projections or sighs of the oppressed. Whether basically impersonal as in Buddhism or personal as in Christianity, such symbolic expressions of an ego-transcending Ultimate appresent a lifelong process or Way toward redemption or release from the bonds of the ordinary, pragmatic world of selfish concern. In the perspective of sociology of knowledge there seems to be no solid reason to believe that these dynamic schemes are any more illusory than schemes of law or kinship. All such "multiple realities" or "finite provinces of meaning," as Schutz has so brilliantly disclosed, have their own special "tension of consciousness." But I wish to contend that unlike other finite provinces of meaning—such as dreams, fantasies, play, and the like—healthy, nonneurotic religious knowledge is thoroughly integrated into the primary reality of the everyday life-world in the same manner that law, science, and systems of art and literature are. Individual groups may strive to thoroughly reject the "iron cage" built by science and technology and live in communal freedom within a "world of nature." Other groups may strive to create similar worlds free from all taint of religion. However, the everyday life-worlds of all persons, it would seem, are simply not the real life-world without an integration, in some form or another, of both scientific and religious notions.

The conclusions pertinent to the present Buddhist and Christian encounter which can be taken from such an analysis seem to be fairly obvious. First, faith as traditionally understood in the mainstream traditions of both Christianity and Buddhism is certainly not the narrowly cognitive belief which the social scientists in Rome found to be epiphenomenal and an inappropriate object for empirical investigation. Secondly, genuinely religious faith is a commitment to symbolic synthesis of apperceptions of an ultimate ground and of the consequences for the living of human life. In light of this fact it becomes provincial and unnecessary for Buddhists and Christians to contend that authentic religion must be confined within the boundaries of a single symbol system. An ever great theological appreciation of this fact within both communities would seem to be the most solid basis on which to build a deep encounter between Buddhism and Christianity with the kind of genuine and deep mutual respect and reverence that can be accorded only to equals. There are many encouraging signs within the various churches and groups of the *sangha* that this realization is growing.

Thirdly, the insight that Buddhist and Christian faith are united by a common anthropology holds out the potential of a new ecumenism between science and religion which is even more momentous in what it holds for Buddhism and Christianity. There are a host of problems and gaps in the above sketch of the sociology of religious faith and knowledge. To say that it is in its present state acceptable to any one of the mainstreams of Buddhist, Christian, or scientific thought would be optimistic to say the least. Nevertheless, I would submit that such a cross-cultural application of the principles of sociology or knowledge to the theological systems of religious self-understanding holds out enough potential for a future religio-scientific reunification of human consciousness to warrant very serious consideration by all parties concerned.

NOTES

1. Thomas Luckmann, *The Invisible Religion* (New York: Macmillan, 1967).

2. Robert N. Bellah, *Beyond Belief* (New York: Harper and Row, 1970); and *The Broken Covenant* (New York: Harper and Row, 1973).

3. See especially Peter Berger and Thomas Luckmann, *The Social Construction of Reality: A Treatise in the Sociology of Knowledge* (Garden City, N.Y.: Doubleday Anchor, 1966); and Berger's subsequent work, *The Sacred Canopy: Elements of a Sociological Theory of Religion* (Garden City, N.Y.: Doubleday Anchor, 1967).

4. The major lines of Alfred Schutz's thought appeared in 1939. This work has been translated under the title, *The Phenomenology of the Social World*, trans. George Walsh and Frederick Kehnert (Evanston, Ill.: Northwestern University Press, 1967).

5. Edmund Husserl, *The Crisis of European Sciences and Transcendental Phenomenology: An Introduction to Phenomenological Philosophy*, trans. David Carr (Evanston, Ill.: Northwestern University Press, 1970), pp. 132-147.

6. Rocco Caporale and Antonio Grumelli, *The Culture of Unbelief: Studies and Proceedings from the First International Symposium on Belief Held in Rome, March 22-27, 1969* (Berkeley: University of California Press, 1971), p. 242.

7. Ibid., p. 247.

8. Paul Tillich, *The Dynamics of Faith* (New York: Harper Torchbooks, 1958).

9. Wilfred Cantwell Smith, *Faith and Belief* (Princeton: Princeton University Press, 1979).

10. Dōgen Kigen, *Shōbōgenzō*, ed. Eto Sokua (Tokyo: Iwanami, 1939-43), 3:131.

11. Shinran Gutoku Shaku, *Kyōgyōshinshō*, trans. D.T. Suzuki (Kyoto: Eastern Buddhist Society, 1973), p. 85.

12. Eric H. Erikson, *Childhood and Society* (New York: W. W. Norton, 1963); and Lawrence Kohlberg and Carol Gilligan, "The Adolescent as Philosopher," *Daedalus*, Fall 1971, pp. 1051-1086.

CHAPTER 3

The Hermeneutics of Practice in Dōgen and Francis of Assisi

John C. Maraldo

INTRODUCTION

One of the central questions in the dialogue between Buddhists and Christians concerns the necessity of establishing or following a daily religious practice. There is no lack of suggestions as to what that practice might be: prayer, meditation, spiritual reading, almsgiving, and other private and social activities. But there is considerable confusion about what religious practice means. What is its role in one's personal life and in the life of society? What is its intent and its value? What use is it? These questions are intensified in the case of contemplative, seemingly private religious practice. Practitioners of meditation, for example, are often asked what meditation does for them, and what good it does for others. This kind of question arises from the notion that practice is an activity directed toward some end or objective outside that activity, a notion which derives from the ancient distinction between theory and *praxis*. Often this type of question will dissolve of itself when one actually engages in religious practice. Nevertheless, it is worthwhile to examine the presuppositions of such questions, for hidden assumptions condition the way we actually experience as well as the way we express what we are doing.

Relevance to the Christian-Buddhist Dialogue

How is this examination relevant to the dialogue between Christians and Buddhists? Let us reflect for a moment on three predominant patterns of the Zen-Christian dialogue.[1] One pattern, the first to occur historically, has been an attempt to confront sophisticated metaphysical views articulated or presupposed in traditional scriptures. At its extreme, this approach comes to an impasse when a dogmatic Christian monotheism confronts a Buddhism "monism," "pantheism," or "atheism." A second pattern discovers comparative structures, symbols, and stories in the history of two traditions. Yet many a metaphysical question still haunts academic comparisons and the approach of a history or phenomenology of religions. What, after all, is to be made of the insistence on the "truth" of the respective teachings?

A third approach has been to eschew metaphysical questions and locate truth in religious experience. If the first two approaches can be said to be biased toward Christian or Western methods, the third appears to lean toward the Zen insistence on experiential truth. Much good work in this approach has gone into comparing the rapture of the medieval Christian mystics with the enlightenment experience of Zen adepts.[2] Yet even if this approach is metaphysically neutral (e.g., with regard to such issues as identity with the Absolute or God), I believe it to be hermeneutically naive in two respects. First, for purposes of dialogue, which occurs via language, it too often assumes that expressions common to the two sides are already shared meanings, and that differences in expression result from adventitious interpretations attached *post factum* to a core experience. It underestimates the degree to which tradition shapes (and sometimes beguiles) communication. Secondly, it tends to forget that our tradition and society see mystical experience as the inner sanctum and enjoyment of the rare adept (or perhaps as the psychological "peak experience"), remote from the usual exegencies of life in a secularized age. Hence it may be said to be naive about the ways in which traditional meanings have already limited the scope and wider relevance of the dialogue.

Perhaps by discovering what is actually done in exemplary instances of religious life, and how that doing is understood, we may find an approach which is metaphysically neutral but not hermeneutically naive. What I offer in the following is a brief examination of some texts of two (among many possible other) practitioners in the Zen and Christian traditions. These texts of Dōgen Kigen Zenji (1200-1253) and St. Francis of Assisi (1181-1226) are exemplary in the sense that they suggest precisely how religious practice shapes the meaning of a textual tradition and the intersection of tradition and concrete life. My point of view may be somewhat overstated as a form of the hermeneutical circle: to understand a text (and tradition), one must practice what it enjoins; and to know how to practice, one must be informed by the tradition (and text).

THE SENSE OF PRACTICE

When we hear the word practice we are likely to be influenced by the meaning that is predominant in the West and wherever Marxism has made inroads. This meaning opposes practice to theory: theory and theoretical knowledge is an end in itself; practice is a means to an end outside itself.[3] It is clear that if we were to apply this notion of practice to the endeavors of Zen and Christian life, practice would appear simply as the means to the goal of enlightenment or salvation. That this is a misleading notion of religious practice, at least for Dōgen and Francis, I shall document later. But there is another consideration which precludes the oversimplified view of religious practice as a means to an end. This is the fact that theory, by way of its Latin translation, has been associated with contemplation and the purely contemplative, that is, apolitical life—the life later associated with religious meditation. Thus we are confronted with a view which would take the theoretical life paradoxically as the life of religious practice.

If an instrumental notion of practice as a means to an end outside itself is inadequate to grasp the sense of contemplative religious life, then what approach to understanding is open to us in a secularized world?

The Experiential Sense of Practice as Performance

In order to anticipate the proper sense of practice in religious life, let us consider the notion of practice as disciplined performance. This notion is akin to the notion of *askēsis*, from which the word asceticism derives. The original meaning of *askēsis* did not connote self-mortification or subjugation of our corporeal nature. Rather it indicated the practice which most fully expressed that nature for the Greeks, namely athletic training. It was an affirmation and positive evaluation of bodily existence and the repeated exertion required for athletic prowess. But one need not take activities specifically identified with athletics to see the point I would like to make about "ascetic" practice. Any activity that "takes practice" to be performed proficiently will do. Let us recall such activities as practicing piano or dance, learning a language, doing floral arrangement, or the tea ceremony. To say that any of these takes practice means that it requires repeated effort and concentrated performance. Such activities are daily disciplines exercised for no other goal than their performance. When we give a piano recital or communicate in a new language we are performing the same kind of activity in the end as we did during our practice sessions. And when the activity becomes "practiced," that is proficiently performed, then there is no gap between what we will and what we do. It may even be said that during any practice there is no room for desires or intentions which separate our present performance from an imagined ideal, what we are doing from how we wish we were doing it.

The sense of practice which follows from the original Greek *askēsis*, as opposed to the sense of practice derived from the *theōria-praxis* distinction, cannot be adequately understood in terms of a means-end relationship. It takes as its model athletic training, but can also be seen to include any activity which requires training, repeated exertion, and concentration of body and mind. Hence, it covers our most ordinary and even routine daily activities.

Might not one object, however, that this notion of practice undermines the specifically religious quality of acts traditionally identified with asceticism. Is there not something special about the practices of the religious ascetics that transcends such mundane pastimes? Does not an implied comparison of playing the piano for amusement with fasting for purgation smack of sacrilege? It will be the burden of my interpretation of texts by Dōgen and Francis of Assisi to show that this is a misguided way of thinking.

THE SENSE OF COMPARISON OF DOGEN AND FRANCIS

The texts which I will examine derive from historically separate traditions. Therefore it is necessary to say a few words here about the sense of reading them together. A comparison of texts or their authors would seem somehow to put them on a par with one another, to seek out their similarities and differences and perhaps a way to reconcile those differences. With regard to the lives and writings of Dōgen Kigen and Francis of Assisi, we might discover a series of similarities ranging from the superficial to the profound. Both were early thirteenth-century founders of religious orders which were novel and yet conservative or long-existing traditions; both had experiences which converted them to a life of austere practice, apolitical and perhaps even nonworldly in their nature; both devoted their lives to teaching others and exemplifying their teachings, and thus were able to transform religious history. Their way of life continues to be practiced today, over eight hundred years later. Differences are no less striking. When we read them, even in English translation, it is still as if we were reading two different languages. Writings of and about Francis abound with piety and praises directed to a transcendent God; severe mortifications of the flesh, states of ecstasy, and miracles are described. Moreover, if we read Bonaventure on Francis, we must read through an epistemology ascending from the sensible to the intelligible and a metaphysics where the creaturely is a sign of the divine. Dōgen, on the other hand, plunges us into a world of Buddhist terms and Zen sayings where words often clash with sense, at least common sense; where a nondualistic metaphysics, denying any ultimate difference between self and Absolute, is suggested. Furthermore, differences in the type of texts to be compared seems overwhelming. On the one hand, we have eulogistic biographies and *legendae* of the life of Francis, as well as poems of praise and versions of fraternity rules by his own hand. In the case of Dōgen we have expositions of Zen koans from Dōgen's own unique point of view and language, and exhortations to follow the example of the buddhas and patriarchs, that is, the enlightened teachers of old.

However, what I propose here is not a comparison of personalities, historical circumstances, enlightenment experiences, nor even types of texts. Rather I want to offer an experiential probe into texts of two traditions which emphasize the significance of practice in order to discover what notion of practice is presented therein, and to anticipate how living out that sense of practice may revolutionize the reading of texts. If we need to turn to the texts for support, inspiration, or corroboration, we also need to return the texts to the world we live in.

THE PRACTICE OF DOGEN ZENJI

An introduction to a hermeneutic of practice in Dōgen can be found in a comment by a contemporary American Soto monk.

> The word *practice* has many rich implications in Zen. In a narrow sense it refers to the activity of sitting meditation we call *zazen*. To practice means to sit in meditation, concentrating with all our effort until the gap between ourselves and others is eliminated.

> In a broader sense, practice refers to the activity of completely involving ourselves in whatever we are doing or experiencing so that there is no gap or separation between ourselves and that activity or experience. It is the extension of *zazen* into our lives from moment to moment.[4]

The English word "practice" renders several terms in Dōgen, each of them having historical connotations and capable of varying translations.[5] But rather than explore the notion of practice via a linguistic account, I believe we can go to the heart of the matter by referring to the first two works Dōgen composed: the *Fukanzazengi* (Universal Promotion of Zazen, 1227, revised 1243) and the *Bendowa* (Discourse on Negotiating the Way, 1231). In these works Dōgen both specifies the concrete form and locus of practice and indicates its universal application. The *Fukanzazengi* begins by proclaiming that the "Way," that is to say, enlightenment or ultimate reality, is manifested unconditionally. But since mankind's discriminating mind separates him from the Way, no one can dispense with efforts to "negotiate the Way." Dōgen writes, "If you want to attain suchness, you should practice suchness without delay."[6] Immediately following this injunction are instructions telling one how to practice *zazen*, giving details regarding the mental attitude, physical posture, and preferred environment.

Zazen as the Locus of Practice

In the *Bendowa*, Dōgen defends his teaching that *zazen* is *the* normative practice for attaining the Way, calling it alone the right path *(masashiki michi)*,
the right entrance *(shomon)* and the "Dharma gate of repose and joy: *(anraku
no homon)*."[7] *Zazen* assumes a particular form which we associate with sitting
in the cross-legged position and letting go of thoughts. But Dōgen insists
that *zazen* cannot be reduced to a mere techinique, exercise, or even portion
of practice when we refuse to count it among the four attitudes, the six *pāramitās* (perfections), and the three learnings.[8] "The *zazen* I speak of is not
learning meditation. It is . . . the practice-realization *(shusho)* of totally culminated enlightenment. It is the manifestation of ultimate reality
(koangenjo)."[9]

   Zazen then is the embodiment of the Buddha-Way as well as the specific
form of human effort to "negotiate the Way." Realization and practice
cannot be separated:

> This Dharma is amply present in every person, but unless one practices,
> it is not manifested, unless there is realization, it is not attained. . . . As
> it is already realization in practice, realization is endless; as it is practice
> in realization, practice is beginningless.[10]

Dōgen's own realization came in a moment of *zazen* practice under Ju-ching
in China, when the master reputedly shouted "Cast off body and mind!"
(shinjindatsuraku) to a drowsy monk.[11] Dōgen frequently uses this phrase to
express the essence of *zazen* practice. Perhaps we may say that to drop body
and mind is to put one's whole body and mind into *zazen*, and further to drop
zazen as a separate activity, so that the field of practice is all existence.[12]
Zazen may be seen as the specific locus of practice, where one learns how to
practice living (and dying). But to restrict practice to the times when meditation is performed would be, in effect, to maintain the very kind of separation
that *zazen* is meant to overcome. For Dōgen, when one totally practices
zazen, dropping body, mind, and separation, there is nothing that is not
practicing.

> Then the land, the trees and grasses, fences and walls, tiles and pebbles,
> all the various things in the ten directions, perform the work of buddhas
> . . . the trees, grasses, and land involved in this all emit a bright and shin-
> ing light, and preach the profound and incomprehensible Dharma, and
> it is endless.[13]

Practice as Universal Manifestation

Practice thus comes to mean the spontaneous manifestations of all reality. There are numerous allusions to this meaning throughout Dōgen. Water practices and realizes itself as water.[14] ". . . the sounds and forms of the valley streams and the forms and sounds of the mountains all become the myriad verses of the sutras"; "it is nothing more than the green of pines in the spring and the glory of chrysanthemums in the autumn."[15] A passage in the *Gyōji* (Continuous Practice) formulates it thus:

> By virtue of this continuous practice . . . *(gyōji)* there are sun, moon, and stars. By virtue of this continuous practice, there are earth, sky, and heart within and body without, the four elements and the five skandhas.[16]

The view that all phenomena are manifestations of practice-realization implies a notion of practice which is *not instrumental and not representational.* Practice is not conceived as a means to an end, and it is not objectified as something separate from the activity of the world or of oneself. Hence, in examples Dōgen cites in various writings, Huang-po sweeps out all the rooms in the monastery, not "for the sake of sweeping out the mind, nor . . . performed to cleanse the light of the Buddha (but as) continuous practice for the sake of continuous practice."[17] And master Pao-ch'e continues to fan himself when asked why fanning (practice) is necessary since the wind (Buddha-nature) reaches everywhere.[18] Masao Abe and Norman Waddell, translators of the *Fukanzazengi,* note that Dōgen may have felt compelled to write yet another manual of Zen practice *(Zazengi)* to counteract other teachers' emphasis on *zazen* as a "*means* for strengthening mental concentration."[19] Hence Dōgen instructs the practitioners to "have no designs on becoming a buddha. Zazen has nothing whatever to do with sitting or lying down."[20]

This latter statement is expressive of the nonrepresentational thinking which, we may say, sees practice from the standpoint of practice. The entire work called "The King of Samādhis Samādhi" *(Sammai O Zammai)* is, I believe, composed from this point of view. There again Dōgen identifies practice as *zazen,* sitting cross-legged, and again he states that this practice is beyond any formalization:

> Rare are those who understand that sitting is the Buddha Dharma and the Buddha Dharma is sitting. Even though some may have known experientially that sitting is the Buddha Dharma, no one has known sitting as sitting. . . . Therefore, there is a mind sitting and it is not the same as a body sitting. There is a body sitting and it is not the same as a mind sitting. There is sitting with body and mind cast off, and it is not the same as sitting with body and mind cast off.[21]

In his book *What is Religion?*, Keiji Nishitani aptly characterizes the standpoint which does not objectify practice:

> The moment you see 'practice' *[gyō]* in a representational fashion, you
> have already attached to the form. On the field where practice is truly
> practice, phenomena such as man moving his limbs, clouds moving
> across the sky, water flowing, leaves falling, and blossoms scattering, are
> formless. Their form is a formless one. And to adopt this 'formless form'
> as one's own form—is none other than the standpoint of 'practice.'[22]

Because this notion of practice is noninstrumental and nonobjectifying, it
signifies not the self-serving activity of the individual but a practice of self-
enlightenment qua enlightening others. Dōgen can therefore unite his exclusive insistence on *zazen* with the general Mahāyāna philosophy of compassion
for all.

The Everyday Character of Practice

In the same way, because this practice is not conceived as a means to an end
nor discriminated as a separate, solely individual activity, it can manifest
itself continuously in everyday life. Practice-realization is to be found in such
everyday, ordinary activity as eating rice, drinking tea, fanning oneself, or
sweeping the hallway. At the same time, emphasis must be put on the efforts
of every day as well as the ordinariness of the activity. To say that continuous
practice means the realization of one's own true nature and the manifestation
of the universe is to say that it demands the totality of one's efforts. To hold
that "even avoiding continuous practice is itself continuous practice . . . is a
half-hearted continuous practice, and it cannot be considered seeking continuous practice."[23] This statement, from the *Gyōji*, is followed by some
twenty-three stories recounting the everyday efforts of practitioners of the
Way. Beginning with Shakyamuni, Dōgen writes: "The teaching and conversion activities of his whole lifetime were nothing but continuous practice,
keeping his robes clean and begging for his food were nothing but continuous
practice." This is also the point of Pai-chang's saying, "a day without work is
a day without eating." There was not a day Pai-chang did not exert himself
on behalf of those studying under him, Dōgen writes. Everyday should be
valued and respected; everyday is a priceless jewel which we should value
highly.[24] Dōgen can thus integrate the Zen predeliction for the commonplace
with the rigorous demands of his own discipline.

Practice as a Hermeneutical Principle

The practice of everyday activities, that is, routine things performed in a concentrated spirit, is itself seen as the content of the Buddha's teachings and instructions of the patriarchs. In the *Kajō* (Everyday Life), Dōgen recounts the
story of Tao-k'ai, who asks his teacher, Master T'ou-tzu, "Are the words
which the patriarchs use the same as their daily life of drinking tea and
eating rice? Are there any other words different from these which are used to
teach people?"[25] Of course, the means or "words" the patriarchs use for
transmitting the teaching are inseparable from their everyday actions. But is
there not another, strictly verbal message transmitted from teacher to
disciple? This is the question not only of the priority of action over speech
(or good works over scripture), but of everyday practice as the source of the
meaning of scriptures. When Tao-k'ai asked his question, he used words;
when Dōgen recounts the story, he passes on a verbal tradition, and when we
repeat it here we remain within the realm of language. However parsimoni-
ous Zen masters may be with words, it is not the case that language is always
rejected in favor of nonlinguistic action. The point is that, if practice supplies
the foundation of the meaning of the linguistic expression, then the linguistic
expression must be carried out to be "understood." Hence Dōgen exhorts the
reader to penetrate the inner meaning of Tao-k'ai's question and then to transcend this inner meaning. That is, Dōgen transmits the story properly as a
koan, to be accomplished by the reader.

Perhaps many of Dōgen's own statements, as well as the numerous stories
he recounts from the Chinese Buddhist tradition, are intended to be taken in
this sense. They are not historical accounts, enigmatic descriptions, or dogmatic formulas, but enjoinders to clarify and enact their meaning. The hermeneutic of practice in Dōgen challenges us to see practice as the principle
through which the text is to be understood. If the text can give one spiritual
inspiration and concrete instruction for daily practice, then how much more
can actual practice open up the meaning of the text.

THE PRACTICE OF ST. FRANCIS OF ASSISI

When we turn to the life and writings of Francis of Assisi, we find the same
insistence on a practice whose universal significance is rooted in, but far
outreaches, the particular forms it takes in everyday discipline. The concept
of practice is itself not an object of Francis's reflection; but it is abundantly
evident from the biographies that Francis is above all a practitioner (L,
professor) and an exemplar of what he understands as the Gospel life, and
from his own writings it is clear that this is what he expects of his followers.

In the prologue of Bonaventure's spiritual biography, the *Legenda Major,* Francis is eulogized as a "practitioner, a leader and a herald of Gospel perfection."[26] In his own *Testament,* composed shortly before his death and intended as "a reminder, admonition, [and] exhortation," he describes how God inspired him "to embark upon a life of penance."[27] What does the life of penance concretely entail, and what does it reveal to us?

In formulating an answer to this question I shall concentrate on the sparse writings of Francis himself, and draw upon the much more voluminous biographies only to add perspective. If one were to focus on Bonaventure's elaborate *Life of Francis,* for example, our attention could easily shift from the practice Francis recommends for all, to the unique saintliness of his own person; moreover, the tradition has tended to interpret his writings in the light of later works and not within their own context.[28] Naturally the exposition here will be very brief, but will, I hope, go to the heart of the matter.

Francis's Asceticism: Obedience, Poverty, Selflessness

The biographers (Thomas of Celano, Julian of Speyer, Bonaventure, among others) discuss Francis's asceticism in detail, but it is noteworthy that he himself does not enjoin his own extreme practices of bodily mortification upon his followers.[29] This would lead us to believe that the mortification of the flesh is by itself not to be taken as the normative practice but rather as based upon another sense of asceticism. The asceticism called for is the continual surrender of oneself to others, and thereby to God. Thus, in the *Admonitions* Francis says the truly poor in spirit are not necessarily those who "spend all their time at their prayers and other religious exercises and mortify themselves by long fasts and so on."[30] Rather, they are those prepared to take upon themselves the abuses of the world. The *Rule of 1221* states that

> no matter where they are, the friars must always remember that they have given themselves up completely and handed over their whole selves to our Lord Jesus Christ, and so they should be prepared to expose themselves to every enemy. . . . (Chap. 16)

and

> Nothing, then, must keep us back, nothing separate us from [God], nothing come between us and him (Chap. 23).[31]

Let us look to the pronouncements on obedience and poverty for a condensation of Francis's sense of practice. Obedience, of course, means following the Rule of the Order and the directives of one's superiors; poverty requires living without poverty. But the root meaning of obedience is submission to all creation:

> Obedience puts to shame
> all natural and selfish desires.
> . . . it subjects a man
> to everyone on earth,
> And not only to men,
> but to all the beasts as well . . .

and poverty is whatever

> . . . puts to shame
> all greed, avarice
> and all the anxieties of this life.[32]

True obedience consists not primarily in simply obeying one's superiors, but of making an offering of one's will to God, even being willing to suffer persecution for *not* obeying a command against one's conscience rather than be separated from one's fellow man. Similarly, true poverty means not simply living without property and money, but freely taking upon oneself the condition of the poor in the world.[33] It means dispossessing oneself of the fear that separates. Francis has these startling words to say of the practice requisite to possessing these and other virtues:

> In all the world there is not a man
> who can possess any one of you
> without first dying to himself.[34]

But before we go into the concrete, everyday dimension of this practice, let us comment briefly on its universal manifestation, as expressed in *The Canticle of Brother Sun.*

The *Canticle* has three sections, composed separately but sequentially in the last year of Francis's life.[35] The major section, which is the first nine of fourteen verses, proclaims the presence of God in his creation. The sun reveals the light of God; and the moon, stars, wind, air, water, fire, and earth all reflect God's light in their own way. God is praised *with, through,* and *in* each and all of them; the *cum* and *per* of the original Umbrian signifies that they themselves are the means by which God is glorified, and not the object of praise nor the cause of our praising God *for* them.[36] Or better, they are the very embodiment of God's glory, just as they are—the weather fair or stormy, the water useful, lowly, precious, and pure; fire full of power and strength; the earth who sustains and governs us. The personifications "brother sun," "sister moon," "brother wind," "sister earth," and so on place all creation on the same level as the human.

The second section of the poem, consisting of verses 10 and 11, specifies how the human manifests God's praise: by granting pardon out of love of God and enduring infirmity and tribulation. Thus we are enjoined to practice forgiveness and to embrace suffering freely, so as to embody what the rest of creation embodies naturally. Such human action reveals the glory of God as that glory is also enacted in the natural being of creation. We would not go too far, I believe, to say that the sun, moon, stars, wind, water, fire, and earth manifest the universal practice of being selfless ("To you, alone, Most High, do they belong"). They can know no separation from their creator.

The concluding three verses of the poem speak of death as the dividing line of human life. No living person can evade "sister death," but there are two ways to meet her: the death of "mortal sin" or ultimate separation from God, and the "second death," of those who have first died to themselves and overcome their separation from God. Sister death, the death of the body (*morte corporale*), then, is not portrayed as a consequence of sin, but as the point of realization of a first death, either to God or to oneself. Those who repose in God's most holy will need fear nothing from their "second death." As such, death, however we accept it, is also the praise of God. The *Canticle* ends with an exhortation to serve God selflessly.

In this reading of *The Canticle of Brother Sun* it is important to reiterate that the works of God, the sun, moon, wind, water, fire, earth, and the like, do not symbolize but actually manifest the light of God. We are not enjoined to praise God for them, and they are not called upon to praise God;[37] they *are* the praise of God, the Lord is praised with and through (*cum, per*) them. Later stories also indicate that Francis experienced the elements not first of all as things in themselves which could then take on a secondary function of pointing to their creator, but rather directly as embodiments of divine life. The manuscript of 1311 called the *Legend of Perugia* relates incidents of Francis's seemingly bizarre attitude toward fire, water, and stones. They are living, sentient creatures to Francis; he treats them so as not to harm them, but accepts them as they are, regardless of their potential danger or benefit to him. He deeply respects them, but has no designs on them; as they exist they reveal their creator. They are addressed as brother and sister, but to address them so requires that one first die to the selfishness of seeing them as created for one's own sake or as a threat to one's own possessions. ("I sinned through avarice by not wanting my Brother Fire to consume [my cloak].")[38] Francis also speaks of the "obedience" of the elements and exhorts humankind to imitate this way of being. To *be* revelatory of God they exist in relationship with God, and not simply of themselves nor for humanity. And how is humanity revelatory to God?

Humanity manifests this mode of being by way of submission to all creation (obedience) and the dispossession of self (poverty/humility). To show that this universal manifestation is realized through concrete, everyday practice is the next step.

The Everyday Character of the Rule

The specific form of practice initiated and exemplified by Francis may be said to have four aspects. It is learned by following a normative Rule with specific injunctions; it is actualized in ordinary, everyday actions and situations; it is persistently and consistently applied; and it itself is the proclamation of the Gospel life, and not a means to an end.

All the versions of the Rule Francis wrote[39] have maintained the spirit as expressed in the opening chapter of the version of 1221: "to live in obedience, in chastity and without property, following the teaching and footsteps of our Lord Jesus Christ." "To follow in the footsteps" (*vestigia sequi*) specifies the guiding priority for Francis: to do what one perceives Christ would do. Francis understands that one learns to perceive this by leading a disciplined life.

The particular content and interpretation of regulations may vary through time and place, but the basic Rule for the friars and the Gospel life it enjoins are never without a specified form. The Rule is transmitted through rules, specific forms of practice. Traditionally these have urged such injunctions as obeying the precepts of the guardian or local minister, praying and worshiping together according to the schedule of the local friary, working and sharing prescribed duties, and serving the wider community in specified ways. Francis forbade his own community to accept or deal with money and exhorted his friars to be as strangers and pilgrims in the world, walking to visit various churches, claiming no ownership of a place for themselves, and gathering under the roof of a stranger to be with others.[40] A typical Franciscan house of formation today might regulate the daily practice in a core schedule of praying the psalms together at seven in the morning and again in the evening, celebrating the Eucharist before supper, and joining together for meals and other meetings. Preparations for the liturgy, house duties, and service to the community at large would be required as well and determined individually.

It would be wrong to conclude that the literal execution of such rules exhausts the meaning of the Gospel life; but it would be equally mistaken to suppose that this life is learned and led in the absence of concrete regulation. Once again we find a practiced way of life that is normative in the double sense of prescribing norms of conduct and establishing a universal dimension of a human life that reveals God as all creation does.

For Francis this normative practice pervades everyday life and consistently applies to it. Work is one concrete manifestation of this practice, encouraged in the *Rule* and in Francis's *Testament,* and according to every major biography, exemplified by him.[41] But whether working, praying, traveling, or eating, the practice is to be continuous:

> Nothing must keep us back, nothing separate us from [God], nothing come between us and him. At all times and seasons, in every country and place, every day and all day, we must . . . keep him in our hearts.[42]

In his *Life of St. Francis,* Bonaventure mentions how Francis continuously practiced this nonseparation through prayer:

> Francis strove to keep his spirit in the presence of God, by praying without ceasing . . . whether walking or sitting, inside or outside, working or resting, he was so intent on prayer that he seemed to have dedicated to it not only his heart and body but also all his effort and time.[43]

Finally, everyday practice is seen as the very proclamation of the Gospel life, not as a means to a personal goal of salvation. The friars are to bear witness and give example by their actions, not to work in order to "get something for their efforts."[44] The verse of the *Canticle* which expresses how humanity reveals the light of God, proclaims, "All praise be yours, my Lord, through those who grant pardon for love of you. . . " and not for self-serving ends. For Francis the presence of God is to be found everywhere; he sees the Son of God in all (including the corrupt clergy he alludes to in his *Testament*[45], and thus can declare that to envy one's brother is to envy God, "who is the only source of every good."[46] But it is our practice which makes this presence visible—to ourselves and to others.

The Hermeneutic of Practice in Francis

We conclude our reading of Francis with a brief comment on how Francis himself saw practice as the norm for understanding the word of God, that is, as a hermeneutical principle.

It is said that Francis was first able to hear the Gospel after he had embraced the lepers. Thereupon he left the world (i.e., the *saeculum,* or realm of selfish desire) and embarked upon the life of penance.[47] In turn, his life of strict discipline continued to illumine the word of God for him. Bonaventure writes:

> His wearied application to prayer
> along with his continual exercise of virtue
> had led the man of God
> to such serenity of mind
> that although he had no skill in Sacred Scripture
> acquired through study,
> his intellect,
> illumined by the brilliance of eternal light,
> probed the depths of Scripture
> with remarkable acumen.[48]

According to Bonaventure, practice and scripture stood in a reciprocal relation for Francis: the scholars should study "in order to practice what they have heard and when they have put it into practice themselves . . . propose it to others." Francis himself "received from God an understanding of the Scriptures, since through his perfect imitation of Christ he carried into practice the truth described in them . . . ."[49]

A pragmatic understanding of the Gospel underlies Francis's frequent use of scriptual quotations, particularly in the *Rule of 1221* and the *Admonitions.* Throughout Francis's writings it is clear that the scriptures are not quoted as embellishments to the text, but as practical injunctions to be lived. The performance of the Gospel first grants it meaning and conveys its truth. The same is true for the Rule, which teaches how the friars are to live the Gospel concretely:

> I entreat the friars to grasp the meaning of all that is written in this Rule
> . . . putting it into practice, as they repeat and perform what is written in
> it for our salvation.[50]

A NOTE ON THE MYSTICAL EXPERIENCE

In this paper I have focused on everyday practice in its universal dimension and its normative forms. I have deliberately underplayed the specific experiences of Dōgen and Francis which some would call experiences of mystical union. Yet Dōgen undoubtedly had a profound enlightenment experience while practicing under Ju-ching in China. And he continually alludes to that experience in exhorting the practitioner to "drop body and mind." The identity of realization and practice proclaimed in the *Bendowa* and elsewhere does not necessarily imply that there is no need for actual attainment, for *kenshō* or satori experience.[51] Likewise, it is obvious from the connotations of the very titles *Bendōwa* (Discourse on Negotiating the Way, or on Making Endeavors to Practice the Way) and *Gyōji* (maintaining one's course in "Perpetual Practice") that Dōgen does not lapse into the view, popular during this time in Japan, that since man is inherently enlightened (*hongaku*) there is no need for practice.

Similarly, Francis of Assisi had a powerful conversion experience, went into rapture time and again, and is held to have received the stigmata as evidence of his perfect union with Christ, the object of his contemplation. The biographers relate how Francis's process of conversion culminated one day when, praying alone in the church of San Damiano, he heard the voice of the Lord coming from the cross, was awestricken and fell into a "state of ecstasy" (*mentis excessus*).[52] Francis's contemplative attainment had a deep impact on Bonaventure, who describes how the saint exemplified the stage of perfective union in the eleventh, twelfth, and thirteenth chapters of his *Life of St. Francis*. And Bonaventure sought in Francis's experience the way by which he himself could reach "the state of contemplation"; the miracle of the stigmata was the inspiration for his *Intenerarium Mentis in Deum*.[53]

Yet I believe it to be profoundly significant that neither Dōgen nor Francis spend any time describing their experiences to their disciples. What we repeatedly find in their writings is an insistence on continual practice, and not a psychology of mystical experience. We surely cannot discount the experiential basis of their writings, but we also cannot expect to find in them instruction for repeating their own experiences. Rather, Francis and Dōgen focus their attention on a way to teach others how to find a continuing experience for themselves — and lose themselves in it.

SUMMARY

I have suggested a way of seeing religious practice as the constant performance of a particular activity which does not aim at, but embodies unconditioned truth. Specified and transmitted forms of practice, however historically or culturally conditioned, are indispensable. The reach of a specific practice may extend far beyond the particular posture of rule, but the particular form signifies, or better incorporates the whole.

I have proposed that the notion of practice to be found in the writings of Dōgen Zenji and St. Francis of Assisi (among many possible others) is precisely of this sort: the everyday enactment of something universal. Finally I have suggested that practice in this sense can function to discern the meaning of religious pronouncements and to guide the interpretation of texts.

IMPLICATIONS FOR INTERRELIGIOUS DIALOGUE

This view of practice as a hermeneutical principle naturally raises certain questions and has implications for interreligious dialogue. We might apply our earlier formulation of the hermeneutical circle and ask: Does one need then to practice *zazen* to understand Dōgen? Do I need to take the Franciscan vows in order to appreciate *The Canticle of Brother Sun?* On the other hand, might it not be that one could practice *zazen* all one's life and still not understand Dōgen? Or, perhaps one could give away all possessions, live a celibate life, obey superiors, and still not be practicing the Franciscan Rule. Our initial question, Does one need to practice in order to . . . has too much of an instrumental flavor. Instead, we might inquire into the actual practice of reading certain texts (and not of doing something else first in order to interpret them). This of course is the traditional business of hermeneutics — but with one fundamental difference. In such practice of reading texts we would be continually challenged to "return the text to the world," to incorporate the message as it is continually discovered into one's concrete life. When practice becomes a hermeneutical principle, the text to which it is applied becomes the whole world; application is not a separate moment of interpretation; and appropriation does not follow upon but forms truth.

I have not clarified just what sort of texts are amenable to this practice, and under what circumstances. Certainly some texts give explicit indications that, at least in part, they are to be read as directives and not assertions. Other texts imply they are not so much describing reality as challenging one to realize their descriptions. But perhaps all texts ask to be heard. Obviously these implications need a much more thorough examination than is offered here. But perhaps I may be permitted to mention one possible application to religious dialogue.

Part of the way we transform the chaos of sounds in a foreign language into meaningful utterance is by actually venturing to speak in that language. We learn to hear clearly by practicing speaking. Sometimes a religious tradition appears to speak in foreign language, and we learn to translate by practicing within that tradition. But the problem of understanding does not obtain only between different religious traditions. Within one's own "language," one often faces the task of hearing what a person or a text has to say. If that task is made easier because we have learned to perform proficiently in our "mother tongue," or to practice a tradition as our own, then perhaps our greatest opportunity in interreligious dialogue is this: to teach others how we have come to understand our own tradition and its texts, and to learn from others how they articulate and live theirs.

NOTES

1. For a review of the difficulties of these approaches and a development of their positive aspects, see Heinrich Dumoulin, *Christianity Meets Buddhism* (LaSalle: Open Court, 1974).
2. One of the most thorough examinations using this approach is that of Hugo M. Enomiya (a.k.a. Enomiya Lassalle), *Zen Buddhismus* (Cologne: J. P. Bachem, 1966); see also H. M. Enomiya Lassalle, *Zen Meditations for Christians* (LaSalle: Open Court, 1974).
3. There is not space here even to sketch the broad outlines of the theory-*praxis* distinction from Aristotle on. For detailed explorations of this distinction in the history of Western philosophy, see Nicholas Lobkowicz, *Theory and Practice* (Notre Dame, Ind.: University of Notre Dame Press, 1967); and Richard J. Bertstein, *Praxis and Action* (Philadelphia: University of Pennsylvania Press, 1971), esp. pp. *ix-xii*. For a sample of the way this distinction has found its way into the East, see the pamphlet by Mao Tse-tung, *On Practice* (Peking: Foreign Language Press, 1968).
4. From the "Introduction," by Stephen Ikko Bodian, in *The Way of Everyday Life: Zen Master Dōgen's Genjōkōan with Commentary* by Hakuyu Taizan Maezumi (Los Angeles: Center Publications, 1978).
5. Some frequently used terms and suggested connotations are: *shugyō* (religious practice, discipline); *gyō* (Buddhist practice); *gyōji* (continuous practice, activity unremitting); *bendō* (negotiating or enacting the Way); *sangaku* (going and studying, penetrating study); and *sankyū* (going and scrutinizing, penetrating investigation). All of these occur in Dōgen's essay *Gyōji* and are translated by Francis Cook as "practice." See Cook's *How to Raise an Ox, Zen Practice as Taught in Zen Master Dōgen's Shōbōgenzō* (Los Angeles: Center Publications, 1978). For alternate translations see Hee-Jin Kim, "Existence/Time as the Way of Ascesis—An Analysis of the Basic Structure of Dōgen's Thought," *Eastern Buddhist* 11, no. 2 (October 1978): pp. 43-73. The Japanese texts I have consulted are in *Shōbōgenzō and Shōbōgenzō Zuimonki*, annotated by Minoru Nishio et al. (Tokyo: Iwanami, 1975). All of the above terms contrast with *jissen*, the word for *praxis* as opposed to theory. However, the term *renshu* covers some of the basic connotations I sought in the experiential notion of practice as performance.
6. Dōgen, *Fukanzazengi*, trans. Normal Waddell and Masao Abe, *Eastern Buddhist* 6, no. 2 (October 1973): p. 121f.
7. Dōgen, *Bendōwa*, trans. Waddell and Abe, *Eastern Buddhist* 4, no. 1 (May 1971): pp. 133, 137, 143.
8. Dōgen, *Fukanzazengi*, p. 122, and *Bendōwa*, p. 143. The "four attitudes" are walking, standing, sitting, and lying; the six *pāramitās* or "perfections" are: charity, morality, patience, vigor, meditation, and wisdom; the "three learnings" are *sīla* (morality), *samādhi* (meditation), and prajña (wisdom).
9. Dōgen, *Fukanzazengi*, p. 123.
10. Dōgen, *Bendōwa*, pp. 129, 144. See also the opening of *Gyōji*: "Arousing the thought of enlightenment, practice, bodhi, and nirvana have not the slightest break, but are continuous practice . . . *[gyōji]* which goes on forever" (trans. Cook, *How to Raise an Ox*, p. 175).
11. Cf. Dōgen, *Bendōwa*, p. 130, no. 21.
12. For a development of this idea, see Keiji Nishitani, "Emptiness and History," *Eastern Buddhist* 12, no. 1 (May 1979): 67.
13. Dōgen, *Bendōwa*, p. 136.
14. Dōgen, *Sansuikyō*, in Nishio et al., *Shōbōgenzō and Shōbōgenzō Zuimonki*, p. 306.
15. "Keisei Sanshoku" (The Sounds of Valley Streams, the Forms of the Mountains), in Cook, *How to Raise an Ox*, p.112.

16. Dōgen, *Gyōji*, p. 175 (translation slightly modified). Kim, "Existence/Time," pp. 59ff, exposes the relationship between *gyōji* (activity remitting) and *engi* (dependent origination).

17. Dōgen, *Gyōji*, p. 198.

18. Maezumi, *Dōgen's Genjōkōan*, no page.

19. Dōgen, *Fukanzazengi*, introduction, p. 117. Waddell and Abe also note that Dōgen apparently shifted his own emphasis in his revision of the text (c. 1243): ". . . in the later version the idea of *dhyāna* or *samādhi* as a means to enlightenment has totally disappeared, and in its place there is a corresponding accentuation of the oneness of practice and realization" (p. 118f).

20. Ibid., p. 122.

21. "The King of Samādhis Samādhi. *Dōgen's Shōbōgenzō Sammai O Zammai*," trans. Waddell and Abe, *Eastern Buddhist* 7, no. 2 (May 1974): pp. 119f.

22. Dōgen, "Emptiness and Time," trans. Jan van Bragt, *Eastern Buddhist* 10, no. 2 (October 1977): p. 9 (translation slightly modified. Cf. the original version, Keiji Nishitani, *Shūkyō to wa Nanika?* [Tokyo: Sōbunsha, 1961], p. 220).

23. Dōgen, *Gyōji*, p. 177.

24. Ibid., p. 177f, 183, 194.

25. Dōgen, *Kajō*, in Cook, *How to Raise an Ox*, pp. 205ff.

26. "The Life of St. Francis," in *Bonaventure*, trans. Ewert Cousins (New York: Paulist Press, 1978), p. 179; see also pp. 203, 298.

27. *St. Francis of Assisi Omnibus of Sources*, ed. Marion A. Habig (Chicago: Franciscan Herald Press, 1973), p. 688. The original language versions of the writings are found in *Opuscula Sancti Patris Francisci Assisiensis*, ed. Caientanus Esser, O.F.M. (Rome, Grottaferrata: Collegii S. Bonaventurae Ad Claras Aquas, 1978).

28. Cf. Regis Armstrong, "The Spiritual Theology of the 'Legenda Major' of Saint Bonaventure" (Ph.D. diss., Fordham University, 1978), p. 10.

29. The friars are expected to fast and to shun expensive clothing, but not to wear abrasive cord under their tunics, to mix ashes with any cooked food, or to sleep sitting up, as Francis is said to have often done. See, for example, *Bonaventure*, pp. 190, 218f.

30. *Omnibus of Sources*, p. 83. Cf. Matt.5.39-42. The *Admonitions* were compiled after the death of Francis, but are considered authentic.

31. Ibid., p. 44, 52.

32. Ibid., p. 133f: "Praises of the Virtues." See also *Bonaventure*: "Because [the friars] possessed nothing that belonged to the world, they were attached to nothing and feared to lose nothing" (p. 211).

33. Ibid., p. 80: *Admonitions* 3; p. 61: *Rule of 1223*, Chap. 6.

34. Ibid., p. 133: "Praises of the Virtues."

35. Cf. Ibid., p. 128.

36. Cf. Ibid., p. 130, n. 1. Ewert Cousins reads this differently and translates *per* as "for," e.g., "Praised be you, my Lord, for Brother Wind." Cf. *Bonaventure*, pp. 27f. Generally, however, Cousins is more accurate, translating from the Umbrian original, whereas the *Omnibus of Sources* appears to translate from a later Latin version. See the *Opuscula Sancti Patris Francisci Assisiensis*, pp. 84-88, for both versions.

37. This reading would also seem to contradict Bonaventure's own reading of the *Canticle*: "and like the prophet David, [Francis] sweetly exhorted them [all creatures] to praise the Lord" (*Bonaventure*, p. 263). But perhaps we may say that Francis exhorted them to be no other than what they already were.

38. See the *Omnibus of Sources*, pp. 1027ff (secs. 49-51 of the *Legend of Perugia*) for such incidents. Again, this reading contrasts with the proclamation in the same source that "every creature says . . . 'God has created me for you, O man' " and that man should

therefore praise God for all creatures. Cf. p. 1029 and no. 92, p. 1096. I believe this view of mankind's domination is inconsistent with Francis's own writings and even with the tenor of the stories related in this source. My interpretation finds support in Eloi Leclerc, *Le cantique des creatures ou les symboles de l'union* (Le Signe/Fayard, 1970).

39. A short, simple Rule (no longer extant) was composed in 1209 and approved orally by the Papal See; this was gradually expanded over the next decade as the Order grew and a revised version was made in 1221; two years later it was replaced by the papally approved *Rule of 1223* (the *Regula Bullata*), which was a briefer and legally more precise expression. See *Omnibus of Sources*, pp. 28-31.

40. See the *Testament*, p. 68, and the *Rule of 1223*, p. 61 in the *Omnibus of Sources*. I am grateful to Steven McMichael and Wayne Hellman, O.F.M., for pointing out to me the pilgrim practice of Francis and for many other insights into the Franciscan life.

41. See for example, the *Rule of 1221*, chap. 7, in ibid., pp. 37f.

42. *Rule of 1221*, chap. 23, in ibid., p. 52.

43. *Bonaventure*, pp. 272f; see also p. 303.

44. Cf. the *Rule of 1221*, chap. 16, p. 43, and the *Testament*, p. 68, in the *Omnibus of Sources*.

45. Ibid., p. 67.

46. *Admonitions* 8, in ibid., p. 82.

47. *Testament*, in ibid., p. 67.

48. *Bonaventure*, p. 280. See also Armstrong, "Spiritual Theology," pp. 182f.

49. Ibid., p. 281.

50. *Rule of 1221*, in *Omnibus of Sources*, 52f.

51. Cf. Kōun Yamada Rōshi, "Dōgen Zenji and Enlightenment," in *On Zen Practice II* (Los Angeles: Center Publications, 1977), p. 7-12.

52. Cf. *Bonaventure*, p. 191.

53. Ibid., pp. 19f.

The Canticle of Brother Sun

Most high omnipotent good Lord
Yours are the praises, the glory, the honor and all blessing.
To you alone, Most High, do they belong,
And no man is worthy to mention you.

Praised be you, my Lord, with all your creatures,
Especially Sir Brother Sun,
Who makes the day and through whom you give us light.
And he is beautiful and radiant with great splendor,
And bears the signification of you, Most High One.

Praise be you, my Lord, through Sister Moon and the stars,
You have formed them in heaven clear and precious and beautiful.

Praised be you, my Lord, through Brother Wind,
And for the air—cloudy and serene—and every kind of weather,
By which you give sustenance to your creatures.

Praised be you, my Lord, through Sister Water,
Which is very useful and humble and precious and chaste.

Praised be you, my Lord, through Brother Fire,
By whom you light the night,
And he is beautiful and jocund and robust and strong.

Praised be you, my Lord through our sister Mother Earth,
Who sustains and governs us,
And produces various fruits with colored flowers and herbs.

All praise be yours, my Lord, through those who grant pardon
For love of you; through those who endure
Sickness and trial.

Happy those who endure in peace,
By you, Most High, they will be crowned.

All praise be yours, my Lord, through Sister Death,
From whose embrace no mortal can escape.

Woe to those who die in mortal sin!
Happy those She finds doing your will!
The second death can do no harm to them.

Praise and bless my Lord, and give him thanks,
And serve him with great humility.*

*English translation by Matthew J. O'Connell, from Eloi Leclerc, *The Canticle of Creatures: Symbols of Union* (Chicago: Franciscan Herald Press, 1977), pp. *xvii-xviii*. Reprinted by permission.

PART II

PROPOSALS FOR UNDERSTANDING
THE NATURE OF DIALOGUE

CHAPTER 4

Interfaith Dialogue as a Source of Buddhist-Christian Creative Transformation

Paul O. Ingram

If I had but little knowledge
I should, in walking on a broad way,
Fear getting off the road,
Broad ways are extremely even
But people are fond of by-paths.
Tao Te Ching, 53

Whatever else might be said about the nature of human existence, it seems to be empirically evident that human beings possess a profound need to believe that the truth she or he apprehends is rooted in, and thereby corresponds to, the structures of the universe as "they really are." For were this not so, could any of the truths which persons believe motivate, guide, and give understanding and perhaps even pleasure to lived experience be really important? Yet how can this be so when human beings have always experienced, apprehended, and propositionally formulated truth so differently in spite of sharing the same planet? Primal mankind, enveloped in limited geographical dwelling spaces and surrounded by tribal mythology, did not have to struggle with this issue to any significant degree. At this level of human experience, such questions remain largely isolated in mankind's prereflective consciousness. But even contemporary "civilized" human beings have largely been spared the pain of explicitly wrestling with this problem, for until very recently the civilizations of the world have also been self-contained. It is we who are what C.G. Jung called "modern" who experience this problem most accurately—the problem of discovering a unified sense of meaning within the context of religious and secular pluralism. For the modern person is by no means the average man. He is rather the man who stands upon a peak, or at the very edge of the world, the abyss of the future before him, above him the heavens and below him the whole of mankind with a history that disappears in the primal mists. The modern man, or let us say, the man of the immediate present — is rarely met with . . . . Since to be wholly in the present means to be fully conscious of one's existence as a man, it requires the most intensive and extensive consciousness. It must be clearly understood that the mere fact of living in the present does not make a man modern . . . . He alone is modern who is fully conscious of the present.[1]

Being modern, then, should not be equated with merely being contemporary. "Modernity" is a frame of mind, a psychological attitude, a mind-set which radically and personally separates a person from the normally accepted, conventional traditions and beliefs of his or her culture. The modern person existentially stands on the fringes of his culture's values and conventions, and in so doing is *in* but not *of* the traditional world view of his culture. In this sense, modern persons have always existed, the classical examples perhaps being Jesus, the Buddha, Mohammed, Marx, Gandhi, or Martin Luther King, Jr.

The psychological dynamics of modernity as a mind-set noted by Jung over forty years ago have also been observed more concretely and more recently by Peter L. Berger in terms of the sociology of knowledge. Because contemporary modernity is situated within the context of immense technological power and the impersonal forces of secularization, at least in Western culture and those non-Western cultures now undergoing the process of modernization, today the modern situation is marked by a nearly inconceivable expansion of the areas of human life open to choice. For this reason modern consciousness has a powerfully relativizing effect on all world views because modernity pluralizes both institutions and world views (plausability structures). Consequently, in a way undreamed of in premodern cultures and societies, the contemporary modern person dwells within a world of choices on all levels of his or her life, ranging from what to eat and wear, to what world view to believe among several competing world views. The result is that the contemporary modern person is one whose understanding of himself and the world he must inhabit is radically relativized by the experience of having to choose between not only the competing gadgets of technology but, more profoundly, between different religious, secular, and social systems and beliefs, none of which can claim a monopoly on the "truth." Of course, not everyone experiences the relativism and pluralism of contemporary modern existence as a problem, which is another way of saying, in agreement with Jung and perhaps Berger, that modern persons are always in the cognitive minority. Most persons either ignore or are unaware of the areas of choice available to them in today's world of secular and religious pluralism. Therefore they do not choose, but merely accept what the traditions of a culture will tolerate and/or allow. But the modern person experiences relativity and the need to choose as fundamental to human growth and development, and for this individual religious and secular pluralism becomes an issue of ultimate importance.[2]

The problem has many interrelated dimensions. Most generally, and perhaps most fundamentally, it is a metaphysical and epistemological issue, for the question involves the nature of knowledge as such and how one can know that he or she possesses knowledge that as corresponds to reality—"the way things really are." It is at this level that the theological issues posed by modern religious and secular pluralism are encountered, for it is here that we are confronted most directly with different and often competing visions of reality. Less generally, the question involves how it is possible to determine whether or not *any* of our specific beliefs in regard to the more specialized concerns of human knowledge—scientific, social, political, aesthetic, historical, or religious—possess any validity. This form of the problem is, of course, rooted in its most general metaphysical-epistemological dimension.

It is within this context that I hope to demonstrate the thesis of this essay, namely, that dialogue between the religious traditions of the world is the most appropriate means of understanding and confronting the theological and philosophical issues posed by the facts of modern religious (and secular) pluralism. As such, interfaith dialogue is the most important means of achieving religious renewal that we possess at a time when the world's religious traditions are everywhere challenged by the various secular, economic, political, and technological ideologies which dominate most persons' lives in our present "cosmic epoch."

Consequently, the following will focus upon how process theologians have pursued Buddhist-Christian dialogue as a source of Buddhist-Christian renewal. By so doing, I hope not only to illustrate my general thesis in a concrete way, but also to offer some suggestions concerning the problems and possible directions of continuing Buddhist-Christian dialogue encounter. To accomplish this it will first be necessary to clarify the conceptual framework which informs my reflections as well as what I mean by "dialogue" and "creative transformation."

I

A conceptual framework is, among other things, a means by which a disciplined scholar in any field of inquiry, in my case history of religions, interprets the nature and meaning of whatever he is investigating. As such, in the words of the philosopher-scientist Michael Polanyi, ". . . the power of our conceptions lies in identifying new instances of certain things that we know. The function of our conceptual framework is akin to our perceptive framework which enables us to recognize ever-new things as satisfying to them."[3] Among other things, this means that any conceptual framework is grounded, tacitly and explicitly, in a wider philosophical vision of reality. My own particular conceptual framework has been informed by that tradition of process thought which has its roots in the philosophical vision of Alfred North Whitehead. While it is not necessary or possible to spell out the specific details of Whitehead's system, a consideration of the meaning of "process" will perhaps clarify what is to follow.

Process philosophy affirms that process is fundamental to existence. But it does not assert that everything is in process, for that would mean that even the fact that things and events are in process is subject to change. There are unchanging principles as well as unchanging, but abstract, forms of process. But anything which is not a process is an abstraction, not a full-fledged actuality. In other words, to be *actual* is to be *in* process.

Whitehead's rather detailed and technical account of the structures of process had its own distinctive character. The temporal process, he affirmed, is a "transition" from one "actual entity" or "actual occasion" to another. An actual entity is a momentary experiential event which immediately perishes upon coming into existence, a state he called "objective immortality." However, perished actualities mark the transition to succeeding actualities, for they become part of the total past which becoming actual entities incorporate into themselves (through positive and negative, physical and mental, and hybrid "prehensions") in their own process of reaching "satisfaction" or completeness. At the moment of their completeness *they* become objectively immortal, perish, and become elements of future becoming actual entities, *ad nauseam,* or in Whitehead's words, "till the crack of doom." In short, true "individuals" are momentary experiences, and the implication is that what we normally call individuals, for instance, particular things, persons, or the sorts of things we perceive as remaining self-identical through time, are not true individuals but "societies" of continually becoming actual entities, including personal human existence (which Whitehead categorized as a "serially ordered society" or occasions of experience).[4]

Besides the process of transition from occasion to occasion which constitutes temporality, Whitehead wrote about another type of process. The real actual entities or occasions which constitute the temporal process are themselves processes of their own momentary becoming. Whitehead called this becoming "concrescence," which means becoming concrete. In other words, the individual actual entities which comprise the world of things and events (societies of actual entities) are themselves dynamic acts of concrescence.[5]

The details of Whitehead's analysis of these processes are, of course, much more technical and complex than I have outlined. But for the purpose of this essay, it is only necessary to note that Whitehead was envisioning a universe in which all the entities which constitute it are what they are because of their interrelation and interdependency. In other words, the universe is not a collection of "pill-like atoms," insulated substance, and isolated minds. Whitehead's vision of reality was his interpretation of the picture of the universe emerging within the natural sciences. That is, he thought of all organizations—biological, social, and even of space-time—as open systems of interdependent relations which are interpenetrated by other systems. In short, we do not live in and experience an amorphous, static universe, but a dynamic universe of open forms and interrelated possibilities. As the natural sciences have been increasingly demonstrating since Einstein, whose work and conclusions greatly influenced Whitehead, the principle of relativity (in the sense of interdependently relational) is at the heart of things.[6]

If this is indeed the case, then the fact of religious pluralism should be thought of as an element of our general metaphysical situation. Consequently, human beings have perceived and understood the Sacred, however it is named, from culturally, biologically, and historically conditioned standpoints, as everything must be perceived and understood. We "see through a glass darkly" and we will continue to do so. And yet human beings will also continue to believe that what has been encountered and apprehended truly corresponds to the "way things really are" apart from the limitations of standpoint and frame of reference. It is here that we are confronted with the epistemological problem of the relativity of belief, not just in terms of our religious faith and beliefs, but in terms of all our beliefs. In light of this, John Cobb has formulated a number of highly suggestive propositions concerning the relativity of belief which might prevent this relativity from becoming debilitating.[7]

First, there can be no standpoint from which to think other than the radically particular standpoint that is oneself here and now. Every aspect of this particular here-now momentary standpoint is interdependent and interrelated with, and therefore relative to, every other here-now standpoint, so that no standpoint and consequently no belief, is free from the influences of biology, biography, culture, and history. At the same time, none of these influences is unaffected by the rational, critical, and creative activity that may or may not occur in the here-now standpoint we occupy.

Secondly, our very awareness of this conditionedness can only be partial since we ourselves are participants in it. As Cobb has noted about this aspect of universal relativity:

> Sociologists of knowledge rarely reflect deeply on the sociology of the
> sociology of knowledge. Those who explain belief psychologically rarely

reflect deeply on the psychoanalytic explanation of their psychoanalytic explanations. Still more rarely do sociologists of knowledge take adequate account of the psychoanalytic explanation of the sociology of knowlege, or psychoanalysts sufficiently consider the sociological explanation of psychoanalytic activity.[8]

The point is that even if these and many other specific limitations are overcome, our knowledge in any field of inquiry will always remain partial, since any one of these reflexive explanatory methodologies and points of view can in principle be pursued endlessly.

Thirdly, analysis of the relativity of beliefs, including this analysis, is itself relative, as is the judgment that it is relative. This may indeed be a vicious regress, but it is a regress to which finitude condemns us. Once more, the charge that a relativist must assert relativity as a "hidden absolute" is false, for the relativist can also recognize the relativity of relativism.

Finally, the relativity of the here-now moment presupposes that there have been, are, and will be other here-now moments. Relativism presupposes realism, meaning that the objects of our knowledge are not merely mind-dependent, but are independently, as well as interdependently, existing entities. It is our belief *about* these entities that is relative to the particular here-now standpoint we occupy.[9] The alternative is "solipsism of the present moment," which is a way of absolutizing the present here-now moment as all there is. But as a realist, I cannot absolutize even the present here-now moment. Against solipsism, I am a convinced realist who recognizes that this conviction is also relative.

There are several important implications of this view of the relativism of belief bearing on the subject of interfaith dialogue which require clarification. First, the relativity of belief does not make it unimportant. Some beliefs are, in fact, trivial, and there are consequently no reasons to attend them. But to recognize this also implies that trivial beliefs can be distinguished from important beliefs. For this reason, the relativity of our beliefs is compatible with concern about whether our beliefs adequately and clearly approximate reality.

Secondly, the relativity of belief does not make it false. It is the opposite that is most likely, for it is doubtful that we are capable of believing totally false propositions. Even the distorted beliefs of insane persons probably possess degrees of truth. The point is that in all likelihood the important beliefs that have compelled human beings most profoundly embody varying degrees of positive relation to reality. Universal relativity entails that this should be the case.

Thirdly, the relativity of belief is compatible with decisive action. There is always tension between cognitive uncertainty and the either/or of action. But since nonaction is a form of action, as the *Bhagavad Gita* tells us, there is no escape from the necessity to act. Once more, it is foolish to contrast this situation with some other conceived condition and then lament its absence. Relativity implies constant readiness to alter the course of action as beliefs are reformed. But there are no reasons for not decisively acting as such.

Finally, the encounter with beliefs other than our own is an opportunity for reformation. Since beliefs, religious or otherwise, are never merely true or false, but more or less adequate, clear, and free from distortion, the encounter between divergent beliefs should not be viewed as an either/or confrontation, but as an occasion to achieve clearer, more adequate, and less distorted beliefs. It is here that dialogue between different systems of religious beliefs becomes a source of renewal. Within the context of universal relativity, dialogue is not only the "key to understanding"[10] and increasing tolerance of religious traditions other than our own, it is itself a source of gaining knowledge and new insight, perhaps the main source of knowledge available to us in our present "cosmic epoch."

The question is, therefore, how one should conceive of the structure and goal of interfaith dialogue. Here, the following observation of the Roman Catholic theologian John S. Dunne becomes pertinent in a rather poetic way:

> The Holy man of our time, it seems, is not a figure like Gotama or Jesus or Mohammed, or a man who would found a world religion, but a figure like Gandhi; a man who passes over by sympathetic understanding from his own religion to other religions and comes back again with new insight to his own. Passing over and coming back, it seems, is the spiritual adventure of our time.[11]

According to Dunne, the structure of interfaith dialogue, or of any dialogue for that matter, involves two movements: "passing over" and "returning." It is an adventure which begins with a departure from the conditioned homeland of one's own religious standpoint, and ends up in the re-conditioned home of one's own faith. It is, in Dunne's words, an "odyssey." But much depends upon the religious perspective where the odyssey begins and ends. The Christian will begin and end with Christianity, a Muslim with Islam, a Buddhist with Buddhism. But more deeply understood, the starting point of dialogue as "passing over" is one's own life in its totality, and the ending point is one's own life in its totality, but changed from what it was before the dialogue began. This is so because in dialogue we do not pass over into abstract entities or things called religions, for religions are not things.[12] Rather, in dialogue we pass over to the lives of persons whose religious standpoints as visions of the Sacred are other than our own, appropriate what we can, and return to our own living standpoints enriched and wiser. We thereby renew or creatively transform our own religious standpoints, because the standpoint of our lives before dialogue is not the same during and after dialogue. And because the whole point of interfaith dialogue, or of any sort of dialogue, is renewal in the sense of creative transformation (otherwise why engage in dialogue at all?), there are at least four conditions which must be present before passing over into another person's religious standpoint can occur and creative transformation result.[13]

First, there must be no ulterior motive of any kind instigating the dialogue. To approach another person's religious standpoint in this way can provide only limited results, usually more negative than positive. For example, to study Buddhist faith merely with the intention of comparing it with Christian faith in order to increase a Christian's awareness of his faith will of necessity undermine the integrity of Buddhist faith. Likewise, to study Buddhist faith with the intention of showing the superiority of Christian faith undermines the integrity of Christian faith. This implies, secondly, being engaged by the faith of persons dwelling in religious standpoints other than our own. Nothing can emerge out of dialogue unless our perspectives have been genuinely challenged, tested, and stretched by the faith of our dialogical partner. On the other hand, when we approach persons of other religious standpoints as advocates, or if we believe that our own particular formulation of religious belief is the only correct one or the most valid one, then genuine dialogue is replaced by a series of monologues. Some form of religious imperialism is the usual result.

Thirdly, interfaith dialogue demands that we possess an adequate, critical, and articulate understanding of our own religious standpoint. Part of the willingness to be engaged by others' claims of truth involves willingness to be engaged by the claims of truth of our own faith. For without a point of view, dialogue with others becomes a formless sharing of ideas in which one person states what he believes and the other reciprocates in kind, with nothing worthwhile being achieved. On the other hand, a person who understands and is open to the truth-claims of his own religious standpoint is more apt to be open to the truth-claims of other perspectives, and is thereby better able to pass over to these claims and appropriate what he can into his own transformed standpoint when he returns to it. This is possible precisely because he has made his own ultimate commitments and has experienced the significance, the "music," of his own religious standpoint. As a friend can understand the experience of love or suffering of another person because of his own experiences of these same realities, so the religious person is able to experience the meaning of the faith of a friend because of his own faith perspective.

Finally, truth must be explicitly understood as relational in structure. This is especially necessary for those of us who find ourselves in varying degrees informed by a Christian perspective. The Christian understanding of God's involvement in human history as witness to by the Bible has more often than not been reduced to a set of unchanging doctrinal propositions which served the needs of the institutional Church and its bureaucrats more than Christian persons. The truth which cannot be named became circumscribed by the creeds and confessional statements of the Church and by the limited understanding and good will of individual Christians. But this is, in fact, contrary to the Biblical tradition, and is a Christian form of *maya*, delusion. Truth can have no institutional or confessional boundaries, so that the Christian in dialogue can share his or her faith or ultimate concerns without having to see the faith of his or her, for example, Buddhist colleagues as inferior or less true. It is the contrary that is most likely the case. In dialogue, it becomes possible for the Christian to find in the perfection of the faith of another a challenge to his or her own self-awareness as a religious person. In short, interfaith dialogue becomes possible and meaningful when it grows out of our common humanity as persons whose sense of what it means to be human finds expression through our various religious perspectives as embodiments of different but real encounters with the Sacred. Dialogue does not occur and truth is not found when we relate to each other merely through such abstract labels as Christian, Buddhist, Hindu, or Muslim.

II

The most persistent and coherent Western attempt to engage in interfaith dialogue of the sort I have described is to be found in process theology, the most important figure of which is John B. Cobb. The motivating factor of process theology's concern for interfaith dialogue is its conviction that Christianity needs to continually submit itself to creative transformation by assimilating not only new aspects of Western culture, but to open itself to still more radical transformation through dialogue with the non-Christian Ways. This task is being carried out individually with each of the great Ways, but dialogical encounter with Buddhism has been especially fruitful. There is good reason for this. Whitehead's thought, which has its origins within the specifically Western intellectual tradition and which was in many important ways informed by the Christian religious perspective despite that Whitehead himself was not a "confessing Christian," contains a special congeniality with some forms of Asian philosophy and religion and especially with Buddhism.[14] The result is that process theologians have appropriated Whitehead's philosophical categories as a hermeneutical tool by which to translate Buddhist insights into Christian faith, thus creatively transforming the Christian Way.

At the same time, process theologians have appropriated Whitehead's categories as a hermeneutical device whereby Christian insights can be translated into language more easily grasped by Buddhists. The hope is that critical Buddhist understanding of Christian faith will be fostered and Buddhist faith might be creatively transformed through incorporating into itself whatever insights it can from Christian faith. In short, the dialogue between process theology and Buddhism has been essentially a very critical and analytical process of passing over and returning. Within this context, Buddhist-Christian discussion and encounter has involved many interrelated themes, but the most difficult and perhaps most controversial involves the question of God. Therefore, the remainder of this discussion will focus on this issue, after which I will conclude with what I believe to be several important observations.

One of the important results of process theology's encounter with Buddhism has been that it has forced process theologians to more clearly apprehend the extent to which Whitehead's philosophy was influenced by specifically Christian interests. That is, when a Buddhist analyzes human experience in a distinctively Buddhist way, informed as it is through the discipline of meditation and unencumbered by Whiteheadian categories, different results are obtained. As Cobb explains it:

> The two sets of results need not be contradictory. Everything the Buddhist finds may be there to be found, and everything Whitehead finds may be there to be found. For this reason the encounter with Buddhism can lead to a creative transformation of process theology that does not deny its insights but incorporates them into a larger whole.[15]

The issue centers on the fact that Buddhist thought is usually quite negative about notions of God. This negativity is bound up with Buddhism's traditional rejection of notions of personal, separate, substantial selfhood. For this reason, Buddhist thought is normally unconcerned with those features of human experience that lead Christians (as well as Jews and Muslims) to place emphasis upon purpose, accountability, qualitative novelty, and gradations of value as issues of primary importance.[16] However, there are also degrees of difference in this regard between Buddhist schools. For example, the Pure Land tradition of Shinran (Jōdo Shinshu) places great importance on just these questions, while at the same time not concerning itself with the question of God.[17] Even so, Buddhists are not usually led by their experience to belief either in Whitehead's God or any of the traditional Christian affirmations of God.

At the same time, Cobb and others also believe that it would be an over-statement to say that Buddhism denies the existence of God in any absolute way, because by "God" Buddhism normally understands either an ultimate ground of being or substance underlying and relativizing the flux of events and things, or a static substantial essence transcending the flux of concrete space-time. However, process theologians have, following Whitehead, denied the existence of God in these two senses as well.

In place of speaking of God as an ultimate ground of being, Whitehead spoke of "creativity" as categorically ultimate.

> Creativity is the universal of universals characterizing ultimate matters
> of fact. It is that ultimate principle by which the many, which are the
> universe disjunctively, become the one actual occasion, which is the uni-
> verse conjunctively. It lies in the nature of things that the many enter
> into complex unity.[18]

But because creativity was also part of Whitehead's categorical scheme through which he understood and appropriated Einstein's theory of relativity, creativity did not have for him an existence or actuality apart from concrete actual occasions of experience. That is, creativity has no existence in itself, and is to be found only in actual instances of the "many becoming one and increased by one." In this sense, creativity is much like the Buddhist notion of "dependent co-origination" *(pratitya-samutpada)*.

Process theology's reflections on God have faithfully followed Whitehead at this point. Instead of a substantial, static being underlying or transcending the flux of temporal process, God is spoken of as a formative element, indeed the chief example, of this flux. So that while it is true that Whitehead spoke of a "primordial nature" of God (God's envisagement of the entire multiplici-ty of "eternal objects" or "pure possibilities"), this is an abstraction from the actual process of what God is in his "consequent nature" (the concrete exis-tence of God that includes not only his conceptual envisagement or "prehension" of all "eternal objects," but also his physical prehensions of every concrete actual occasion).

It is for these reasons that Cobb and other process theologians who have followed his lead have concluded that since the questions to which God is the answer in Christian faith are not normally Buddhist questions, White-head's God is not to be explicitly found in Buddhism. Tacitly, however, the question may be open because of the presence of entities called bodhisattvas which play somewhat analogous cosmological and religious functions in Mahayana Buddhist teaching and practice. Accordingly, process theology has affirmed that the question of a nonsubstantial divine reality remains a metaphysically open possibility for Buddhism. Whether or not Buddhism can affirm this possibility remains problematic.

Conversation with Buddhist thinkers has also led process theologians to reflect more fully on the question of how adequately they have conceived the meaning of the nonsubstantial character of God, and on this point process thought has been profoundly illumined by what it has appropriated from Buddhist thought and experience. For example, the Mahāyāna Buddhist doctrine of emptiness (śūnyatā) has played an important role in this regard. The question is, what does Buddhism mean when it teaches that an event, for example, a moment of human experience, is empty? According to Cobb's interpretation, which in fact is a very accurate interpretation of the Buddhist meanings involved, it means first of all that the experience is empty of

substance.[19] That is, there is no underlying self or "I" that remains self-identical through time and which unites the separate moments of experience. Thus, there is no separate subject, even in a single moment, to which the experience "belongs." There is only a momentary event or happening. Secondly, the experience lacks all possession, for that which constitutes it does not belong to it, for the constituent elements of the experience, in Buddhist language its *dharmas,* are a coming together of what is other than the experience. Thirdly, the experience is empty of form because it does not possess a form which it imposes on what constitutes it. Rather, the form is the result of what constitutes it. Finally, the experience is empty of being. There is not, in addition to the coming together of the constituting elements of an experience, something else which is the being of the new experience. Instead, the constituting elements *become* the new experience, this becoming *is* the experience. At the same time, the constituting elements do not have being either, for they are also empty in the same way. The resulting conclusion that Buddhists draw is that, because there is no being, there are "no-things." There is only emptiness.

The ideal for some schools of Mahāyāna Buddhism is therefore to experience, through the practice of meditation, the self as empty or void of self-definition and to allow whatever is to fill it. The aim is to achieve maximum fullness by imposing no principle of selection. Or in Whiteheadian language, the individual actual occasion is to meditatively realize itself as a void which imposes nothing on the many that constitute it as one and increases the many by one.

Cobb finds remarkable affinities between Whitehead's account of the consequent nature of God and the Buddhist view of emptiness. Because the dominant thrust of God's consequent nature (God in his relation to the temporal process in its entirety) is his aim at the realization of all possibilities

in their proper season, God imposes no principle of selection upon his consequent nature. As Whitehead expressed it:

> Thus the consequent nature of God is composed of a multiplicity of ele-
> ments with individual self-realization. It is just as much a multiplicity as
> it is a unity; it is just as much an immediate fact as it is an unresting ad-
> vance beyond itself.[20]

Or as Cobb has interpreted Whitehead on the point:

> That is, God is 'empty' of 'self ' insofar as 'self ' is understood as an es-
> sence that can be preserved only by excluding 'other' things, or at least
> not allowing them to be received as they are.[21]

And what applies to God's consequent nature applies to all actual entities in
their becoming, since God, for Whitehead, was not an exception to the
principles of process and creativity that constitute the becoming of all actual
entities. Indeed God is the chief example of these principles.

Conceiving God in this way in dialogue with Buddhism has led to a creative transformation of process theology that is not foreign to Christian faith.
And while the idea of God is not a central concern in Buddhist faith, a Whiteheadian notion of God is not foreign to Buddhist faith and experience.
Buddhist appropriation of such a notion of God, in a way that does not erode
the basic religious integrity of Buddhist tradition, can lead to its creative
transformation as well. But the specific directions and outcome of such a dialogical process cannot be foretold since process thought is still in process.
But in all probability, the result will not be some final and complete
synthesis, but only the emergence of new processes of creative
transformation.

III

I do not wish to conclude with an evaluation of the strengths, the
weaknesses, or the specific conclusions process theologians have drawn about
Buddhism in their dialogical encounter, nor do I wish to critique the specific
ways in which process thought has creatively transformed Christian faith.
While I find myself generally within the process theological camp, I am not a
camp follower. I only wish to make a few observations concerning the process
of dialogue itself in order to point out some future possibilities. At the same

time, I want to point out what I believe to be real, but not insoluble, problem areas.

First of all, if Whitehead's interpretation of existence adequately corresponds, as I believe it does, to the picture of the universe now emerging within the natural sciences — "things" are what they are because of how they have interrelated with and interpenetrated every other thing in the universe at a particular moment of space-time — then "creative transformation" is a process that is rooted within the very structure of nature itself. That is, it is the way the universe operates regardless of human knowledge or cooperation. But if this process is understood, acknowledged, and cooperated with, then human imagination and the freedom to structure human existence around centers of meaning can be transformed by a lucidity of vision and a new openness to what we see. In other words, creative transformation is that process around which human existence is best organized. Interfaith dialogue is perhaps the most important means of realizing and appropriating this process because it can provide a center of human unity within which the many centers of meaning and existence that have grasped the human imagination can be appreciated, encouraged, appropriated and integrated. In short, as process theology demonstrated more radically than any other form of Christian thought, openness to the other great religious Ways of mankind can lead to a deepening of Christian existence and faith. But it can also lead to a deepening of Buddhist, Confucian, Hindu, Jewish, or Muslim faith as well. It is this sort of "renewal" we should be dialogically seeking and which I have called "creative transformation."

My second observation is a negative one. The goal of interfaith dialogue is emphatically not that of trying to discover which insights and practices of the different religious traditions of mankind can be mixed together in order to create a new religious way more universal than any of the particular historical religious traditions. The Hindu sage Rāmakrishna notwithstanding, the historical evidence suggests that all paths do not lead to the same summit. Thinking otherwise is playing fast and loose with the facts and is a rather subtle form of religious imperialism. After all, it is very easy to affirm the unity of all religions if all religious teachings and practices look like your own, as they apparently did to Rāmakrishna, who perceived them as forms of his own brand of Advaita Vedānta. The point is that "creative transformation" is likely to occur only if interfaith dialogue is carried out in a critical spirit that recognizes both the differences and the similarities in the religious Ways of humanity. Uncritical syncretism should be avoided, for not all religious ideas and practices are of equal value, as the Old Testament prophets have warned us. Some are in fact quite destructive, as the terrible event that occurred with the People's church in Jonestown so tragically demonstrated. Just because something is religious does not make it worth appropriating.

Thirdly, as matters now stand, Buddhist-Christian dialogue at the level of philosophy and doctrine appears to be one-sided. At least in Japan, the initiative in interfaith dialogue has almost completely come from the Christian side,[22] in spite of the fact that Buddhists are usually pictured as extremely open and tolerant in their attitudes toward other religious faiths. But the fact is that Buddhist-Christian dialogue is almost a Christian monologue. It is true that there exist Buddhist study centers which occasionally arrange lectures and discussions with Christian thinkers, and that there are important circles of interest in studying and learning from Christianity. But apart from the Eastern Buddhist Society, no Buddhist center seems to make dialogue with Christian faith a matter of ultimate importance. It is therefore very difficult to perceive how Buddhist faith has been creatively transformed through contact with Christianity. Individual Buddhists have expressed interest and admiration for Christian ethical and social concerns and stress the need to learn from Christianity on these points, but there does not as yet appear to be a similar challenge from Christianity on the doctrinal and philosophical level. The interesting fact is that even though Christians are usually regarded as more doctrinally intolerant than Buddhists, it is Christians who have more openly and systematically responded to the challenge of Buddhist religious experience through interfaith dialogue. In short, the process of creative transformation has been more evident in Christian faith than in Buddhist faith. I do not mean this observation as an indictment of the Buddhist Way. Dialogue and creative transformation cannot be forced. But surely creative transformation is just as necessary and important for Buddhism as it is for Christianity in an age of religious and secular pluralism.

A related point must be made on the Christian side of the encounter. Christian dialogical encounter with Buddhism has mainly focused on the Japanese Zen tradition and somewhat on Pure Land teachings and practice. More concerted efforts should be made to encounter other forms of Japanese Buddhism such as Shingon and Tendai, as well as a more in-depth encounter with Pure Land faith. Along with this Christians should seek out non-Japanese forms of Buddhist faith as well, especially the Theravāda and Tibetan traditions. Buddhism, like Christianity, is a highly complex tradition the whole of which needs to be dialogically encountered.

Fourthly, interfaith dialogue is a very risky business for at least two reasons. From a sociological perspective, Buddhist-Christian dialogue has mostly been an elite movement led by the more "liberal" professionals of each faith. Very little interfaith dialogue has taken place on the grass roots level. Part of the problem is whether or not people are capable of preserving a sense of identity if the boundaries of their religious faith are weakened by the process of creative transformation. Interfaith dialogue, in awakening persons to the reality of their being human, might become a "dysfunction" because persons need "discernible identity boundaries."[23] The problem is that interfaith dialogue does delimit the boundaries between the various religious Ways, and therefore Christian and Buddhist persons run the risk of losing the limits that protect and define their self-identities and sense of meaning. And if we are insensitive to this, the whole enterprise may become quite harmful and not worth the effort. This is not to say that the enterprise ought to be given up, but that it should help persons open themselves to the process of creative transformation within the limits of discernable boundaries in order not to be self-destructive.

On the other hand, it is precisely because dialogue with other religious persons and perspectives changes us that there are no guarantees that we will or can or should remain labeled as Christian or Buddhist. Here lies the greatest risk and adventure of the process of creative transformation. After passing over to Ways other than our own, we may find ourselves returning to a completely different point from where we started. And if Whitehead was right in his belief that things are in process of interdependent and interrelational becoming, the Christian or the Buddhist or the Jew or the Muslim in dialogue with traditions other than his own may find himself or herself so completely transformed as to be outside the pale of his or her original faith perspective altogether. In fact, it is possible that each of the Ways of mankind may be so creatively transformed as to become "objectively immortal" and be replaced by novel, more inclusive, and universal Ways. This is not meant to be a prediction of the future, but in a world of process, relativity, and radical finitude, nothing is permanent if it is alive, including the various religious Ways of mankind. Historically, religious traditions have died and been replaced by more inclusive religious visions, as Christian faith replaced the mystery religions of the Hellenistic world or as Buddhism replaced the ancient Bon tradition of Tibet. There is no reason to suppose that the contemporary religious Ways of mankind do not face a similar future.

There is, finally, an ultimate temptation which process theologians must avoid at all costs. It is very tempting to perceive the affinities between Buddhist faith and process thought, along with the obvious Christian interest which forms part of the background of Whitehead's philosophy, as a verification of Whitehead's philosophical vision. This might be a valid judgment if one is doing philosophy, although I doubt it. But if one is seeking interreligious understanding and creative transformation through dialogue, absolutizing Whitehead's system in this way becomes a distortion of Buddhist and Christian faith, as well as of Whitehead's philosophical vision. This means that the conceptual problem, the problem of language, becomes extremely important. Whitehead's philosophy is a highly technical, Western philosophy based on a scientific world view with a language meant to explicate *his* interpretation of what this world view means. The use of this technical language—terms such as "actual entity," "prehension," "causal efficacy," "presentational immediacy," the "primal" and "consequent" natures of God—ought to be kept at the barest minimum. Otherwise Buddhist and Christian faith may be too easily transformed into an inferior form of the process thought that was articulated more coherently by Whitehead. The end result is likely to be that dialogue between Christians and Buddhists will become a series of Whiteheadian monologues. Process theologians need to be more sensitive to this than they are, for a theoretical vision such as Whitehead's should not be confused with an existential religious faith (Cobb's terms is "structure of existence") such as Buddhism and Christianity. But if care is taken at this point, Whitehead's process vision may be an important heuristic means of opening us up to the insights of both the Buddhist and the Christian Way which will not falsify either one and yet allow for the creative transformation of both.

NOTES

1. C.G. Jung, *Modern Man in Search of a Soul* (New York: Harcourt, Brace, and World, 1933), pp. 196-197.
2. These points are more fully developed in Peter L. Berger, *The Heretical Imperative* (Garden City: Doubleday Anchor, 1979).
3. Michael Polanyi, *Personal Knowledge* (New York: Harper Torchbooks, 1964), p. 103.
4. See Alfred North Whitehead, *Process and Reality* (New York: Macmillan, 1967), pp. 136-167.
5. Ibid., p. 165.
6. "The principle of universal relativity directly transverses Aristotle's dictum, '(a substance) is not present in a subject.' On the contrary, according to this principle an actual entity *is* present in other actual entities. In fact if we allow for deeper relevance, and for negligible relevance, we must say that every actual entity is present in every other actual entity. The philosophy of organism is mainly devoted to the task of making clear the notion of 'being present in another entity'" (ibid., pp. 79-80; see also pp. 76-77, 224-226, 532.)
7. John B. Cobb, Jr., "Further Reflections on the Relativity of Belief," in *John Cobb's Theology in Process,* ed. David Ray Griffin and Thomas J. J. Altizer (Philadelphia: Westminster, 1977), pp. 165-170.
8. Ibid., p. 165.
9. See Whitehead, *Process and Reality,* pp. 62-89.
10. See Donald K. Swearer, *Dialogue: The Key to Understanding Other Religious Beliefs* (Philadelphia: Westminster, 1977).
11. John S. Dunne, *The Way of All the Earth* (Notre Dame, Ind.: University of Notre Dame Press, 1978), p. *iv.*
12. See Wilfred Cantwell Smith, *The Meaning and End of Religion* (New York: New American Library, 1966), pp. 7-8. The thrust of Smith's argument is that religion is not a "thing" that can be defined in the same way that nouns are "things" capable of definitions. He is certainly correct in pointing out that it is perfectly possible for human beings to live according to a religious faith without the benefit of a definition of a thing called religion. In fact, this seems to be the normal situation among religious persons.

13. Similar points have been discussed by Swearer, *Dialogue,* pp. 40-51.
14. For a clear and readable account of this point, see John B. Cobb, Jr. and David Ray Griffin, *Process Theology: An Introductory Exposition* (Philadelphia: Westminster, 1976), pp. 136-142. See also Cobb's *Christ in a Pluralistic Age* (Philadelphia, Westminster, 1975), and especially Chap. 4 for an example of how Buddhist religious experience and insight, understood through Whiteheadian process categories, have been appropriated in the development of a rather distinctive process Christology. See also my response to this in my "To John Cobb: Questions to Gladden the Atman in an Age of Pluralism," *Journal of the American Academy of Religion* 50 (June 1977):753-788.
15. Cobb and Griffin, *Process Theology: An Introductory Exposition,* pp. 139-140.
16. Cobb makes this the center of his analysis of Buddhism in his *The Structure of Christian Existence* (Philadelphia: Westminster, 1967), pp. 60-72.
17. See my study, *The Dharma of Faith: An Introduction to Classical Pure Land Buddhism* (Washington, D.C.: University Press of America, 1977).
18. Whitehead, *Process and Reality,* p. 31.
19. See Cobb, "Buddhist Emptiness and the Christian God," *Journal of the American Academy of Religion* 45, No. 1 (1977):11-25.
20. Whitehead, *Process and Reality,* p. 53.
21. Cobb and Griffin, *Process Theology: An Introductory Exposition,* p. 142.
22. Notto R. Thelle, "Prospects and Problems of Buddhist-Christian Dialogue: A Report," *Japanese Religions* 10, No. 4 (July 1979):53.
23. See Jan Swyngedouw, "Interfaith Dialogue: A Sociological Reflection," *Japanese Religions* 10, No. 4 (July 1979):7-26.

CHAPTER 5

Śūnyatā and Religious Pluralism

Shohei Ichimura

INTRODUCTION

American society has experienced a new era of religious pluralism in the last quarter of this century, especially in relation to the Asian traditions in general and Buddhism in particular. Practically every surviving Buddhist tradition, such as Zen of East Asia, Theravada of South Asia, and the esoteric Tibetan tradition, has increasingly assumed a more visible presence in the United States. This trend, however, has by no means been confined to North America. There also exists an impressive growth of interest in Buddhism among Europeans. In light of the facts of modern religious pluralism, illustrated by the presence of Buddhist movements in Western cultures, especially in America, interreligious dialogue would seem to be both a necessity and an opportunity for religious persons of differing cultural and religious perspectives.

My first interest in interreligious dialogue was aroused by an article written in January 1971 by Harvey Cox in *Christianity and Crisis* in which he wrote about his participation in a seminar at a Tibetan Buddhist center in Colorado. According to Cox, the Asian religious movements pose a serious theological challenge to the mainline religious traditions of America. He warned Christians in particular that these movements should neither be ignored, contemptuously dismissed, nor enthusiastically welcomed, but carefully assessed with the attitude of "a little yes, a little no, and a little maybe." I think Cox was correct in foreseeing that the nontheistic Buddhist traditions could pose a serious challenge to the theistic Judeo-Christian tradition. But the present status of Buddhist tradition in America does not as yet seem conducive to interreligious dialogue either, for what is lacking on the Buddhist side is a theoretical understanding of the potential contributions of Buddhist faith to Christian experience and faith. This essay is therefore an attempt to formulate a theoretical understanding of the possible forms of Buddhist participation in interreligious dialogue with Christianity.

It is my contention that a theory of interreligious dialogue should primarily do justice to the paradoxical nature of religious experience. Living religions are involved in a wide range of worldly activities, but they also possess elements of nonaction or introspective withdrawal from the world. The empirical scholarly disciplines, such as anthropology and the other social sciences, have greatly advanced religious studies by analyzing religious phenomena in reference to the correlation between symbol systems and goal-directed activities. On the other hand, there has been little progress in theoretical attempts at clarifying the paradoxical aspects of religion or the critical examination of symbol usage. Yet it is precisely the introspective, experiential dimension of religious faith that has been the primary focus of contemporary Western interest in Buddhism. Therefore, interreligious dialogue with Buddhism will produce its most fruitful results if it emphasizes the experiential dimensions of religious faith.

Any theory of interreligious dialogue should assume a common ground which theistic and nontheistic religions can equally accept as their dialogical starting point. Moreover, the scope of this common ground should be relevant to both the religious and the secular dimensions of modern human life. I have chosen teleology as the universal feature of human experience, be this religious or nonreligious, as the common ground from which interreligious dialogue can proceed. Consequently, this essay is an attempt to clarify this teleological common ground as it relates to the use of language and the goal-seeking nature of action. Here, the insight of the ancient Indian grammarians will serve as our starting point. We shall also demonstrate, with the aid of the Buddhist concept of *śūnyatā,* that religious teleology stands in a paradoxical relationship to secular teleology.

THE TELEOLOGICAL FORMULA OF RELIGIOUS DIALOGUE

The Teleological Formula in Symbolic Terms

After his visit to Japan in the early sixties Paul Tillich began to develop what was for him a new interest in interreligious dialogue. Because of the difference between theistic Christianity and nontheistic Buddhism, he found it necessary to develop methodological principles applicable to both traditions. He came to the conclusion that interreligious dialogue should not begin with traditional Christian concepts such as God, man, history, or salvation, which had hitherto been the foci of comparative studies. Rather, he proposed that dialogue begin with a more fundamental problem, namely, the true goal of existence which the various religious traditions conceptualize in their specific doctrinal formulations. In other words, the goals of each religion should be compared, such as the Buddhist concept of nirvana with the Christian concept of the Kingdom of God. He called the focus of dialogue of this sort its "teleological formula."[1] Although I intend to borrow Tillich's terminology, I have formulated the structure of dialogue somewhat differently because I have also been guided by the more inductive approach of William James.

Nearly eighty years ago William James in effect predicted the behavior of many contemporary young Westerners when he lectured to his students at Harvard University that there were ways of experiencing religion that they were unaware of, and that these new ways were intuitive inner paths leading toward supernatural kinds of happiness.[2] Experiences of this sort, he believed, would become the urgent goal of their lives when they realized that their normal modes of existence were not as satisfactory as they thought. This is the underlying theme of his work *The Varieties of Religious Experience* where he most clearly tried to show that religious phenomena can be inductively studied and defined in reference to religious experience. The following two ideas from this work are especially helpful: (1) religious ideas can be scientifically generalized as having a "teleological formula" that involves two different stages of life, and (2) any religiously motivated action is a process in which one stage of life is transformed into another.[3]

From ancient times, Buddhists applied the term nirvana and samsara as teleological symbols referring to the two modes of human existence. Likewise, Christianity uses the symbols of heaven and earth in symbolizing its notions of the two modes of human existence. The humanists and Marxists also apply equivalent symbols to guide their actions toward specific goals. Since there is no difference between religious and nonreligious forms of teleology in terms of how symbols are employed to structure human experience, it is necessary to discuss why dialogue should begin with the question of how two-term relationships can be more meaningfully and adequately activated in human consciousness.

The Teleological Formula of Buddhist Symbolism

Anthropologists such as Clifford Geertz regard religions as systems of meaning embodied in the symbols which constitute a particular religion proper. On this basis they relate religious systems to socio-cultural and psychological processes.[4] Since action motivated by religious faith is controlled through symbols, social-scientific studies of religion can clarify the social and psychological aspect of life in which religion plays a determinate role. In this respect, I agree with Geertz that religion is a form of culture whose historically transmitted patterns of meaning are embodied in symbols. In other words, religion is a system of inherited symbolic forms through which we communicate, perpetuate, and develop our knowledge and attitudes about life. This is very close to the Buddhist understanding of religious symbols, for the ancient Buddhist masters taught that nirvana, the goal of religious faith, experience, and practice, had to be sought within the structure of symbolic processes as such. For it is through these structures that symbols acquire the meanings that guide human action (karma). Consequently, by analyzing the structural mechanism of the symbolic process, it is possible for a person to bring about the cessation of action, that is, to achieve liberation from all symbolic processes as such during moments of meditative insight.

In Buddhism, therefore, the symbol of nirvana embodies the ultimate goal of religion. It is the universal emancipation *(mokṣa)* to which every individual is entitled. However, even though the concept hardly receives any positive meaning in relation to its doctrinal formulation, the symbols of nirvana refer to a positive experience which the Abhidharmists defined as a transempirical mental state *(asaṃskṛta-dharma)*.[5] This has been clearly seen by Isaline Blew Horner, who believed that the experience of nirvana is most suitably denoted by the term *parā* (yonder). The compound term *parā-gata,* for example, has been translated to as "gone beyond" until Mrs. Rhys Davids and Horner determined that the term is a present and not a past participle, that is, "going beyond" instead of "gone beyond," and that the term implied the possibility of an infinite going, an infinite improvement and enrichment, or even an expansion of the microcosm in depth and height toward the macrocosm.[6] According to these Pali scholars nirvana should be understood in the sense of *parā,* meaning the process of unending and dynamic becoming of a person continuously going beyond what he is in the present. For the term *parā* is always used in reference to an object "gone beyond," for instance, "cross over to the other shore of sorrow," "cross to the further shore beyond darkness," "the safe shore of fearlessness," "having crossed beyond the limited," or "cross to the shore beyond ignorance." Thus *parā* is used as either an adjective or an adverb denoting "beyond," "higher in space," "further in time," and as a neuter noun, "another" or "others."

To restate this in the language of William James, there seems to be a "teleological polarization" at work here between the experiential, subjective core of religious experience and its symbolic expressions through language and symbol. The concept of nirvana, which originally pointed to a process best expressed by *parā,* was eventually transformed to mean a final state of being. Similar teleological polarizations are invariably found in every religion, as for example expressed in references to the moment of consciousness when one experiences "life and death," "being and nonbeing," "hope and despair," or "light and darkness." One might question whether a moment of consciousness is the relevant reference for teleological polarization since it lacks an objective reality. However, there is in fact only the moment of consciousness since the goal embodied in symbols such as nirvana has no independently objective place beyond the mind in time and space. In the *Theravā-din* system, the introspective path consists of the eight stages, that is, four pre-liminary practices of meditation *(dhyāna)* and four advanced stages of concen-tration *(samādhi)*.[7] Through these steps a person perfects the process of empty-ing the objects of his consciousness externally as well as internally. They are designed to guide the meditator beyond the layers of stages and, in the process of emptying his consciousness, lead him toward the ultimate goal of imperturbability, that is, the stage of nirvana, singularly attributed to the arhat. As such, stages do not represent time duration or space extention, but varied depths of consciousness. In other words, the teleological polarization involved in the nirvana-samsara relationship has its reference nowhere but in a given moment of consciousness.

Teleological Formula as Existential Polarization

The concept of nirvana underwent a further change in *Mahāyāna* tradition. Nirvana was withdrawn behind the grandeur of the Buddha-realm *(buddha-loka)*, the macrocosm envisioned by the enlightened. The concept of nirvana was never given much positive description in the Abhidharmist system, but *Mahāyāna* literature magnified nirvana as a grand, supernatural, unearthly realm. The major *Mahāyāna* textual groups, for example, the Hua-yen *(Avatamsaka)*, the Lotus *(Saddharmapuṇḍarika)*, the Pure Land *(Sukhāvatīvyūha)*, and the *Prajñā* Insight *(Prajñapāramitā)* all allude to such a supernatural realm visible to no one but the enlightened. The best example is the Hua-yen text.[8] This text pictures the wondrous Buddha-realm as an external, immutable macrocosm utterly transcending our unstable phenome-nal world. The presiding buddha, Vairocana, more luminous than the sun, is said to be forever immersed in contemplation and hence forever beyond the reach of ordinary human perception. The main effect of such notions was that the meditative disciplines evolved ever more difficult practices for ob-taining even more miraculous, transcendental experiences. This can be easily seen in the *Daśabhūmiśvara* chapter, which sets forth ten stages of perfection to be accomplished by the aspiring bodhisattva, beginning with the first called "delightfulness" *(pramuditā)* and ending with "Dharma cloud" *(dharmamegha)*.[9]

In spite of this, the underlying theme of the ultimate identity of the super-natural and the natural worlds remains, as is suggested through images that compare the Buddha's cosmic contemplation to a totally quiescent ocean. In this ocean all the possibilities of phenomenal occurrences are said to be simultaneously present in their prototype forms or in their basic patterns *(mudrā)*, like constantly active waves.[10] Even though ordinary persons cannot perceive it, beings of heroic aspiration, such as the bodhisattva determined to attain enlightenment, are said to be able to have a glimpse of it. The point is that not only in this text, but also in all other *Mahāyāna* texts, the realms of samsara and nirvana are declared to be totally identical. This bipolar structure, by which I mean any teleological scheme in which two symbols, for instance, nirvana and samsara, are unified, is characteristic of *Mahāyāna* philosophy. It is the identity of samsara and nirvana that is the definitive insight involved in *śunyatā* (emptiness), and which at the same time is frequently alluded to in a number of antitheses, such as "Buddha and human," "heaven and hell," "emancipation and fetteredness," and "light and darkness."[11]

Another example of teleological polarization in *Mahāyāna* Buddhism occurs in the Pure Land texts which teach the doctrine of salvation through the grace of *Amitābha* Buddha. The striking resemblance between this doctrine and that of some forms of Protestant Christianity has been frequently noted. In the Pure Land texts the goal of life is rebirth into the Land of Happiness, a realm whose nature is totally opposite to the phenomenal world of pain and suffering. Salvation is said to come exclusively from *Amitābha,* who vowed in the immemorial past to realize universal salvation for all sentient beings. The only thing required from the devotee is genuine faith in his vows and the sincere desire to be reborn in his Buddha-land. The Land of Happiness is described as filled with gold and its citizens uniformally endowed with a golden complexion. There is no more effective a polarization than that which is expressed in the Pure Land texts. Yet here too, the redemptive insight of *śunyatā* is hypostatized as the Buddha of Immeasurable Compassion, whose sole purpose is to help persons miraculously cross the transcendental boundary from this world to the Land of Happiness. What arouses our curiosity is the polarity of *Mahāyāna* insight, which, on the one hand, magnifies the gulf of teleological polarization, while on the other hand, simultaneously bridges that gulf in terms of complete identity. Although this appears to be logically contradictory and psychologically paradoxical, I believe that it can become the starting point for Buddhists who engage in interreligious dialogue.

The reason for this assertion is that historically the *Mahāyāna* movement surfaced a few centuries after the establishment of the orthodox professionalist system and intensified their confrontation with the orthodox Abhidharmists. The various *Mahāyāna* movements began with the common intention of revitalizing the original Buddhist symbols through the incorporation of a secular symbol system. For by this time, the institution of monasticism and the older goal of seeking nirvana through monastic isolation from the secular world had lost contact with the needs of persons living outside

the monastic establishment. The champion reformers were those who compiled the *Prajña* Insight texts and who advocated the concept of universal
emptiness *(śūnyatā)* in distinguishing reality from empirical concepts, along
with repudiating the monastic system and its teachings of nirvana.[12] The underlying insight was that the monastic institution was essentially no different
from the teleological systems of secular society, because in spite of all the differences between their respective intended goals, that is, one intending to
free persons from all goal seeking while the other emphasizing the pursuit of
worldly goals, they were fundamentally identical in terms of their symbol
usage. The implications of this were vast, and they are important for understanding the nature of religious dialogue in the contemporary world. For the
concept of *śūnyatā* can allow us to analyze not only theistic and nontheistic
religious systems, but also humanist and Marxist systems of teleology as well.
And it is for this reason that I propose the concept of *śūnyatā* as a worthy
Buddhist starting point for a theory of religious pluralism and interreligious
dialogue.

THE TELEOLOGY OF LANGUAGE

The Antithesis Between Revealed and Natural Theology

There is an assumption at the heart of most Western religions and philosophies that existence is grounded in the tension between dualities such as the
supernatural and the natural, the religious and the scientific, or faith and
reason, and that ultimately persons must choose either one or the other
alternative, but not both unless one is logically simple minded. In fact the
contemporary religious crisis is the result of this antithesis. Therefore, since
we accept religious pluralism as a fact of modern existence, the secular and
the religious dimensions of human experience are integral aspects of modern
existence. But why have modern religious and secular traditions in the West
been so incompatible? I believe the root causes of this conflict in the West
can be traced back to the clash between the Judeo-Christian anthropomorphic
conception of casuality and the Greco-Roman conception of natural law. Yet
it must be recognized that in the history of civilization this clash has not
been a universal phenomenon, but rather a regional one since it has been
absent in most other parts of the world, especially in those areas whose cultural traditions are Buddhist. That is to say, the "religious" and the "natural"
are not necessarily incompatible.

    Nature, as conceived of in classical Western philosophy, was fundamental-
ly teleological. Philosophers were concerned in part with the ultimate stan-
dards guaranteeing the validity of knowledge and the norms of action, and in

part with the perfection of moral and political wisdom. For they were convinced that wisdom enables persons to choose right goals and to execute
right actions, and that these practical virtues lead to the eventual fulfillment
of human nature. It is at this point that natural law was conceived of as a
guide for teleological causation. In the Greco-Roman world, however, this rational outlook with its humanistic optimism about the capacity of reason was
successfully challenged by Judeo-Christian tradition. The Christian concept
of the living God as the Supreme Person was not the result of philosophical
reflection, but was grounded in the historical experience of the Christian
community. Christian faith is centered on the experience of personal relationships with this Supreme Person, who is at the same time the source of everything in the universe. And because of this experience of personal relationship
with God, Christians are led to affirm the importance of personal relationships with others as the major ethical implication of faith. This anthropo-
morphism implied a new concept of teleology and freedom in that acts of
free will on the part of mankind can be affirmed over against a history
governed by impersonal natural laws of efficient causation. As understood by
the Stoic philosophers, natural law was thought to govern the morally
teleological cosmos as the all-compelling power and inviolable necessity of
nature. The antithesis was, therefore, between belief in the existence of an
anthropomorphic supernatural being or belief in the existence of unalterable
natural efficient causation.

Western philosophers and theologians have been accustomed to interpreting this classical confrontation in terms of antithesis and complement. In the
case of Augustine, history was seen as a conversion process by which mankind
is led from the natural to the supernatural, as illustrated by his distinction between the City of God and the City of Earth. For Thomas Aquinas, this hori-
zontal antithesis was changed to a complementary vertical formulation.
Reason and faith each possess their respective domains, although faith is the
umbrella under which reason guides the natural life of mankind. Subsequent
history, however, amply proves the case that the medieval arrangement was
not really an adequate system for doing justice to faith and reason, and that
faith and reason were once again separated during the Renaissance and the
Reformation as two incompatible modes of mentality. The problem with
which contemporary scholars are now confronted is the question of what pro-
motes belief in one form of causation to the exclusion of the other. In light
of this, I wish to propose that it is the use of language itself that reinforces
both anthropomorphic and naturalistic casual conceptions because both types
of teleology are inherent in the very structure of language. Thus it is necessary that we examine the nature and function of language, and it is in this
connection that the Buddhist notion of *śūnyatā* might prove promising.

The Teleological Structure Inherent in Language

The grammarians of ancient India were convinced that perfected knowledge of their science was necessary for achieving the goal of religious emancipation.[13] The grammarians of India divided the world of phenomenal experience into three categories: external events, internal ideals, and mediatory language. In so doing, they created the science of linguistics, which became the ground of not only grammarian epistemology, but the epistemological ground of all orthodox systems of Hindu philosophy. However, the Buddhist schools in general and the Mādhyamika school in particular, through the doctrine of *śūnyatā,* gave only limited recognition to the linguistic structuring of experience in their analyses of the phenomenal world, while at the same time denying any relevance whatsoever to language in relation to the Absolute. It is my contention that this attitude toward language can be applied to the problem of how to deal with the linguistic reinforcement of anthropomorphic and natural conceptions of casuality.

The fact that action is invariably purposive and teleological was known by philosophers and theologians in both the East and the West. But the insight that sentence structure implies teleology originated with the grammarians of India. Whether written or spoken, they argued, language consists of a series of sentential symbols which, in turn, contain a series of word symbols (parts of speech). In human consciousness, these symbols rapidly come and go, creating the existential context of each given moment of consciousness. This dynamic flow of symbols which constitutes the stream of consciousness occurs in our minds in two different, but interrelated, sets of order. Our speech, for example, carries not only meanings which words express, but also bears the underlying syntactical relations which the word order reveals. In regard to this, Pāṇini, the great grammarian of the fifth century B.C., theorized that it was the *verb element* expressing action which called for syntactic relations for the fulfillment of action.[14] Here lies the linguistic source for teleology, namely, the fulfillment of action.

To illustrate, suppose we have numbers of noun bases stripped of any affixes or case endings. These barren symbols are completely meaningless but once affixes are attached to them, they express a particular meaning through the configuration of case endings. For example, when the root system *kṛ* (the root form of "to act," "make," or "do") takes on an affix such as *karoti* (third person, singular, present), a whole group of syntactical categories, *kāraka* in Sanskrit, evolve involving an agent of action and an object toward which action is directed. Pāṇini understood *kāraka* as "anything that helps towards the accomplishment of some action," and he identified six forms of *kāraka:* nominative, accusative, instrumental, dative, ablative, and locative.[15] In the action of cooking, for instance, the fire, the furnace, the vessel, and the cook are all helpers in the accomplishment of the action. In applying these terms, we say "Rāma cooks food in a vessel by the fire in the furnace for his master." Here Rāma is an agent *kāraka*, food an object *kāraka*, the vessel a locative *kāraka*, fire an instrumental *kāraka*, and the master a dative *kāraka*. All six of these occasions are required in order to complete the goal of the act of cooking.

Although Hindu philosophers characterized Buddhism as heterodox and nihilistic, it is ironic that later Buddhist tradition was in some sense more in accordance with the grammarian tradition at this point than was Hindu philosophy. For example, Nāgārjuna critically examined the conviction that the phenomenal world possesses independent reality external to perceiving minds. His dialectical treatise on motion in the second chapter of this *Mādhyamika-kārikā* clearly shows that he was undeniably aware of the grammatical arrangement of names (noun bases) and their relations (case endings).[16] Here, in reference to the action of "to go or move" *(gam)*, he demonstrated that real movement cannot be found in either the passage supposed to have been traversed *(gata)*, or in the passage not yet traversed, neither can motion be found in the passage where an actual movement is proceeding *(gamyamāna)*. His dialectic concludes that the relationship between the agent goer and the actual movement *(gamana)* cannot be established either in terms of identity or difference.[17] The result is a collapse of the teleological system expressed in the *kāraka* structure, for since all *kāraka* terms are symbolic structures *(prapañca)*, the conviction that language has the power to reveal reality as it really is is an illusion. The truth of whatever reality is must therefore be sought in the processes of the practical application of linguistic structure to experience itself.

It is at this point that grammatical knowledge of *kāraka* would seem to be imperative for making sense of Nāgārjuna's repudiation of *kāraka* terms, such as *gantṛ* (goer) and *gantavya* (what is gone to), precisely because the *kāraka* structure implies teleological goals within itself, especially in the accusative case *(karma-kāraka)*. Pāṇini defined this syntactical case as "that which is intended and which should be most affected by the action of the agent."[18] One of the commentaries rephrases this more clearly as "that which is especially desired by the agent to be accomplished by the action."[19] This illustrates the point that teleological polarization is potentially inherent in the *kāraka* structure. For once one attaches a concrete meaning, such as nirvana, heaven, or any of the common realities of ordinary life, to a particular *kāraka*, it is easy to see that the whole structure, while previously inactive, will be set into motion to create teleological polarizations in man's consciousness, thereby generating forces of motivation toward action. Contemporary philosophers are fully aware of the fact that the use of words has its origin in the desire to achieve some human end,[20] so that if Nāgārjuna's criticism has any truth to it, it must have something to do with the goal-bound *kāraka* structure and its inherent potency. But what is it that transforms an inactive structure into an active one? The Buddhist concept of *śūnyatā* suggests that it is semantic attachment.

The Naive Realism Inherent in the
Teleological Structure of Language

Mahāyāna Buddhist texts frequently allude to the doctrine of illusion *(maya)* in describing how the use of language creates a naively realistic sense of external forms in our stream of consciousness, and thereby the illusion of causality. Although what we actually experience is the constant process of transiency, our ingrained teleology seems to create a system of transcendental forms or immutable ideas, which in turn fools us into believing in an unchanging, stable, referential world. This has been pointed out in the West by the linguistic studies of Saussure and Ogden and Richards, who analyzed semantic structure in terms of the triangular relationship between word (symbol), its meaning (reference), and its object (referent).[21] When we use a word, we have its meaning in mind, and in this sense, there is a direct correlation between linguistic symbols and their respective meanings. But there is only an indirect relationship between symbols and their external objects. The reason that the proponents of certain systems of Hindu philosophy, such as the Nyāya logicians and the Mīmāṃsā ritualists, are generally regarded as naive realists is that both schools upheld that there is precise one-to-one correlation between the external objective world and the way this world is related to persons through the linguistic symbols of Sanskrit language. It was this sort of naive realism that was rejected by Buddhism in general, and the Mādhyamika school in particular, in terms of the notion of *śūnyatā*.

Generally speaking, there are two necessary conditions for a realistic view of the world to be valid: (1) the external world must have stable and lasting forms to which linguistic symbols can be meaningfully applied, and (2) the mind must be constituted so as to process correlative conceptual categories that correspond to perceived forms in the external world. The systems advanced by the Nyāya logicians and the Mīmāṃsā ritualists were somewhat different from each other. The logicians argued that *"sabda* [vocal word] is impermanent, because it is a product, just as a pot is," whereas the ritualists argued that *"sabda* is permanent because it is audible, just as any audible sound is." The logicians noted that vocal words were a temporary modification of a substantial ether *(ākāsa)*, and that the symbolic power of words was contingent on a given linguistic community's fixed usage. Nevertheless, they were convinced that words could actually correspond to the structures of the external world because their theoretical formulation assumed in part the metaphysical categories of being, such as "substance" and "quality," and in part the effective power of *kāraka*. The ritualists, on the other hand, postulated semantic paradigms *(sphoṭa)* as transcendental ideation principles, and then theorized that, on account of their symbolic power, any audible word or intelligible sound carries its respective paradigm, thereby enabling human beings to accurately communicate inner thought and precisely express the external world they believed to evolve into consciousness as sounds, and at the same time to project themselves as forms extraneous to consciousness. In other words, the word-object relationship is a necessary relationship.

Most students of Indian philosophy and religion generally assume that the Hindu schoolmen were directly in the line of the grammarian tradition, whereas the Buddhists rejected this tradition outright. This is probably not an accurate characterization. For the grammarians themselves, such as Patañjali, held two types of interpretation in regard to semantic relationships. The problem involved explaining the way a postulated semantic paradigm manifests itself as an actual linguistic form. For example, in analyzing a word into grammatical elements, such as syllables, the grammarians faced the difficulty of explaining how these symbolic elements could bring about the specific meaning supposed to correspond to the permanent word paradigm. One interpretation, which resembles that of Plato, claimed that the word-essence *(sthānin)* somehow manifests itself as an appearance *(ādeśa)* in the world of change.[22] This is the evolutionary theory *(pariṇāma)* which was later developed into a full-fledged system of metaphysics by the medieval grammarian Bhartṛhari. The Mīmāṇsā and the later Vedānta systems generally accepted this interpretation. The grammarians noticed, however, that each *kāraka* form did not affect the grammarical elements of a base term, but it did affect the psycho-linguistic unity in the act of cognition, bearing its particular meaning as nominative, accusative, or instrumental. In the evolutionary theory, modification is considered to take place in the grammatical elements themselves in relation to the permanent word-paradigm, whereas here the modification is transferred to cognition because of the correlation between cognition and *kāraka* form, although the cognitive modification may be radically different from the actual transformation of the external world.

This type of interpretation is a "functional theory" of meaning because it explains the coming into existence of unified meaning in terms of the functional interdependence of syllabic elements in their totality. However, there are also parallel Buddhist interpretations, such as the Sarvāstivādin. The merit of a functional interpretation of meaning is that the correlation between words and objective fact can be explained exclusively in reference to the inner stream of consciousness without postulating the transcendental word-paradigm or the metaphysical category of being. This is what the Buddhist concept of *śunyatā* accomplishes as one of its two major tasks. Its other task is to repudiate the metaphysical basis of any two-term relationship, be this logical, syntactic, or semantic, in relation to the momentary states of consciousness. Contemporary linguists, grammarians, and behavioral scientists have been theorizing on the nature and function of language in similar ways. According to the advocates of generative grammar, for example, syntactical relations are innate in the human mind, while the behavior scientists insist that all verbal behavior is dependent upon the stimulus-response mechanism. But if a sequence of symbols, ordered by logical, syntactical, and causal relationships is understood to be fixed in *any* way, there is no hope of realizing liberation from any symbolic structure. On the other hand, if symbolic usage depends only upon habit formation, we cannot determine the ultimate criteria for valid knowledge and action. It is precisely at this point that the Buddhist teaching of *śunyatā* can free us from the bondage of symbolic determinism inherent in both "generative" and "behavioral" theories of language.

SUNYATA AND TELEOLOGICAL SYSTEMS

Śunyatā: Identity and Differences in Two Related Terms

Whether in the East or the West, the nature of human consciousness has usually been understood in reference to the momentary passage of time. For it is here that we perceive sequences of change and continuity, along with the symbolic processes that link one moment of experience with the next. It is this referential moment, as I have been discussing above, that is the source of the existential and teleological polarization of experience into dualities such as samsara and nirvana, earth and heaven, or secular and religious. It is also the source of every religious person's expectation of some form of change or transformation from ordinary to "enlightened" or "revealed" experience. In this regard, Nāgārjuna's dialectical analysis of motion can be a model through which to examine the core symbolic structure that underlies linguistic convention. His treatment is remarkably therapeutic in the way in which it demolishes linguistic convention. Yet, by means of the notion of *kāraka*, it is also possible to perceive something more in Nāgārjuna's method, for here we can see the workings of the specifically Buddhist notion of causation, by which any two related symbols are simultaneously identical and different.

Since the grammarians considered *kārakas* and action as interdependent, without *kārakas* no actions can occur nor can the *kārakas* exist apart from action. This necessary relation leads to an insurmountable difficulty, however. Suppose, following Nāgārjuna, we have three *kārakas* as agent goer, instrumental motion, and desired goal, and then analyze instrumental motion into an actual movement (gamana) and an equivalent passage being traversed by this movement (gamyamāna). Here in the light of the kāraka structure, we visualize that an "agent goer" proceeds on the passage by an actual movement from one point to another. The problem is how change can take place from moving to stopping. Linguistic convention allows us to change the expression from "the goer goes" to "the goer stops." Nāgārjuna argued that the convention wrongly separates an agent and a movement as mutually dependent, incorrectly abscribing the movement to the agent in

kāraka.[23] That is to say, since without movement no kāraka can exist, we cannot find the beginning point of stopping either in the passage already traversed (gata), in the passage not yet traversed (agata), or in the passage where movement is actually proceeding.[24] Nor can we find the beginning point of motion anywhere in these referential passages. Moreover, since agent and motion are differentiated in linguistic convention, they are supposed to possess mutually independent existence and reality, which is impossible. Nor does their identification save linguistic convention from collapsing, because this would mean identifying the agent kāraka with the instrumental one which is impossible as well. The only conclusion is that the agent and the motion cannot be related either in terms of difference or identity, and the same also holds in the case of change from moving to stopping and vice versa.[25]

The seriousness of this critique may be more clearly grasped in reference to the necessary relationship between an agent of perceiving and an object of perception. We take it for granted that a perceiving agent and an object of perception must be co-present at the moment of perception because vision requires the direct contact of the visual faculty with its object. In the Vigrahavyāvartanī, another important work by Nāgārjuna, he applied a similar dialectical argument in his conclusion that the relationship between subject and object makes it impossible to change successive occurrences of cognition, so that the subject-object relationship cannot be understood either in terms of difference or identity. This particular conclusion was directed against the Nyāya logicians' realistic faith in the power of language as a valid means of knowledge. Since the Nyāya and the Mīmānsā thinkers equally relied upon linguistic convention as an ultimate means of knowledge, it is not difficult to understand why Nāgārjuna's critique of their position created such a negative reaction on their part. But Nāgārjuna's method was not intended merely as a means to undermine their doctrines so as to demonstrate the superiority of Buddhist philosophy. The kārakas are the formal foundation of sentiential construction and hence of linguistic convention as such, so that

Nāgārjuna's real purpose was to demonstrate how all forms of linguistic convention, Hindu as well as Buddhist, operate in human consciousness.

Śunyatā: The Logical and Dialectical Contexts

From the foregoing analysis we can discover two clearly different contexts within which a sense of truth can develop. In one, linguistic convention is operative, while in the other it is not. The first we shall call the "logical context," the second, the "dialectical context." The best way to demonstrate their difference is to transcribe the dialectical context into symbolic notation in parallel to the logical context. When someone observes smoke rising on a distant hill, he normally concludes that the hill is on fire. Indian logic requires that this conclusion be demonstrated deductively by means of similar and dissimilar examples of the relation between the presence of smoke and fire, such as a kitchen where smoke and fire are observed to occur together, along with dissimilar examples where neither smoke nor fire occur together. Let the class of similar and dissimilar examples be transcribed as variables x and y, the two predications "is smoky" and "is fiery" as as P and Q, and their contrapositions "is not fiery" and "is not smoky" as $-Q$ and $-P$. Applying these notations, we have similar and dissimilar examples symbolized as $(x)\{P(x) (x)Q\}$ and $(y)\{-Q(y) -P(y)\}$ respectively.

In applying similar symbolic notation to Nāgārjuna's dialectic, it can be readily seen how ingeniously he treated the relationship between cognition and its object by means of the metaphor of light and darkness. The Nyāya logicians held that any valid means of knowledge such as language must be self-luminous and require no secondary cognition. A perception enables a cognizer to obtain visual self-understood by the cognizer. In parallel to any given cognition, the light of a candle should be capable of illuminating itself as well as other objects. In contrast, darkness is also supposed to be capable of obstructing itself as well as other objects from illumination. Let us transcribe the class of light as variable x and that of darkness as variable y, the two related predications "illuminates itself" and "illuminates others" as P and Q, and "obstructs itself from illumination" and "obstructs others from illumination" as $-Q$ and $-P$. We now have similar and dissimilar examples to the ones noted above, but with one difference. In this example of "dialectical context," both light and darkness are required to possess the identical spatio-temporal reference. This is obvious because the visual faculty and its object must be co-present before cognition can occur. This is precisely the first formula of Nāgārjuna's argument in *karika* 36 of the *Vigrahavyāvartanī*. The following parallel columns are simplified translations with corresponding symbolic notations of *karikas* 36-39.

Where light x illuminates
itself and darkness $(P.Q)$;
Darkness y also obstructs $(x)\{P(x).Q(x)\}.(y)\{-Q(y).-P(Y)\}$
illumination there $-Q.-P.$ (k.36)

Where there is light
there is no darkness; $(x)\{P(x).Q(x)\}.-[(y)\{-Q(y).-P(y)\}]$
How can light illuminate
anything? (k.37) $= (x.y)\{P(x.y).Q(x.y)\}$

When there is darkness
there is no light; $-[(x)\{P(x).Q(x)\}].(y)\{-Q(y).-P(y)\}$
How can light illuminate
anything. (Supplement) $= (y.x)\{-Q(y.x).-P(y.x)\}$

Does light illuminate
darkness at its moment of arising;
No, light does not reach it $(x)\{P(x).Q(x)\}.(y)\{-Q(y).-P(Y)\}$
from the beginning. (k.38)

If light here illuminates
darkness without reaching it; $(x)\{P(x).Q(x)\}.-[(y)\{-Q(y).-P(y)\}]$
This light illuminates
all the world. (k.39) $= (x.y)\{P(x.y).Q(x.y)\}$

If darkness here destroys
light without reaching it; $-[(x)\{P(x).Q(x)\}].(y)\{-Q(y).-P(y)\}$
This darkness destroys light
in all the world. (Supplement) $= (y.x)\{-Q(y.x).-P(y.x)\}$

The predicament created by the dialectic in *kārika* 36 is an unexpected contradiction. This feature is suddenly disclosed by the dialectical context in which two contrary entities, "light" and "darkness," are juxtaposed over the same moment of illumination. There is no sophistry here, however, because the co-presence of the agent of illumination and its object is a priori grounded in the structure of language itself, and thereby in our linguistic conventions. This fact does, however, point out that our linguistic conventions find no objective reality, such as referential interaction of light and darkness, to account for the lack of illumination. This peculiar situation, namely, the absence of a real object of reference, is further demonstrated in the subsequent *kārika*. Suppose we follow our ordinary experience, thinking that light and darkness cannot occur together within the same space and time. This means that light cannot reach darkness and vice versa, and illumination becomes impossible, which *kārika* 38 and my supplement demonstrate. Although it is not directly detectable in ordinary spoken language, our symbolic notation can reveal a significant insight behind the apparent absurdity. *Karikas* 37 and 39 show that in the case in which illumination alone is present, two different variables are also co-present as *x.y.* In the same way, as shown in both supplements, both variables are co-present as *y.x.* This means that in spite of the fact that *x* and *y* are mutually exclusive, they co-exist as contrary functions. This in turn means that there is only one condition such that *x* and *y* are identical while simultaneously different. This amounts to saying that *x* and *y* can reciprocally assume each other's nature.

Śūnyatā: The Theoretical Basis of
Religious Pluralism and Dialogue

Although the above demonstration appears to be reductionistic, in fact it is not. First, the dialectical context which Nāgārjuna developed can be more easily distinguished from the logical context. Second, the dialectical context can be clearly paralleled to those of the logical context. Third, Nāgārjuna's dialectical method can be shown more meaningfully in contrast to the grammarian tradition. Similar and dissimilar examples deductively and inductively work in our minds as simultaneous processes. On the one hand, their operations differentiate contrary variables *x* and *y,* and at the same time, calculate their truth values in terms of verification and falsification as *PQ* and *-P-Q.* In the dialectical context, on the other hand, the two classes of variables are juxtaposed over the same spatial-temporal context, resulting in an inevitable contradiction. Nāgārjuna usually ended his dialectic with the conclusion that the agent of action and the action itself cannot be related either in terms of identity or difference. Since this means a collapse of all symbolic systems, Nāgārjuna was in effect challenging his hearers to demonstrate exactly what it is that enables our linguistic conventions to meaningfully function. My symbolic notation is designed to demonstrate the fact that two mutually contrary variables *x* and *y* can also exchange their own identities, so that the reciprocal co-presence of these variables as *x.y* and *y.x* lead to affirmative and negative sentential construction respectively. This reciprocal context obviously embodies the limit or boundary of linguistic constructions of truth and reality, and therefore should provide a promising theoretical basis for understanding modern religious pluralism and interreligious dialogue.

Despite the merits of linguistic convention, its power of reinforcing teleological thought and action is formidable. The grammatical structure of *kārakas* is the primary source of this power, especially in terms of anthropomorphic causal conceptions. The semantic structure that links words and meanings is no less powerful an agent of reinforcement over human thought patterns, such as the notions of causation involved in theories of natural law. The Mādhyamika dialectic demonstrates that categories and systems are neither absolute nor ultimate precisely because they have neither self-identity nor any referential foundation, (i.e., *niḥsvabhāva*) is another expression of *śūnyatā*.

Modern scholarship, both Eastern and Western, has analyzed the relation between language and external phenomena from a number of linguistic and nonlinguistic perspectives. For example, sociologists and anthropologists have extended their disciplines to include the analysis of religions in terms of symbol and action systems. But until now, very little modern scholarship has been directed toward analyzing the paradoxical dimensions of religious faith and experience captured in religious language as such. I am convinced that doing justice to the paradoxes of religious experience linguistically expressed is crucial for an understanding of religious pluralism, interreligious dialogue, and the renewal of religious faith in the modern secular world. The boundaries of the Mādhyamika critique of language seem to suggest that the renewal of religious faith, whether in Christian or Buddhist form, can be accomplished by means of reexamining the process of the linguistic structuring of human experience.

NOTES

1. Paul Tillich, "The Significance of the History of Religions for the Systematic Theologian," in *The Future of Religions*, ed. J. C. Brauer (New York: Harper and Row, 1966), pp. 80-94.
2. William James, *The Varieties of Religious Experience* (New York: Collier Books, 1961), p. 78.
3. Ibid., p. 393.
4. For instance, the following is Clifford Geertz's definition of religion: "A system of symbols which acts to establish powerful, pervasive, and long-lasting moods and motivations in men by formulating conceptions of a general order of existence and clothing these conceptions with such an aura of factuality that the moods and motivations seem uniquely realistic" ("Religion as a Culture System," *Anthropological Approaches to the Study of Religion*, ASA Monographs 3, ed. Michael Banton [London: Tavistock Publications, 1966], p. 4.) See also Robert N. Bellah, "The Sociology of Religion," in his *Beyond Belief, Essays on Religion in a Post-Traditional World* (New York: Harper and Row, 1970), p. 12. In this essay Bellah incorporates Geertz's ideas into his theory.
5. See Th. Stcherbatsky, *The Central Conception of Buddhism and the Meaning opf the Word 'Dharma'* (Calcutta: Susil Gupta, 1956), pp. 43-44.
6. Isaline Blew Horner, *The Early Buddhist Theory of Man Perfected* (Amsterdam: Philo Press, 1936), p. 284.
7. Majjhima-Nikāya 3. 121-122: Cūlasuññatasutta and Mahāsuññatasutta (London: PTS, 1899), pp. 104-118; and the English translation by I. B. Horner, "The Lesser Discourse on Emptiness," in *The Collection of the Middle Length Sayings III*, PTS Translation Series no. 31 (1955), pp. 147-162.

8. The Sanskrit original was called Buddha-avataṃsaka-nāma-mahāvaipulya-sūtra, of which two chapters still exist, "Gaṇḍavyūha" and "Daśabhūmi." The Chinese translation has two versions, one in 60 chuans and one in 80 chuans, Ta-fan-kuan-fu-hua-yen-ching (Taishō Daizōkyō), IX and X respectively. The text may be regarded as the Buddhist book of practices and disciplines par excellence.

9. The doctrine of the ten stages of bodhisattvahood initially appeared in *Mahāvastu*, developed in the Prajñāpāramitā textual tradition, and were completed in the Avataṃsaka textual group. The remaining eight stages are:

2. the stage of spotless purity *(vimalā)*
3. the stage of radiance *(prabhākarī)*
4. the stage of bright light *(arciṣmatī)*
5. the stage of overcoming the most difficult *(sudurjayā)*
6. the stage of immediate proximity *(abhimukhī)*
7. the stage of far-reaching *(dūraṅgamā)*
8. the stage of being immovable *(acalā)*
9. the stage of holiness *(sādhumatī)*

See J. Rahder, *Daśabhūmika-sūtra et Bodhisattvabhūmi* (Paris: Paul Geuthner, 1926).

10. The Sāgara-mudrā-samādhi (Hai-yin-san-mei) is the state of concentration equated to the Second Body of the Buddha theorized in the Mahāyāna Buddhology as the state of beatitude (Sambhogakāya, or "Body of Enjoyment"). This is the ultimate goal to be achieved through all the Hua-yen samādhis which are supposed to embellish the Buddha's macrocosmic world.

11. See R.A.F. Thurman, trans., *The Holy Teaching of Vimalakīrti: Mahāyāna Scripture* (University Park: Pennsylvania State University Press, 1978), introduction.

12. The best example of this textual group is the ultra short version known as The Heart Sutra (Prajñāpāramitā-hrdaya-sūtra) which repudiates the enter system of the orthodox Sarvāstivāda, i.e., from the existential basis, such as the "five skandhas," up to the raison d' être of the system itself, "fourfold truth," "arhat status," and "nirvana."

13. For an excellent comprehensive introduction to the tradition, see L. Renou, *L' Inde Classique* (Paris: 1947), pp. 86ff.

14. Pāṇini, *Aṣṭhādhyāyī* 1.4.23 (on *kāraka);* or in S. C. Vasu, trans. (Delhi: Motilal Banarsidass, 1962), 1:327ff.

15. The definition is actually given in *Pāṇiniya-vyākaraṇa-sūtra-vṛtti.* Pāṇini did not include the genetive case because it can never be directly related to an action and hence can never stand in the relation of a *kāraka* to a verb.

16. The following passage clearly points to the *kāraka* structure centered upon action and the verb element. *Mādhyamika-kārikā (=MK)* 2.2, 7, and 9: "Where there is a physical movement *(ceṣṭā),* there is motion *(gati).* Since motion is (only) in the passage being traversed *(gamyamāna)* by an actual movement *(gamana),* there is no physical movement in any completed passage *(gata),* nor is it in the passage not yet traversed *(agata).* Hence, motion is in the passage being traversed *(gamyamāna).* (k.2.) In the absence of an agent *(gantṛ),* an actual movement is not possible. In the absence of an ongoing movement *(gamana),* there should neither be an agent." (k.7)

17. *MK* 2.24, 25.

18. Pāṇini, *Aṣṭhādhyāyī,* 1.4.49.

19. Vasu, *Aṣṭhādhyāyī,* p. 328.

20. See A. Kaplan, *The New World of Philosophy* (New York: Random House, 1961), p. 23.

21. F. de Saussure, *Course in General Linguistics,* trans. W. Baskin (New York: McGraw-Hill, 1966), pp. 7-17. Cf. C. K. Ogden and I. A. Richards, *The Meaning of Meaning,* (London:

Harcourt, Brace and Co., 1938), chap. 1; Kunjuni Raja, *Indian Theories of Meaning* (Madras: Adyar Library and Research Center, 1963), p. 17f.

22. See S. D. Ruegg, Contributions à l'Historie de la Philosophie Linguistique Indienne, (Paris: Ed de Boccard, 1959), p. 36.

23. See J. J. Katz, *The Philosophy of Language* (New York: Harper and Row, 1960), pp. 240-281.

24. Gamana and gamyāmana are respectively the active and passive present participles, i.e., "going" and "being gone." As a part of instrumental action, an actual movement constitutes the instrumental kāraka, while objective reference, a passage traversed by it, constitutes the accusative kāraka. See MK 2.3, 4, 5; also n. 5 in sec. 3 here.

25. Ibid., kk. 10, 11; and kk. 15, 16, 17.

CHAPTER 6

The Mutual Fulfillment of Buddhism and Christianity in Co-inherent Superconsciousness

Roger J. Corless

> God is a fox; and he likes fox-cubs.
> G. Christopher Stead

> Playing a flute without holes is very difficult.
> *Zenrin Kushu*

Christianity and Buddhism are both supremely self-confident religions. From small, local beginnings, they have become supranational organizations assured that they alone possess the fullness of truth. Until fairly recently, this was not really a problem, for each religion kept itself predominantly in its own hemisphere. But now they are meeting and interpenetrating, and their mutual perplexity begins. How do two ancient, consummate explanations of totality relate to each other? Three possibilities at once present themselves: segregation, victory of one, or mutual tolerance.

Segregation is becoming increasingly unrealistic, and may be dismissed at once. We live in a pluralistic universe.

Victory of one party is the traditional, or missionary, approach. The spread of Christianity throughout Europe and Russia cannot be attributed solely to its alliance with military might. Paganism simply did not have as many satisfactory answers to human problems. The advance of Buddhism was more peaceful, though not as peaceful as some of its apologists would wish,[1] and can be more clearly attributed to the power of its teachings. Both religions, to varying extents, absorbed rather than destroyed the faiths which they found in their paths. Thus the old European gods were demoted to fairies or converted into saints, or become perforce Christian enantiomorphs within witchcraft; the Asian gods were demoted to *dharmapālas* or converted into bodhisattvas, or became perforce Buddhist emantiomorphs within systems

such as Bönpo in Tibet. The very success of Christianity and Buddhism creates a barrier to their mutual understanding. Having developed such effective
polemics, they then seek to use them on each other, without asking if they
are really appropriate.[2] For example, Buddhism early developed arguments
against the existence of a prime mover, of a sophistication not seen in the
West until quite recently. It now uses these arguments against the Christian
God. But the Christian God is not a prime mover, even though, traditionally,
theologians have tried to use the philosophical idea of a prime mover to
make systematic sense of the God of biblical revelation.

This point is so often overlooked by both sides in Buddhist-Christian dialogue that it needs emphasizing. At least two biblical texts are usually
dragged out to prove that God is an Aristotelian by philosophical preference.
Genesis 1.1 is supposed to prove that God created the world *ex nihilo,* and
Exodus 3.14 is regarded as the statement "I am the Self-Existent One" (i.e.,
someone like the Hindu entity variously called Svayambhū, Paramesvara,
Paramabrahman, etc.). It is time to say that this is nonsense, and that Christians have themselves been responsible for the nonsense, because they wrote
in Greek and Latin but did not study Torah. The verb in Greek and Latin ex-
hibits tense, but the Hebrew verb (like the Japanese verb, curiously enough)
has no tense but expresses completion or incompletion of an action. The
action of God in Genesis 1.1 is *bārā,* "the creative act is complete," and his
words in Exodus 3.14 are *'ehyeh 'asher 'ehyeh,* "I am present as I am present,"
"My presence with you will never cease," "I shall be who I shall turn out to
be." Fr. Stuhlmueller translates the Tetragrammaton, the four-lettered unpro-
nounceable Name of God (YHWH) as "He who is always here."[3] The rabbis
interpret Genesis 1.1 as the perfection of the creative act of God which is
renewed from moment to moment; but in Greek (Septuagint translation, abbreviated LXX) and Latin (Vulgate translation, abbreviated Vulg.) it is
merely something that happened a long time ago (LXX: *epoīesen;* Vulg:
creavit). Again, when St. Jerome (c. 342-420, the originator of the Vulgate,
which became the standard Catholic version for over fifteen hundred years)
rendered Exodux 3.14 as *ego sum qui sum,* he opened a door to Aristotelianism
which, despite the work of the Process Theologians, has even yet not been
closed. A God who says *ego sum qui sum,* "I am who I am," is infinitely
distant, cold, and unfeeling. One who says *'ehyeh 'asher 'ehyeh,* "I am always
present," is profoundly immanent, warm, and caring. They are opposites. If
Buddhists wish to deny the Christian God they must attack at the level of experienced revelation, not *ex post facto* philosophy.

On the other hand, Christians, having developed arguments against
polytheism, pantheism, and atheism, began to use them (with riotous
inconsistency) against Buddhists without realizing that Buddhism is not any
kind of "theism," or indeed any "ism" at all, because *śunyatā* (emptiness,

devoidness, qualificationlessness) is not a thing or a viewpoint, as Nāgārjuna once said quite clearly (*Mūamadhyamaka-kārikā* 13.8). More seriously, some Christians have imagined that they could assess the Dharma in the way they might assess the words of Socrates. European (and therefore Christian) philosophy has been largely an affair of rationalism separating the person from what he or she experiences. Buddhists deny this way of philosophizing. Any thinking which does not proceed from an experience of nonduality is the product of ignorance and is so deluded as to make it impossible to say that it is wrong. European philosophers have, with the exception perhaps of Wittgenstein, held to the binary view that either the universe exists, or it does not. They are thus caught in the *Sutra of the Perfect Net (Brahmajāla Suttanta: Dīgha Nikāya 1)* and thrust through by Nāgārjuna, as we shall shortly see.

Buddhism and Christianity are not opposed to each other. They are irrevelant to each other. Both God and *śunyatā* are, ultimately, beyond analogy. Comparisons of incomparables cannot aspire to meaningful conclusions. Therefore, neither Christianity nor Buddhism can win. Their battle-axes cannot connect. So, can they exist in mutual tolerance? Perhaps. But tolerance becomes, sooner or later, intolerable. A Christian must insist that God in Trinity exists and that it is cosmically wrong, a most appalling insult, to ignore him. A Buddhist cannot see how one could do better than go for refuge in the Three Jewels, and learn from that lion among beings, the teacher of gods and men. As we see in India today, a condition of tolerance is an exercise in brinkmanship which is always in danger of breaking out in squabbles or actual violence. The point is that tolerance implies indifferentism, and neither Buddhism nor Christianity permits indifferentism.

So, our three possibilities for relating Christianity and Buddhism have gone under. A fourth option appears to present itself, unity. This has two aspects: immanent and transcendental. Immanent unity, unity within the visible world, has been tried in China ("the harmonious unity of Confucianism, Taoism, and Buddhism," *san chiao ho-i*) and in Japan ("deities and Buddhas are identical," *shimbutsu shūgō*). Transcendental unity is characteristic of many forms of hinduism. Rāmakrishna (1834-86) says:

> God is one, but many are his aspects. As one master of the house appears
> in various aspects, being father to one, brother to another, and husband
> to a third, so one God is described and called in various ways according
> to the particular aspect in which He appears to His particular
> worshipper.[4]

But unity is not really a fourth option. Immanent unity is an institutionalized form of tolerance, while transcendental unity is a mode of victory (in the case quoted, the victory of Vedāntic Hinduism). If the unity *is* transcendental it must necessarily transcend notions of unity and difference; it cannot be "one" in any comprehensible (numerical) sense. *Chāndogya Upaniṣad* 6.2.1-2 is quite precise: "at the start there was One and Only One, with no Second," that is, the primal one is not a countable number, it is not part of a series, as if we could count up how many Brahmans there are and discover that there is in fact only one but there might have been more. St. Augustine said something very similar when he noted that as soon as we begin to count, we lose the Trinity *(De Trinitate* 15.43 *[xxiii]*). Likewise, Nāgārjuna's *vandana* (invocation) is to the Buddha who proclaimed "nonsingularity and nonplurality." Within plurality, distinctions must be made: it is nonsense (specifically, it is a category mistake) to melt plurality into a monistic syrup.

But there is, I maintain, a real fourth option: co-inherent superconsciousness. Christianity, Buddhism, Islam (to name only a few religions) speak of a two-level consciousness — an everyday consciousness which does not tolerate paradox and which arranges things hierarchically, and an extraordinary or "super" consciousness which transcends paradox and hierarchies. In what follows I shall (1) characterize this duplex of the mind; (2) examine the construction in Buddhism and Christianity of existing notions of co-inherence (i.e., paradox and hierarchy transcendence) with regard to *śūnyatā* and Christ; (3) offer a meditation practice for opening oneself to superconsciousness in which Christianity and Buddhism may be allowed to co-inhere (Part 4); and (4) suggest some of the implications and effects of superconsciousness.

CO-INHERENT SUPERCONSCIOUSNESS

Modern Western philosophy largely presents itself to the historian of religions as a headless giant, a mechanical monster which has escaped incomplete from the mad scientist's basement. It is an affair of truth tables and symbol manipulation which, admirable in itself, has oddly been permitted to fill our epistemological horizon. It startlingly contrives to congratulate itself with an ethnocentric assumption of the value of Western noetics and a chronocentric assumption of manifest intellectual destiny. According to this epistemology, Asians are Easterners. Easterners are mystics. And mystics cannot think.

If we take a less prejudicial and more cosmopolitan view, quite a different situation emerges. Easterners have, somehow or other, contrived to keep complex and sophisticated civilizations going for as long as or longer than Westerners. So they must have had, and still have, considerable savvy. Detroit is now trembling before Tokyo, and Washington, D.C. is smoothing the atomically agitated feathers of New Delhi. Yet, as the youth of Calcutta and

Osaka run after blue jeans and rock music, disaffected Americans are today taking up yoga and Zen. What is the lesson? Wholeness, I would say. It is not my intention here to examine this from the Eastern standpoint, but to inquire into the Western fascination with Eastern Mysticism. There is a feeling that something is lacking. It is, I think, not so much the head in general as the eyes in that head.

At least three spiritual traditions have developed systematic explanations of what we today vaguely call "the mystic experience." Islam states that ordinary knowledge, gained by memorization and reflection, is open to all with the requisite intelligence and application. It is called *'ilm*. With it, the "doctors" *('ulama')* interpret the will of Allah from the texts of the Qur'an, and the Hadith. But the Sufi claims a special gnosis, *ma'rifa*, which one cannot earn, but which descends as a free grace from Allah upon chosen prepared disciples. *Ma'rifa* gives a direct knowledge of Allah, bypassing but not abrogating the information in the sacred texts.[5] Scholastic Catholic Christianity maintained a similar distinction between *ratio*, the knowledge of natural truths, and *intellectus*, the wisdom which gazes upon supernatural truths and is the provenance of that "certainty of invisible things" (Heb. 11.1) called "faith" *(fides)*. St. John of the Cross could therefore intelligibly speak of the development of a new "organ" of mystical insight. Buddhism regards ordinary thinking (Skt., *vikalpa, vijñana;* Gk., *sems*) as deluded and productive only of suffering, and points to Buddha-thinking (Skt., *jñana;* Tib., *rig.pa;* Chin., *wu-hsin*) as "cloudless mind," in turn leading to the development of a new organ called the Dharma eye.

What we appear to have in these three representative religions is a two-level hierarchy of consciousness, whose levels I shall dub respectively "consciousness" and "superconsciousness." Consciousness is binary and distinguishes clearly between this and that, more and less, above and below. Superconsciousness is nonbinary and leads to remarks like "I am in the Father and the Father is in me"; it sees thusness *(tathatā)* rather than this or that; and it has no difficulty hearing the sound of one hand.[6] It allows differences not only to co-exist but to *co-inhere*, nonhierarchically and absolutely, retaining their several integrities. Consciousness can increase its knowledge discretely, by study, but it can understand the nonbinary only by analogy or by tagging it with the label "mystical paradox." Superconsciousness simply happens. It does not happen *to* anyone or *about* anything/one, but, having happened, it floods consciousness with praeternatural light and makes of its ratiocinations a supersense, in a superorder which Tarthang Tulku has called "great space-time."[7]

Steven Rose has tried to resolve the opposition, in his discipline of neurobiology, between holistic (systems explanations) and reductionistic (unit explanations) models of brain and mind by mapping a series of "hierarchies in biological explanation," from the physical up to the sociological. Thus, the statement "he is in love" is patient of many explanations, for instance, changes in the quantum states of the body's atoms or of the subject's social interactions. Such explanations occur across a hierarchy of discrete levels, operationally (not absolutely) defined, which have a correlative (not a linear, causative, and nonreversible) relationship. Events then are observed to occur on different levels in systematic correlation (can one say, Buddhistically, in conditioned co-arising, *pratītya-samutpāda?*) such that either the "top-down" (holistic) or "bottom-up" (reductionistic) model is seen to be incomplete without the other. Translation across levels is then problematic, and may be illegitimate, especially when performed upwards (reductionistically).[8]

Is not this also the controversy between the historians of religions (the holist) and the logical positivist (the reductionist)? The reductionist regards the head as a secondary, and possibly needless, appendage. The holist is all head, and tends to vagueness about the body. A more fruitful approach to religious, and especially mystical, phenomena, would combine scientific data with symbolic structures in a correlative hierarchy, and be suspicious of the legitimacy of a "bottom-up" causative translation, without denying the validity of the "lower order" data.

This would restore the vanished head to Western thinking and allow us to speak of God, of mysticism, and paradox without automatically provoking gales of derisive laughter from our departments of philosophy. For superconsciousness is not unsystematic. It is supersystematic.

An example of the perils of headlessness is the fate of the cosmological argument for the existence of God, in its colorful form of Canon Paley's "watch discovered on the beach." The good Canon told us that because *he* found the cosmos as ordered as a watch, an intelligence must have made it. The standard reply is, we have only one cosmos to work with, so we cannot compare it with a hypothetical chaos, as we can compare functioning watches with disassembled ones—so, the cosmological argument fails. But another answer, which transcends the standard controversy, is that reality appears as part cosmos and part chaos to consciousness, but to superconsciousness it appears as supercosmos which is beyond binary models of order and disorder and may be understood only by God or by Buddha-mind.

It is my contention that only to superconsciousness does anything make ultimate "sense" or "nonsense;" that this has been the opinion of many great minds throughout history; and that it is only comparatively recently that we have become epistemologically trapped in a headless monster which cannot see this.

In this essay I wish to begin with the clearly understood proposition, already stated, that Buddhism and Christianity are doctrinally incompatible in every respect. But I do not mean by this to put myself out of business as a comparer of religions. The incompatibility is on the lower hierarchical level of *this* and *that*. *Either* God *or* the Buddha. At the level of superconsciousness, of thusness and both-and, this incompatibility does not disappear, it is not resolved, but it is understood differently, so differently that Sino-Japanese Buddhists call this level of the mind's function "no-mind" *(wu-hsin/mushin)*. I propose to show that this superconsciousness, the mind of God and the Buddha-mind (two minds which, being beyond analogy, cannot be said to be either the same or different) is the modality in which, for Christians and Buddhists, Christ and *śunyatā* are respectively understood, and that only when Christian and/or Buddhist persons have contacted superconsciousness can there be any compatibility between the two religions. This supercompatibility in the superconsciousness of the participant I wish to identify as an Einsteinian shift from the Copernican universe of quasi-objective compatibilities in either a Teilhardian omega point or an Aurobindan *purosottama,*[9] and from the Ptolemaic universe of quasi-subjective compatibilities in some form of psychological reductionism. Co-inherent consciousness escapes the limitations of absolute objectivity, absolute subjectivity, or some combination of the two.

The compatibility I propose is non-, or super-, conceptual. A persistent problem with modern Westerners is conceptualization (reductionism).

> My friend Father L, who lives in Japan . . . practices zazen. Still he understands nothing of Soto Zen. Christian Zen, yes. But not Soto Zen. Christianity is Christianity, Zen is Zen, and though we can find similarities between the two, one should go beyond them both. It is not necessary to become attached to Zen, to Buddha, God or Christ . . . Father L is always making categories.[10]

Let us recognize once and for all that Buddhism is Buddhism, Christianity is Christianity, and that any meeting is beyond them. But the beyond is neither "out there" nor "in here." It is in superconsciousness and great space-time.

Both Christians and Buddhists have searched for and found a superconsciousness in great space-time, from which perspective their several ambiguities (God/man; nirvana/samsara) display an identity-in-difference *(bhedabeda)*. These superconsciousnesses are respectively ontological and epistemological, and are called Christ (to post-Nicene orthodoxy) and *śunyatā* (to post-Nāgārjuna Mahāyāna). To discover their structural similarities, their doctrinal incompatibilities, and their several authenticities, the process of their construction needs to be investigated.

CO-INHERENCE: THEORY—EXISTING MODELS IN
CHRISTIANITY AND BUDDHISM

Ontological Co-Inherence According to Nicene Christianity

The monotheistic statement, as made by Parsis, Jews, Christians, and Muslims, that God is one, is subject to two internal dangers: it may fall into monism or plain theism. The *mono*theistic God is simultaneously immanent and transcendent, personal and transpersonal. Nirguṇabrahman (life-force without qualities) is immanent and transpersonal, while the Trimūrti (Brahmā-Viṣṇu-Śiva) or Harihara (Viṣṇu-Śiva) or Ardhanārīśvara (Śiva-Devī) or whatever combination is transcendent and personal. The philosophical quest of the monotheist is to make sense of an experience that, on the face of it, is nonsense. ". . . the being of God needs to be justified to reason alike as transcendent, as creative, and as immanent."[11] The Council of Nicaea (A.D. 325) adopted the term *homoousios,* "of the same nature," to express the relationship of the visible Christ with the invisible Father. We need to unwrap this a little, and see how close is its logic to that of the term *madhyama-pratipad,* "middle path," as used by Nāgārjuna.

The early followers of the Way (as Christianity was first called) got themselves into trouble with their fellow Jews, and eventually became a separate religion. I wish to suggest that the central problem was monotheism. Christians at first identified Christ as a great rabbi, and then as the Messiah. The identification was controversial, but controversy is the life of Judaism, and quite unlikely characters such as Sabbatai Sevi, who concluded a paradoxical life by converting to Islam, have been hailed as the Messiah.[12] But then Christians decided that the only way to explain the power which they felt flowing from Jesus, now apparently dead, was to say that he was God.[13] This was too much, and they were charged with polytheism, or, more exactly, ditheism. But *because* of the experience of the risen Jesus, Christians could *therefore* understand the oneness of God who is immanent, transcendent, personal, and transpersonal, as never before. For them, the God of the Torah seemed pallid by comparison.

Once separated from Judaism, and enjoying the Peace of Constantine, the identity of Jesus became an in-house problem. Everybody agreed that Jesus was divine in some sense, but nobody agreed on how much he was divine, and whether he had to become divine or had always been divine. The discussion, which was often vigorous, not to say vicious, proceeded in barber shops and led to torchlight processions in favor of a certain side, as well as being the concern of the bishops and the theologians. For a great deal was at stake: was Jesus the sort of being who made the big difference between enmity to and friendship with God? This soteriological concern is often ommitted from the dry, academic histories of the period.[14] The Christian analysis of *la probl̃eme humaine* is ontological. Created in God's image and likeness, we rebelled (sinned) and, while retaining the image (mere existence is the "image" of God) we lost the likeness and became subhuman. Our *being* is not *human*. Thus, a middle must arise to bridge the gap who is a living middle and into whom we can be incorporated so as to regain our likeness to God.

The controversy had many sides. For simplicity, I shall consider Nicene Orthodoxy and Arianism (so called after Arius, its chief exponent Thaleia or "Banquet"). For Arius, Christ was a human who "was made God" *(etheopoīethē)* and became God "by participation" *(metochē)*. His unity was first and foremost with fallen man, and he could draw us up to God because he himself had been so drawn. Orthodoxy objected that one who "becomes" or "advances" *(prokoptē)* might also retreat, and the work would fail. But more seriously, Arianism, by allowing a gap between Jesus and God, albeit one that is eventually closed, preached a God who is clearly transcendent but not certainly immanent. Theirs is not a monotheistic God, but a kind of Saguṇabrahman (life-force with qualities).

Nicaea maintained against Arius that Jesus and God participated in the same *ousia*. *Ousia* is normally translated into Latin as *substantia,* therefore "substance," and it is sometimes claimed that the problem with pre-Nicene thought was a fixation on "naive realism," that is, God physically extruded some of his "stuff" to make Christ, producing a kind of ditheism, against which Nicaea taught a monotheistic identity (of God and "Christ-stuff").[15] In fact, however, *ousia* was anciently a much broader term, and could also mean light or spirit.[16] The difference between God and Jesus (called the *idiotes,* "particularity") was explained according to the term *hypostasis,* normally put into Latin as *persona* (theatrical mask) or "person," which I might suggest can be provisionally rendered as "subset." But the subsets of God the Father and God the Son are not in a hierarchy, they are reciprocal. A quote from Prestige states the position well:

> The difference between the Persons, says Basil *(c. Eun. 1.19),* consists in their plurality and in the 'particularities' which characterize each: and again *(ep. 38.8),* everything that belongs to the Father is seen in the Son, and everything that belongs to the Son abides whole in the Father and again possesses the Father whole in Himself; the hypostasis of the Son is, so to speak, the 'form' and presentation (prosopon) [literally 'face'] of the recognition of the Father, and the Father's hypostasis is recognized in the form of the Son; there remains the supplementary particularity with a view to the clear distinction of the hypostasis. These particularities are called by Basis *gnōristikai idiotētes* ('identifying particularities'), and they consist in being *gennetos* ('begotten') and being *agennetos* ('unbegotten') . . . . They are modes of being, not elements in being.[17]

Eventually, a gentleman known mysteriously as Pseudo-Cyril homed in on the term *perichōrēsis*, which became the Latin *circumincessio*. In classical Greek, for example, in Anaxagoras, the word meant "rotation," as of the seasons, and reciprocity of action (always with *eis* "into," or *pros* "toward," never with *en* "in," or *dia* "through,").[18] Prestige illustrates the final Christian meaning of the word by summarizing a passage from a work spuriously attributed to Gregory of Nyssa, *Against the Arians and the Sabellians:*

> If the Father is perfect and fills all things, the writer asks, what is left for the Son, who is also perfect, to contain? His answer is that the Father and the Son are receptive and permeative (*chōrētikos*) of the another, and, as thus 'containing' one another, would be equal in extension; the one is enveloped in the other (periechesthai), but not in like manner with human instances of envelopment, in which the enveloping substance has an empty space in which to hold the substance enveloped; with God the relation is mutual . . . . So far as extension can be conceived in relation to deity, the Father and the Son are mutually interpenetrative like the sciences [in the human mind, and extend over identical space and are receptive of one another, differing only in hypostasis and title,
>
> and reside in one another, like perfume in the atmosphere.[19]

Therefore, what we have is mutual containment of the divine and the human, which allows total freedom and validity to each, does not arrange them hierarchically, and in which they are co-extensive in a nonspatial, imageless fashion, in a person whose co-inherent identity is comprehensible only to God, or to those who in some way participate in the divine consciousness. This sounds very much like a walking, talking *madhyama-satya* (middle truth), that is, like an ontological version of the epistemological middle, as I hope to demonstrate.

Epistemological Co-inherence
According to Mādhyamika Buddhism

Buddhism is a religion of discovery rather than revelation. In monotheistic revelation, God approaches persons and reveals his existence and nature, both of which could otherwise be at most inferred. Since this necessarily concerns itself with ontology, specifically the divine ontology, it is this which forms the basis of monotheistic systematic thought. In Buddhic discovery, however, a finite being moves from ignorance (*avidya*) to knowledge (*vidyā, prajña, bodhi*) and, in some sense or another, infinity. Epistemology is central, for we have to know that we do not know and then know the knowledge when we know it.

Early Buddhism, much of which appears to have survived in present-day Theravāda and to have been preserved in amber within Mayāyāna as a similar but distinct system called Hīnayāna, saw "thinking" as both the problem and the answer. It regarded the liturgical recitation of the Vedas as useless noise, and rejected the spirit-matter dualisms of both Hindu yoga (*puruṣa-prakṛti*) and Jainism (*jīva-ajīva*) as quite simply wrong. All legends of the Buddha insist that, before his enlightenment, he tried a form of yogic enstasis, finally reaching beyond the state of nothing-whatever (*akiñcanāyatan*) to the state of neither-thinking-nor-not-thinking (*naiva saṃjñānāsaṃjñāyatana*), but said, on returning to normal consciousness, that he had merely gone to the subtle fine point of being (*bhavāgra*), without transcending his desires. The legends are also unanimous on the point that he tried extreme asceticism (*tapas*) (almost to starvation) of a type still recommended today by Jainism, but found he had merely become weak without transcending his desires. So he made the decision to care for his body just sufficiently to allow thinking to function smoothly, and attempted to wake-up to what-there-is rather than retreat inward. This is the Middle Path in its simplest expression.

Abhidharma, the first really important classical attempt to make sense of the Buddha's vision, analyzed human experience of the perceived universe into its component parts. For instance, a person appears at first to be a unity. On closer examination she/he is seen to have visible elements (*rūpa*) and invisible elements or mental phenomena (*nāma*). More precisely still, *nāma* is observed to have arranged itself into four clusters (*skandha*), that is, sensory input (*vedanā*),coherent mental images (*saṃjñā*), consciously willed reaction (*saṃskāra*) and consciousness of consciousness (*vijñāna*). Since sensory input requires something to put into it, namely *rūpa*, we now have five clusters as the constituents of a perceived person. These are further examined (in meditation) until a finite list of irreducible simple constituents generating the infinity of perceived universes is obtained. The precise number of simple constituents and their relationships with the five *skandhas*, was a matter of spirited debate between different schools of *abhidharma*. Each simple constituent is called a *dharma* because it grasps (*dhṛ*) a single, unique characteristic (*lakṣana*). This is not an atomic theory, although Western Buddhologists have in the past mistaken it for one. A *dharma* is an element of *the universe as perceived* rather than the universe as such, and it is extremely unstable, lasting, for example, according to one school, a sixteenth part of a hand clap. There is a certain similarity to atomic theory insofar as every *dharma* of a certain class, though evanescent, is indistinguishable from every other instance of a *dharma* of that same class, just as every hydrogen atom is indistinguishable from every other hydrogen atom. When the *dharmas* are observed in altered states of consciousness by the meditator, ignorance can be destroyed, knowledge obtained, and the passage from dualistic existence (samsara) to nondualism (nirvana) is made.

The Mahāyāna tradition pointed to a number of fatal antinomies in the foregoing, and claimed that it did not make sense, indeed that it was unBuddhist (see *Mumadhyamaka-kārikā* 10.16). If nirvana be nondual, how can it be dualistically distinguished from samsara? But if nirvana and samsara be the same, how is liberation possible? Hīnayāna (the Small Vehicle—a derogatory name given by Mahāyāna) claimed that all the *dharmas* arise in dependence upon each other, in a kind of unified field theory in which every *dharma*, or perceived particularity, conditions and is conditioned by every other *dharma* (*pratītya-samutpāda*), "conditioned co-arising"), while retaining its own distinct essence (*svabhāva*) and special being. But if so, a *dharma* is dependent upon all other *dharmas* for its so-called existence, and hence it does not exist in and out of itself. Therefore, how is it possible to get outside of all this and make a statement such as "the *dharmas* exist"? But if we make no statement, the Buddha preached in vain.

Mahāyāna groups its opponents into two main camps: Śāśvatavādins (eternalists) and the Ucchedavādins (nihilists). The Śāśvatavādins maintain that things exist, and that something can therefore be said about them. The Ucchedavādins believe that nothing "really" exists, that everything is an illusion, and so nothing can be said about it. Mahāyāna sets out to show the absurdity of both views, indeed of all views. The classical text is the *Mūlamadhyamaka-kārikā* (Root Verses on That Which Pertains to the Middle, hereinafter abbreviated as *MMK*) of Nāgārjuna (c. A.D. 150-250).[20]

Everything is laid out in the *vandana* (invocation) which opens the work:

> I bow to the Perfectly Enlightened One,
> the Best of Teachers,
> who taught that *pratītya-samutpāda* is:
> unperishing, unarising, nonnihilist, noneternalist,
> not a singularity, not a plurality, not come, not gone,
> and quiescent of discursiveness.

A series of philosophical viewpoints is then examined, and their antinomies are brought out so that they collapse upon themselves. For instance, fuel and fire:

> If fire is fuel, then the doer is the deed; if fire is other than fuel, fire
> exists without fuel. Not having a cause of lighting, fire would burn con-

stantly . . . . If you state that therefore the being-burnt becomes the fuel, by what is the fuel burnt when it along is there? The others will not catch fire, the uncaught will not burn, the unburning will not burn out, the un-burnt-out will endure and possess its own mark. (*MMK* 10.1-2a, 4-5)

Nāgārjuna presents this as a typical polemic, which can be adapted to destroy any pluralistic or monistic viewpoint whatever. Its subtlety, apart from its logical cohesion, lies in the traditional symbolism of fire and fuel as the passions and their objects, the going out of which is nirvana. The "un-burnt-out" in verse 5b is *anirvāṇaḥ*, "that which has not 'nirvanated.'" That a being, having been liberated by achieving nirvana, should still be unliberated, is absurd.

The obvious charge is that Nāgārjuna is a nihilist. But that is precisely one of the views which he rejects. He is arguing for *śūnyatā*, which is not a view but an emptying of views. Setting up *śūnyatā* as a view leaves us where we were at the beginning, in fact worse off than that, for now we think we know the answer (*MMK* 13.8). Whether one affirms or denies *śūnyatā*, it is all *prajñapti* (provisional truth, operational hypothesis) (*MMK* 22.11). The Buddha is called the Tathāgata because what-there-is is *tathatā*, (thusness), and to ask whether the Tathāgata survives death or not is invalid, since the question splits thusness into this and that. The Tathāgata neither exists nor does not exist (*MMK* 22.13). Similarly, nirvana cannot be said either to exist or not exist (*MMK* 25.10). Finally, in a famous and beautifully crafted pair of *ślokas* (Sanskrit couplets), Nāgārjuna says:

> Nothing of samsara is distinct from nirvana.
> Nothing of nirvana is distinct from samsara.
> Nirvana's limit is the limit of samsara.
> Between the two there is not even the subtlest something.
> (*MMK* 25.19-20)

Nirvana and samsara are thus co-extensive although not of course in a naive physical, or even metaphysical, sense, for both are *śūnyatā*. This co-extension, which is called the "middle truth" (*madhyama-satya*) or "middle path" (*madhyama-pratipad*) is in no sense a third truth between or in the middle of eternalism and nihilism, but it is interesting to note that some early Chinese Mādhamikas thought that it was. They regarded the distinction between samsara and nirvana as that between yang and yin, with the middle truth as a kind of compromise within their alternation.[21] This is strikingly similar to the early meaning of *perichōrēsis*, since yang and yin rotate with the days and nights, the seasons, and so forth. As it took Pseudo-Cyril to refine *perichōrēsis* into "co-inherence," so it took Seng Chao (A.D. 374-414) to (re-)discover the non-objectivity of *śūnyatā* in his *Knowledge (prajñā) has no Knowing (Pan-jo wu Chih)*.[22]

Mādhyamika thus presents Buddhism with a mutual containment of the liberated and unliberated states which allows total freedom and validity to each, does not arrange them hierarchically, and in which they are co-extensive in a nonspatial, imageless fashion, in a knowledge whose co-inherent identity is comprehensible only to the buddhas and those who in some way participate in a Buddha-consciousness.

Chronological Co-Inherence in
Buddhism, Christianity, and Physics

In moving toward a model for the mutual containment of Christianity and Buddhism, a temporal difficulty presents itself. Christianity arrives about five hundred years later than Buddhism. It therefore might be said, as indeed it often has been said, that Christianity is the fulfillment of Buddhism,[23] but it seems odd to say that Buddhism is the fulfillment of Christianity. The root of the difficulty is primarily the inescapable feeling, in ordinary consciousness, that time passes, that it has an arrow pointing to the future. That is to say, there is a felt asymmetry between past and future. The problem of time asymmetry has engaged the best human minds in both the East and the West.

For example, Zen Master Dōgen said, in A.D. 1240, that "[time] appears to be passing but the past is always contained in the present."[24] The "Uji" chapter of Dōgen's collected works *Shōbōgenzō* (Looking into the Treasury of the True Dharma) examines the connection between existence and time. Dōgen has taken as his koan the puzzle that although we *are* enlightened (*hongaku*) we must *become* enlightened (*shikaku*). The koan solved itself when he realized that *hongaku* and *shikaku* were nondual, and existence itself *is* time. *Uji* is a mystifying compound normally Englished as "being-time." Although this accurately reproduces the order of the characters, I suggest that it makes better English sense to reverse them: "time-being." This contains two implied puns (Dōgen loved implied puns). It gives a feeling of temporariness, of *uji* as *prajñapti*, as in "leave it for the time being," and it has the sci-fi spookiness of a hypothetical "being who is made of time" — "Attention all personnel: a Time Being has invaded sector five!" Both of these ideas seem to lie behind Dōgen's neologism.

Dōgen makes his point at the very beginning, and then unwraps it: "Time-being means that time is being and being is time. A Buddha image is time. Time is, above all, the effulgence of time."[25] That is, time and being arise together, in dependence on each other, and anything at all that exists (such as the Buddha image in the Dharma hall where Dōgen may have been preaching) is time, and it is the effulgence *(sōgon)* of itself, in other words, it is nirvana and samsara co-inhering. If time is studied only as moving away from us *(hikyo tobi saru)*, we end up with nonsense, for we make a separation *(kangeki)* between us (our existence) and time.[26] Therefore, "my own time-being is dependent upon time-being [itself]."[27] Nāgārjuna had denied temporal flow in the absolute sense *(MMK 19)* — "things do not come or go" *(MMK Vandana)*. Dōgen says, "Thinking and expressing are squeezed between coming and going, and are time-being. Thinking and expressing are not squeezed between coming and going, and are time-being."[28] But this does not imply time travel. It is a change in our consciousness: "Past and present do not pile up on each other" *(Kokon no ji [toki], kasanareru ni arazu)*.[29] This change in consciousness is called "dreaming" by the Australian aborigines: the world was created in dream time, and certain rituals restore the participants to dream time, in which ordinary time and space collapse.[30]

But if I cannot find a Christian who agrees with *uji,* it is my argument that will collapse. Fortunately, the Cappadocian fathers (i.e., Saints Basil of Caesarea in Cappadocia [c.330-79], Gregory of Nazianzus [329-89] and Gregory of Nyssa [c.330-95] read the Bible in Greek, and the Greek Old Testament (LXX) is a very bad, that is to say a very literal, translation of the Hebrew. Genesis 1.5 LXX renders the Hebrew *yōm 'eḥad* as *hēmera mia.* Hebrew *'eḥad* is the number "one" and can be a cardinal, an ordinal, or a distributive. Clearly it is here an ordinal, "the first day," but LXX takes it as a cardinal, "one day." This grammatical oddity occasioned much debate.[31] Following the Pythagoreans, one *(mia)* was understood as the unique monad (the day of creation) and not the first *(prōtē)* of the *hebdomad* (the week). A Christian view of the value of history was introduced against the antihistoricism of the Pythagoreans, and the seven days of the temporal week were regarded as a symbol of flowing time while the "one day" was Sunday, which "returns upon itself" *(anakuklousthai)* as does the aeon (eternity) so that one week is really one day.[32] That is to say, because the week is a circle of which Sunday is both the beginning and the end, it is a temporal symbol of the circle of eternity, the day of the Lord (another name for Sunday) which has no ending. The "one day" is then called the eighth day, which is beyond the temporal cycle. St. Augustine of Hippo (354-430) noticed that the Bible does not assign an evening to the seventh day of Creation (Gen. 2.1-3), and he said it was because it flowed ahistorically into the eighth.[33]

From God's perspective, time does not flow. St. Thomas Aquinas, sometime between A.D. 1266 and 1272, gives us an analogy in his *Perihermenias.* A mind in time is like a person in a procession, seeing a before and an after. But a person "set in a high tower" sees the whole procession "not under the aspect of before and after . . . but he sees all at one time." This latter is how

God sees, for "he is set upon the pinnacle of eternity" wherefrom "all is seen in a glance."[34]

Eido T. Shimano Rōshi once said at a lecture during a retreat which I attended, that the essence of Zen is *nen*. *Nen* basically means "to read aloud so as to remember" and has a rich history as a Buddhist technical term. Eido Rōshi chose to interpret it from its form: it is the heart/mind (*kokoro*) in the present (*ima*). The etymology is fanciful but instructive. "Recollectedness" (the usual meaning of the term in Zen) is the eternal present, the apparition of the buddhas and bodhisattvas of the three times in the mandala in front of the practitioner; it is the "pinnacle of eternity" and *nunc stans* (standing now) of both Christian and Buddhist mystical experiences. The eighth day is the endless Sabbath or Rest, wherein rest and activity are nondifferentiated and the saints "possess a rest which is always awake," as St. Augustine says.[35] This active rest or restful activity of the Christian saints in Heaven is also characteristic of the bodhisattvas in Sukhāvatī (the Western Paradise of Buddha Amitābha which is "located" outside of space-time), according to Master T'an-luan (c. A.D. 488-554):

> These bodhisattvas attain to the goal-oriented consciousness and in the divine power of that consciousness, [remaining] in one place (i.e., in Sukhāvatī), they go throughout the worlds in the ten directions (i.e., all directions) instanteneously and simultaneously . . . and go to the innumerable worlds which lack the Buddha, the Dharma and the Sangha, and, manifesting themselves variously, variously teach-and-transform: completely liberated (*tu-t'o*), they constantly do the work of the Buddha for the sake of beings, themselves quite without notions of 'going and coming,' 'worshipping' or 'being completely liberated.'[36]

But if this is the condition in heaven and Sukhāvatī, it is also said to be possible to enter it directly, this very moment. For Shinran Shōnin *nen* is "the tiny instant in which *shin* (i.e., the realization of the nonduality of Amida Buddha's mind and my mind) manifests, and our minds are filled with inexpressible joy."[37] Augustine speaks of the "Sabbath of the heart," which is the deep tranquillity amidst the trials of life coming from the certainty of salvation: "This joy, in the peace of our hope—this is our Sabbath."[38]

Some cautious support for this extra-spatio-temporal viewpoint may be gathered from modern physics.[39] For Newtonian physics, time is an absolute which is definitely measurable. Our ordinary notions of time are a version of Newtonian time. The clocks we use assume its linearity and absoluteness, and produce for us a mean solar day by which we regulate our lives. The "arrow" of time is taken for granted. But in modern physics, the absoluteness of Newtonian time has been abandoned. Space-time is now seen as a four-dimensional unit and, depending on our motion relative to other objects in space, our measurements of time differ. Physicists are mightily intrigued by this problem, but they do not seem ready to give up the "reality," in some post-Cartesian sense, of time and its arrow. However, it appears that we would have no problem if we could visualize four-dimensional space-time as readily as we can visualize three-dimensional space. It may be that superconsciousness is just a resolution to the problem, and that it is toward this that the pioneering explorations of Fritjof Capra and others are trying to move.

Christianity, Buddhism, and perhaps physics thus conspire to present us with a state of consciousness of the mutual containment of past, present, and future which allows total freedom and validity to each, does not arrange them hierarchically, and in which they are co-extensive in an imageless fashion—a chronological middle.

CO-INHERENCE: PRACTICE

"It's academic" has come to mean it doesn't really matter. Were I to stop at this point, I would be false to both Buddhism and Christianity. I have been exercised by the plurality of religions in general, and by the antagonisms and similarities between Christianity and Buddhism in particular, since my middle teens. I have by turns espoused monistic tolerance, sectarian intrasigence, and a curious metaphysic of superimposed universes, mutually invisible due to their differential frequences of vibration, which I dreamed up while trapped in an examination hall by a Latin test which confounded me. The beginning of a solution proposed itself to me when, nearly thirty years after my original excitement at discovering the mystics, a koan which I had set myself, Are you Christian or Buddhist?, seemed to answer itself.

Others may wish to work with my koan. But koans are not for everybody, and indeed I feel that in my case solving of it was only preliminary to the movement toward co-inherence. I felt I needed both a more public and a more embodied meditation. I have myself been most helped in understanding Nāgārjuna by considering the *Ekākṣaraprajñāpāramitā-sūtra*, "The Sutra on the Nirvanic Wisdom in a Single Syllable." This sutra, as its title suggests, is gnomically succinct. It is the lapidary revelation of the syllable A as the ultimate wisdom. It is so because A is, in Sanskrit, the middle which co-inheres Śāśvatavāda and Ucchedavāda (or any other duality). As the first syllable in the Sanskrit alphabet, it is the origin of all things—since, according to an important stream of Hindu thought, the universe is a precipitation of the sonic energies contained in the Sanskrit alphabet—but it is also used as a negative prefix (as the Greek alpha-privative, or in English words such as "asymmetry"). Thus, from A all things are generated (Śāśvatavāda) and by it all things are negated (Ucchedavāda). Upon this tiny sutra is based the Tantric practice of "Visualization of the Syllable A" *(Ajikan)* in which A is used as a *yantra* by being visualized in what Catholicism would call an imaginary vision[40] and expanded to fill the universe such that everything is experienced as *madhyama-satya.*

A Co-inherence *yantra* needs to be both things at once, as A is. In Figure 1 I offer the yantra for Buddhist-Christian Co-inherence.

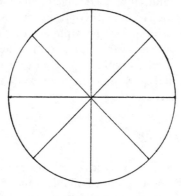

Figure 1

This *yantra* consists of two eight-spoked wheels, one contained in the other. Each wheel represents both Christianity and Buddhism. As a Buddhist symbol, it is clearly the eight-spoked wheel of Dharma. As Christian, it is an ancient symbol for Christ, composed of the equal-armed or Greek cross (✛) combined with the first letter (*chi* X)of the name "Christ" in Greek, so as to produce the figure✱.[41]This is then enclosed in the circle of eternity, and the eight spokes thus resulting may be taken as a symbol of the eighth day. As Christian-Buddhist, it is the ✸ enclosing the ✸ and the ✸enclosing the ✸, a mutual   containment which allows   total freedom and validity to each, and does not arrange them hierarchically.

I would like now to suggest its use. Draw it yourself (it is important that the practitioner execute his or her own *yantra)* in bold black lines on white paper, or bold white lines on black paper. Gaze at it long enough to be able to form an image of it without its aid. Then, as you engage in formless Buddhist meditation (such as *zazen),* visualize it in front of you as the Dharma containing Christ. During formless Christian meditation (such as the silence after Communion at Mass), visualize it as Christ containing the Dharma. Later, try transferring the image to your own chest, mindful of Kōbō Daishi's *sokushin zebutsu* ("This very body is Buddha's Body"), and of St. Paul's "The 'I' who lives is no longer 'me' but Christ who lives in me" (Gal. 2.20). Do not try to visualize the co-inherence (by definition, that cannot be done), simply alternate from one inherence to the other, and wait for the co-inherence to manifest itself. "This very body lives, yet not it, but—lives through it." When that happens, you may find that the Buddha and Christ have been having a good laugh together as you tried to figure them out. Perhaps this is the Zen shout (KA!) and the *risus sanctorium* (laughter of the saints). Or perhaps, in the more sober words of the physicist Niels Bohr, you may discover that although the opposite of a fact is a falsehood, the opposite of one profound truth is another profound truth.

In order to test my model, I took refuge as a Gelugpa Buddhist under Geshela Lhundup Sopa on July 13, 1980, having received prior permission from my Catholic spiritual director and having explained to Geshela what I was doing. Two weeks later I took bodhisattva vows and received a Tantric initiation. I now regard myself as, at the level of superconsciousness, both a Christian and a Buddhist.

I chose Gelugpa over the more popular Zen because I felt that Christians who do Zen most often do *Christian* Zen. *Zazen* is, for them, sitting in *contemplatio* (what the English mystics called "bare beholding") before God. A highly laudable but still a Christian practice. If, however, one is engaged in a Gelugpa visualization liturgy, struggling to relate to all kinds of oddly colored ladies and gentlemen improbably perched upon supportless lotuses, one cannot fool oneself that this has anything in the trichiliocosm to do with God. Similarly, at Mass or Divine Office, there is no time to be thinking of the Triratna. Thus the two incompatibles are forced in the superconsciousness.

Liturgically, there must be an oscillation between my Christianity and my Buddhism. Ethically, there is little conflict, for compassion is emphasized in both, and the Buddhist concern for nonhuman beings can be approximated to a Schweitzerian "reverance for life." I found at first a conflict in constant awareness (*smrti; recollectio*), for I clearly could not simultaneously say the Jesus prayer and the Avalokiteśvara mantra. I have resolved this by allowing the Jesus prayer to go on (since it has, over the years, become difficult to stop) and, while walking, visualize lotuses rising out of *śunyata* to meet my steps.

I must repeat that I am not proposing a new religion nor a new blend of religions, for such would compound rather than solve religious plurality. I am proposing a new consciousness of what we already have, and there is nothing in it of a theosophical attempt to raise relativism to absolute status.

CO-INHERENCE AND THE NEXT STEP

I have been careful to confine myself to comparisons of structural co-inherence and not to wander into the tempting field of comparing Christianity and Buddhism themselves, a perilous and I would say premature operation. If my vision (and it is more of a vision than an argument) has any validity, I think that some of us should try it and see what happens. The evolution of knowledge, or consciousness, is by definition unpredictable: could we predict new knowledge, we would already know it, and it would not be new. But it seems obvious to me that such an intimate contact between Christians and Buddhists (rather than the abstractions Buddhism and Christianity) must result in quite new interpretations of Christ (or the Trinity) and the Buddha (or *śūnyatā*). But more broadly, it is possible that the foregoing model could be expanded toward the co-inherence of all religions, ideologies, sciences, and cultures whatsoever, to produce a world wherein territorial wars and planetary mono-culture alike would be absurd, and the notion of authority would transcend legalism and anarchy. That I leave to the future. In the absence of some such truly cosmopolitan attitude, there will be no future, or not at least one that can be experienced from the *mānuṣya-loka* (human realm). As Pablo Casals once remarked, "We ought to think that we are the leaves of a tree—and the tree is all humanity [all beings, a Buddhist would add] — and we cannot live without the tree, without the others."

NOTES

1. See, for instance, Trevor Ling, *Buddhism, Imperialism and War* (London: Allen and Unwin, 1979).

2. I owe the germ of this idea to Maha Sthavira Sangharakshita, "Dialogue between Buddhism and Christianity" in *Buddhism and Christianity*, Concilium 116 (New York: Seabury, 1979), pp. 55-63.

3. Carroll Stuhlmueller, C.P., *Thirsting for the Lord: Essays in Biblical Spirituality* (New York: Alba House, 1977) p. 13 and passim.

4. *Teachings of Sri Rāmakrishna* (Calcutta: Advaita Ashrama, 7th imp., 1971), p. 7.

5. For refreshing and refining my memory on this point I am grateful to my colleague Harry B. Partin, Department of Religion, Duke University.

6. See Tracy Nichols and Bill Sparrow, *Rastafari: A Way of Life* (Garden City, N.Y.: Doubleday, 1979).

7. See Tarthang Tulku, *Time, Space, and Knowledge: A New Vision of Reality* (Emeryville Calif.: Dharma Publishing, 1977).

8. Steven Rose, *The Conscious Brain*, second edition (New York: Random House, 1976). See especially pp. 23-33 and Chap. 13.

9. For an intriguing comparison of Fr. Teilhard de Chardin and Aurobindo see Beatrice Bruteau, *Evolution Toward Divinity* (Wheaton Il.: Theosophical Publishing House, 1974), especially pp. 156-80.

10. Deshimaru Taisen Rōshi, *The Voice of the Valley*, ed. Philippe Coupey (Indianapolis: Bobbs-Merrill, 1979), p. 193.

11. G.L. Prestige, *God in Patristic Thought* (London: Heinemann, 1936; reprint, London: S.P.C.K., 1952), p. 300.

12. Gershom G. Scholem, *Sabbatai Sevi: The Mystical Messiah, 1626-1676*, trans. R.J.Z. Werblowsky (Princeton N.J.: Princeton University Press, 1973).

13. There is more than a tendency among modern exegetes to feel that this conclusion or realization is subsequent to the mysterious and awesome experience called the Resurrection, and that statements by Jesus in the Gospels concerning his divinity are editorial. See, for example, the essays in *The Myth of God Incarnate*, ed. John Hick (Philadelphia: Westminster, 1977). For a useful summary of the "state of the field" on modern interpretations of the Resurrection, see Gerald O'Collins, S.J., *What Are They Saying About the Resurrection?* (New York: Paulist Press, 1978).

14. See Robert C. Gregg and Dennis E. Groh, "The Centrality of Soteriology in Early Arianism," *Anglican Theological Review* 59, no. 3 (July 1977): 260-278. The following discussion of Arianism is much indebted to this insightful article.

15. Broadly, this is the perspective adopted by Bernard Lonergan in his *The Way to Nicaea: the Dialectical Development of Trinitarian Theology*, trans. Conn O'Donovan, from *De Deo Trino, Pars Dogmatica*, pp. 17-112 (Philadelphia: Westminster, 1976).

16. G. Christopher Stead, "The Concept of Divine Substance," *Vigiliae Christianae* 29 (1975): 1-14. Stead discovers seven basic meanings and proposes a theoretical twenty-eight meanings, only one of which is "stuff." I am indebted to Robert Gregg for alerting me to this article.

17. Prestige, *God in Patristic Thought*, p. 244f.

18. Ibid., pp. 284, 291-94. See also *A Patristic Greek Lexicon*, ed. G. W. H. Lampe (Oxford: Clarendon Press, 1961), which gives "cyclical movement, recurrence" as the general meaning, and "interpenetration" as the later christological and the trinitarian meaning.

19. Ibid., p. 289f.

20. I have used the text of Kenneth K. Inada (Tokyo: Hokuseidō, 1970) but have made my own translations with reference to a privately circulated draft translation by the late Richard Hugh Robinson.

21. Walter Leibenthal, "Shih Hui-yōan's Buddhism as Set Forth in His Writings," *Journal of the American Oriental Society* 70, No. 4 (October-December 1950): 243-259.

22. Translation in Richard H. Robinson, *Early Mādhyamika in India and China* (Madison: University of Wisconsin Press, 1967), pp. 212-221.

23. According to the so-called Logos Christology, based upon the New Testament Johannine corpus, in which Jesus is the enhumanization of God's ordered thinking (his "logic"), anyone, even an atheist, who lives according to ordered thinking and without hypocrisy, is a Christian, though not in the explicit ecclesiastical sense (Justin Martyr, *Apologia Prima*, 46 [Migne, PG 6.397]). Since Vatican II, this has become the official teaching of the Catholic Church (*Conciliorum Oecumenicorum Decreta*, third edition [Bologna, 1973], p. 969, especially lines 28-31).

24. Kōsen Nishiyama and John Stevens, trans., *A Complete English Translation of Dōgen Zenji's Shōbōgenzō* (Sendai: Daihokkaikaku, 1975), 1:69. Cf. Okubo's critical text, *Kohon Kōtei Shōbōgenzō*, ed. Dōshū Okubo (Tokyo, 1971), p. 191.

25. Okubo, *Kohon Kōtei Shōbōgenzō*, p. 189. My translation.

26. Ibid., p. 191.

27. Ibid.

28. Ibid., p. 194.

29. Ibid., p. 191.

30. Mircea Eliade, *Australian Religions: An Introduction* (Ithaca, New York: Cornell University Press, 1973). Index S.VV. *"Altjira," "Djugur,"* "Dreaming," "Dream Time."

31. This paragraph summarizes Jean Daniélou, S.J., *The Bible and the Liturgy* (Notre Dame, Ind: University of Notre Dame Press, 1956; Ann Arbor: Servant Books, 1979), Chap. 16, "The Eighth Day."

32. Daniélou, *Bible and Liturgy*, pp. 263-265. The ideas are taken from Basil, *De Spir. Sancto* 27, and *Ho. Hex.* 2,8.

33. Daniélou, *Bible and Liturgy*, p. 280.

34. Aquinas, *I Perihermenias*, 14, in *Sancti Thomae Aquinatis . . . Opera Omnia*, Fiaccadori edition (New York: Misurgia, 1949), Vol. 18, p. 35, col. 2. My translation.

35. Augustine, "Sermon on the Octave of Easter," quoted in Daniélou, *Bible and Liturgy*, p. 280.

36. Translation adapted from my "T'an-luan's Commentary on the Pure Land Discourse" (Ph.D. diss., University of Wisconsin-Madison, 1973).

37. *Shinran*, Nihon Shisō Daikei, 11 (Tokyo: Iwanami, 1971), p. 321. My translation.

38. Augustine, *En. in Ps. XCI.2*, translation from Daniélou, *Bible and Liturgy*, p. 286.

39. See Gary Zukav, *The Dancing Wu Li Masters: An Overview of the New Physics* (New York: Morrow, 1979), especially pp. 156-176.

40. Translation in Edward Conze, *The Short Prajñapāramitā Texts* (London: Luzac, 1973), p. 201.

41. An imaginary vision is one with an image *(imago)* which is visible to the experient. Beyond it (as beyond Buddhist visualization) is the purer intellectual vision, wherein nothing is visible to the experient but the mental reflex of a vision felt in the *intellectus*.

PART III

DIALOGUE ON SPECIFIC RELIGIOUS NOTIONS: EVIL, SELF, AND RELIGION

CHAPTER 7

The Problem of Evil
in
Christianity and Buddhism

Masao Abe

It is said that human history began with the realization of evil. The problem of evil is indeed one which is deeply rooted in human existence. Throughout human history, both of the East and the West, evil has time and again been regarded as one of humanity's most crucial dilemmas. However, the approach to and the resolution of the problem of evil have in the East and the West not always been altogether the same. To begin with an example of the East, it is a fact that Westerners in general and Christians in particular often express the criticism that Buddhists are rather indifferent to the problem of good and evil. Whether or not their impressions are true must be carefully examined. On the other hand, quite a few Buddhists whose lives are based on the realization of the as-it-is-ness, or suchness, of man and nature often feel somewhat uncomfortable with Christianity's strong ethico-religious character and its excessive emphasis on righteousness and judgment. Whether or not such an impression reaches the core of Christian faith must be carefully scrutinized. Giving up stereotypical understandings of each other, and with receptive and responsive minds, both Christians and Buddhists must try to enter into a deeper understanding of each other's faith by striving to achieve a critical, mutual understanding. They may then be in better position to discover both affinities and differences. In what follows, I shall undertake a comparative study of Christianity and Buddhism from the angle of the problem of evil. Although I am not unaware of the many important attempts at new interpretations of Christianity which are now being written, I will take up here only the traditional form of Christianity. The limitation of space partly encourages this approach but more importantly, I believe that new interpretations cannot be properly understood without the basis of traditional Christianity. Therefore, this paper is a prolegomena to the "problem of evil in Buddhism and Christianity."

I

In Christianity the good is not simply that which is desirable, such as happiness, nor is evil merely that which is undesirable, such as misery. The good in Christianity refers to an act, belief, attitude, or state of mind that obeys and fulfills the will of God. Evil on the other hand is an act or state of mind which disobeys and goes against the divine will. This is precisely because in Christianity God is the creator, the ruler, the law-giver, and the redeemer of all the universe, and the end for which human beings exist consists in establishing and maintaining a relationship with God. The Ten Commandments, which form part of the basis of Judeo-Christian ethics, are described in the Bible as given by God to Moses on Mount Sinai.[1] Moral transgression of the divine law is termed "sin" in theology. Sin is an attitude, act, or inward state of the heart that is offensive to God. As is well known, the origin of sin is to be found in the Genesis story of Adam and Eve partaking, against the word of God, of the fruit of the knowledge of good and evil.

For St. Paul, "sin was not just an act of disobedience to God's will and law; it was open revolt against Him, the result of which was a state that was inimical to God and would lead to death."[2] For Paul then, "sin is something internal and stable in man," that is, "a personal force in man that acts through his body. It entered into the world with Adam's sin and exercised its deadly work by means of the Law."[3] In Romans, Paul declares that sin permeates the whole human race through death, but its power is not equal to Christ's grace and justice: "For if by reason of the one man's offense death reigned through the one man, much more will they who receive the abundance of the grace and of the gift of justice reign in life through the one Jesus Christ. . . ."[4] By being baptized into Christ's death and resurrection, one is freed from sin and begins to live by Christ's life. After baptism the "old man" and the "body of sin" cease to be the instruments of sin. Now the Christian has a new mode of being, a new mode of acting. He is no longer in the service of sin; the Holy Spirit is present in him. The new man is inspired, motivated by the Spirit to fight against the flesh; he passes from the carnal state to a spiritual state. St. Paul's opposition between a life of the flesh and a life of the spirit represents his belief that sinful flesh is God's enemy while the life of spirit is God's divine gift.

Sin, then, is a personal force by which we are opposed to God, and sinful deeds are its fruits. However, if one does not accept Jesus as the Christ and does not believe in his death and resurrection as God's work of redemption, one will be inflicted with eternal suffering. The sufferings of the damned in hell are interminable. This eternal punishment, which is laid upon the souls of the unredeemed at the last judgment, constitutes the largest part of the problem of evil in Christianity.[5] Thus, in the full range of Christian beliefs (from the doctrine of creation to that of eschatology), the problem of evil is a primary preoccupation and one which consists in a dis-relationship with God.

What is the Buddhist view of good and evil? From earliest times, Buddhism had its own "Ten Commandments," or better to say "ten precepts," which are very similar to the Ten Commandments of the Judeo-Christian tradition. These emphasize not killing, not stealing, not lying, not committing adultery, and so forth. A remarkable difference between the Buddhist and Judeo-Christian Ten Commandments, however, lies in the fact that although both equally prohibit the destruction of life, that prohibition appears as the first commandment in Buddhism and as the sixth in Judeo-Christian tradition. In the latter the first commandment is "You shall have no other gods before me," a commandment whose equivalent cannot be found in the Buddhist ten precepts. The differing emphasis in the item of the first position in two lists indicates the strong monotheistic nature of the Judeo-Christian tradition and the I-Thou relationship between persons and God in Christianity on the one hand, and it also shows the Buddhist emphasis on the boundless solidarity of life between persons and other living beings, on the other. Without the notion of transmigration which links human beings to other forms of life, there can be no proper understanding of why the destruction of life in general is prohibited as the first precept in Buddhism. On the contrary, in the Judeo-Christian tradition, not the boundless solidarity with other forms of life, but personal obedience to the will of the one God, and the distinction between creator and creation with humanity at the summit of the created order are essential. This difference naturally reflects upon the different understandings of good and evil in these two religions.

However, the emphasis on the solidarity between humanity and nature does not mean that Buddhism is indifferent to human ethics. In the *Dhammapada,* one of the oldest Buddhist scriptures, there is a well-known stanza: "Not to commit evils,/ But to do all that is good,/ And to purify one's heart — This is the teaching of all the buddhas."[6] This stanza has been held in high esteem by Buddhists throughout their long history and is called "the precept-stanza common to the past seven buddhas," indicating that it is a teaching that was realized and practiced even before Gautama Buddha lived.

In this connection, let me introduce a story concerning this stanza. In China of the T'ang Dynasty, there was a Zen master, Tao-lin, popularly known as Niao-ke, "Bird's Nest," for he used to practice his meditation in a seat made of the thickly growing branches of a tree. Pai Lê-t'ien, a great poet of those days, was officiating as a governor in a certain district in which this Zen master lived. The governor-poet once visited him and said, "What a dangerous seat you have up in the tree."

'Yours is far worse than mine,' retorted the master.
'I am the governor of this district, and I don't see what danger there is in
it.'

To this the master said, "Then, you don't know yourself! When your passions
burn and your mind is unsteady, what is more dangerous than that? "
    The governor then asked, "What is the teaching of Buddhism? "
    The master recited the above-mentioned stanza:

'Not to commit evils,
But to do all that is good,
And to purify one's heart—
This is the teaching of all the buddhas.'

The governor, however, protested, "Any child three years old knows that."
    The Zen master up in the tree responded, "Any child three years old may
know it, but even an old man of eighty years finds it difficult to practice it."
    The point of this stanza lies precisely in the third line, that is, "to purify
one's heart," and the first and the second lines, "Not to commit evils, But to
do all that is good," should be understood from the third line. And "to purify
one's heart" signifies to purify one's heart from *avidyā*, the fundamental ignorance rooted in a dualistic view, and thereby it indicates "to purify one's
heart" even from the dualistic view of good and evil. Eventually the text enjoins us "to awaken to the purity of one's original nature" or "to awaken to
the original purity of one's nature"[7] which is beyond the duality of good and
evil. The problem of good and evil must be coped with on the basis of
awakening to the original purity of one's nature—that is, the teaching of all
Buddhas.
    This Buddhist notion of "the original purity of one's nature," roughly
speaking, may be taken to be somewhat equivalent to the state of Adam
before eating the fruit of knowledge of good and evil. It is to be back where,
according to Genesis, "God saw everything that he had made, and, behold, it
was very good."[8] Therefore, God blessed Adam because he was good. Does
the term "good" in this connection simply mean good in the ethical sense? I
do not think so. The term "good" God used to evaluate his act of creation is
not good as distinguished from evil, but the original goodness prior to the
duality between good and evil, that is, the original goodness prior to man's
corruption of the primordially good nature of mankind and the world. It is
good not in the ethical sense, but in the ontological sense. The goodness of
Adam as created by God is, roughly speaking, equivalent to the original
purity of one's nature as understood in Buddhism. "The original face at the

very moment of not thinking of good or evil" requested by the sixth Zen patriarch, Hui-nêng, is simply another term for one's original nature which is pure, beyond good and evil. Thus Buddhism often refers to our original nature as "Buddha-nature," the awakening to which provides the basis for human ethics to be properly established.

II

The problem of evil in Christianity and Buddhism, however, is not so simple as I have suggested. There is the serious problem of the origin of evil that must be clarified.

The problem of evil in both traditions involves the contradiction, or apparent contradiction, between the belief in the actuality of evil in the world and religious belief in the goodness and power of the Ultimate. This problem is especially serious in Christianity because of its commitment to a monotheistic doctrine of God as absolute in goodness and power and as the creator of the universe out of nothing, *ex nihilo*. The challenge of the fact of evil to this faith has accordingly been formulated as a dilemma: "If God is all-powerful, he must be able to prevent evil. If he is all-good, he must want to prevent evil. But evil exists. Therefore, God is either not all-powerful or not all-good. A theodicy (from *theos*, god, and *dike*, justice) is accordingly an attempt to reconcile the unlimited goodness of an all-powerful God with the reality of evil."[9]

Accordingly, there are at least two questions to be addressed in this connection: Why has an infinitely powerful and good God permitted moral evil or sin in his universe? and Why has an infinitely powerful and good God permitted pain and suffering in this universe? In Christian tradition, there are two main versions of theodicy, the Augustinian and the Irenaean. Limitations of space constrain me to a description of only the essential points of these two types of theodicy in connection with the problem of moral evil.

Rejecting Manichaean dualism, Augustine insisted that evil has no independent existence, but is always parasitic upon the good, the latter alone having substantival reality. "Nothing evil exists in itself, but only as an evil aspect of some actual entity."[10] Thus, everything that God has created is good, and the phenomenon of evil occurs only when beings who are by nature good (though mutable) become corrupted and spoiled. Accordingly, to Augustine evil is nothing but the privation, corruption, or perversion of something good.

How does this spoiling of God's initially good creation come about? Augustine's answer is that evil entered into the universe through the culpable volitions of free creatures, angels and human beings. Their sin consisted not in choosing positive evil (for there is no positive evil to choose), but in turning away from the higher good, namely God, to a lower good. "For when the will abandons what is above itself, and turns to what is lower, it becomes evil—not because that is evil to which it turns, but because the turning itself is wicked."[11]

When we ask what caused the Fall, Augustine's answer is his doctrine of deficient causation. There is no efficient, or positive, cause of the will to evil. Rather, evil willing is itself a negation or deficiency, and to seek for its cause "is as if one sought to see darkness, or hear silence."[12] "What cause of willing can there be which is prior to willing? "[13] According to Genesis, a serpent tricked Eve and Adam to eat the forbidden fruit. Adam's sin was not absolutely the first. The serpent was the evil tempter of Adam's innocence. Augustine was saying that Adam had within himself the possibility of falling and that fallibility is not an evil in itself.[14] However the notion of fallibility explains only the possibility of evil not its reality. Thus, according to Augustine, the origin of moral evil lies hidden within the mystery of human and angelic freedom. The freely acting will is an originating cause, and its operations are not explicable in terms of other prior causes.

This traditional theodicy has been criticized as an account of the origin and final disposition of moral evil. For example, Schleiermacher argued that the notion of finitely perfect beings willfully falling into sin is self-contradictory and unintelligible. A truly perfect being, though free to sin, would, in fact, never do so. To attribute the origin of evil to the willful crime of a perfect being is thus to assert the sheer contradiction that evil has created itself out of nothing. The final disposition of moral evil, that is the eschatological aspect of Augustinian theodicy, has also been criticized. If God desires to save all his human creatures but is unable to do so, he is limited in power. If, on the other hand, he does not desire the salvation of all but has created some for damnation, he is limited in goodness. In either case, the doctrine of eternal damnation stands as an obstacle to a consistent Christian theodicy.

The second type of theodicy was developed by the Greek-speaking fathers, notably by Irenaeus (120-202), prior to the time of Augustine. Whereas Augustine held that before his fall, Adam was in a state of original righteousness, and that his first sin was the inexplicable turning of a wholly good being toward evil, Irenaeus and others regarded the pre-Fall Adam as more like a child than a mature, responsible adult. According to this earlier conception, Adam stood at the beginning of a long process of development. He had been created as a personal being in the "image" of God, but had yet to be brought into the finite "likeness" of God. His fall is seen not as disastrously transforming and totally ruining humanity, but rather as delaying and complicating its advance from the "image" to the "likeness" of his maker. Thus, humanity is viewed as neither having fallen from so great a height as original righteousness, nor to so profound a depth as total depravity, as in the Augustinian theology; rather, humanity fell in the early stages of its spiritual development and now needs greater help than otherwise would have been required.[15]

III

In Buddhism there is no theodicy. There is no theory justifying God because in Buddhism there is no notion of one God whose goodness and power must be justified against the reality of evil in the world. Buddhism has no need of a notion of one God because the fundamental principle of Buddhism is "dependent origination." This notion indicates that everything in and out of the universe is interdependent and co-arising and co-ceasing: nothing whatsoever is independent and self-existing. This is the reason Gautama Buddha did not accept the age-old Hindu concept of Brahman as the sole basis underlying the universe and the accompanying notion *ātman* as the eternal self at the core of each individual. Rather, he emphasized *anātman*, no-self, and dependent origination. The universe is not the creation of one God, but fundamentally is a network of causal relationships among innumerable things which are co-arising and co-ceasing. In Buddhism, time and history are understood as beginningless and there is no room for the idea of unique, momentary creation. Since time and history are believed to be beginningless and endless, there can be no particular creator at the beginning of history and no particular judge at its end. Thus the sacred and the human are, in Buddhism, completely interdependent: there is nothing sacred whatsoever that is self-existing. The supernatural and the natural co-arise and co-cease: there is nothing supernatural whatsoever which is independent of the natural.

The same is true of good and evil. Good and evil are completely dependent on one another. They always co-arise and co-cease so that one cannot exist without the other. There is, then, no supreme good which is self-subsistent apart from evil, and no absolute evil which is an object of eternal punishment apart from good. To Buddhists both the supreme good and absolute evil are illusions. In this respect Buddhism significantly differs from Christianity, in which God is understood to be infinitely good, and sinners who do not believe in God must undergo eternal damnation. In his *Enchiridion*, St. Augustine says: "No evil could exist where no good exists,"[16] but he does not say that No good could exist where no evil exists. This is precisely because to Augustine, evil is nothing but the privation of good. Evil does not exist in itself but is always parasitic upon good, which alone has substantial being. Elsewhere in the *Enchiridion*, St. Augustine says: "Wherever there is no privation of good there is no evil."[17] Here we can see the strong priority of good over evil. This notion is not peculiar to St. Augustine but is common to

Christian thinkers in general. Contrary to this, Buddhists generally talk about the complete relativity of good and evil and reject the idea of the priority of the one over the other. The emphasis is on the inseparability of good and evil and even their oneness in the deepest sense. It is understandable why, given this emphasis on the relativity of good and evil and the consequent rejection of the priority of good over evil, Christians find an indifference to ethics in Buddhism.

Whether or not this is the case must be carefully examined. We human beings must seek good and avoid evil. To be human is to be ethical. Unlike animals, persons can be human only when guided by reason and ethics in place of instinct. This is an undeniable fact. Buddhists accept this without qualification. That is why, as I said before, not to commit evil, but to do all that is good, is emphasized as the teaching of all the buddhas throughout Buddhism's long history, as exemplified, for instance, in the precepts of monks and laymen, including the ten precepts. "To do good, not commit evil" is an ethical imperative common to the Easterner and the Westerner. Wherever persons exist this ethical imperative must be emphasized. A question arises, however, at this point as to whether it is possible for persons to actually observe that ethical imperative. Can human nature be completely regulated and controlled by that ethical code? If we can actually observe that ethical imperative thoroughly only insofar as we try to do so, the problem of evil is very simple. In actuality, however seriously one may try to observe the ethical imperative, one cannot do so completely and instead cannot help realizing one's distance from the good to be done.

This is the reason Niao-ke said to Pai Lê-t'ien, "Any child three years old may know it, but an old man of eighty years finds it difficult to practice it." This is also the reason St. Paul painfully confessed, "the good which I would do, that I do not; but the evil that I would not, that I do." [18] Because persons are flesh as well as soul this is the inevitable conclusion of the ethical effort. To reach any but this conclusion implies a lack of seriousness in one's ethical effort. However strong the ethical imperative may be, we cannot *actually* fulfill it, but rather must fall into a conflict, the dilemma of good and evil. Human nature cannot be completely controlled and regulated by ethics, which is why we must go beyond the realm of ethics and enter that of religion. The limitation of, and the dilemma involved in, ethics are equally realized in Buddhism and Christianity. So far, Buddhists share with St. Paul the painful confession mentioned above.

One primary difference between Paul and Buddhists lies in the following: by saying, "If what I would not, that I do, it is no more I that do it, but sin which dwelleth in me," [19] Paul ascribes the ultimate cause of the problem to original sin and finds the solution, or salvation, in the redemptive love of God working through the spirit of Christ. On the other hand, Buddhists realize the ultimate cause of the problem in karma and find the solution in enlightenment, that is, the awakening to the truth of dependent origination and no-self. Since our present existence is the fruit of a beginningless karma, we are involved in the conflict between good and evil. However, if we go beyond such a dualism and awaken to our original nature, we will be freed from karma as well as from the problem of good and evil. In Christianity, the limitation of, and the dilemma involved in, ethics and its religious solution are grasped in contrast to the absolute nature of God who is all-good and all-powerful. In this sense, the religious solution realized in the context of the collapse of human ethics still finds its orientation in the problem of good and evil, although in a religious rather than an ethical dimension. In Buddhism, on the other hand, the collapse of human ethics is grasped in terms of beginningless and endless karma and its religious solution is found in the realization of no-self which is neither good nor evil.

The Buddhist solution of the problem is not faith in God as all-good but the awakening to one's original nature, which is free from both good and evil. In this sense we may say that Buddhism has primarily an ontological orientation whereas Christianity has primarily an ethical orientation.

This difference may cause Christians to feel an indifference toward ethics in Buddhists and cause Buddhists to feel skeptical about the Christian emphasis on faith. We must, however, inquire into the background of this difference to elucidate the present issue.

IV

The above-mentioned difference between Christianity and Buddhism comes from their divergent understandings of the nature of evil. As seen in St. Augustine, Christians understand evil as the privation of good or as the rebellion of human beings against the will of God, who is viewed as infinitely good. Thus, in Christianity, evil is understood as nonsubstantial, as not existing in itself, and as something to be overcome by good. Accordingly, good has priority over evil not only ethically but also ontologically. This conviction gives Christianity its ethico-religious character and also gives rise to the problem of theodicy: that is, the question of how to explain the reality of evil in relation to God as absolute in goodness and power.

On the other hand, Buddhists base their beliefs and practices not on the ethical dimension but on the ontological dimension by realizing that everything is impermanent and interdependent, and understanding that evil is entirely relative to good. Good and evil are inseparably related to one another. Therefore, what the Buddhist is concerned with is not how to overcome evil by good, but how to transcend the good-evil duality. To Buddhists, the problem of how to overcome evil by good is a "wrong question," based on an unrealistic understanding of the nature of evil and an unjustifiable assumption of the priority of good over evil. Although, ethically speaking, good should have priority over evil, ontologically and existentially speaking, good is not stronger than evil, and good and evil have at least equal strength in their endless struggle with each other. Accordingly, it is necessary for Buddhists to overcome the good-evil dichotomy itself and return to their original nature prior to the divergence between good and evil. This is the meaning of the third line of "the precept-stanza common to the past seven buddhas," "to purify one's heart" — to purify one's heart from the duality of good and evil. It is noteworthy that even in the oldest scripture of primitive Buddhism what is emphasized is the need to go beyond good and evil. For instance, in *Suttanipāta* (547), it is said: "Just as a beautiful lotus flower being not tainted with water and mud, you are not spoiled by either good or evil." In the case of Mahāyāna Buddhism, it is emphasized even more strongly that we must go beyond good and evil and attain the realization of *śunyatā*, or "emptiness," which is neither good nor evil.

As I have indicated, in rejecting the priority of good over evil, Buddhists emphasize their relativity. Buddhism is similar, at least in this respect, to the Manichaean insistence on the dualism of good and evil. The central theme of Manichaeism is that the world is an inextricable mixture of good and evil with each force in constant combat with the other. Thus, Manichaeism proclaims two deities in opposition, a good deity as the author of light and an evil deity as the author of darkness. Insofar as good and evil are understood dualistically as two different principles and as inextricably related to and fighting against each other, there is great affinity between Manichaeism and Buddhism. The essential difference between them, however, can be seen in the following three points:

1. Although Manichaeism emphasizes the fight between two opposed principles of good and evil, it does not carry this opposition to its final conclusion. On the other hand, Buddhism existentially realizes the final conclusion of the contradiction of the two opposed principles as beginningless and endless karma, and tries to overcome it.

2. Buddhism, therefore, comes to a realization of *śunyatā* in which the duality of good and evil is completely overcome and their nondualistic oneness is fully realized. Contrary to this, Manichaeism remains a rigid form of dualism from beginning to end, without any means of overcoming that conflict.

3. In Manichaeism, good and evil are two independent principles which respectively have their reality and substance. In Buddhism, however, although good and evil are two opposing principles, they are not under-

stood as reality or substance but rather as something nonsubstantial. Accordingly, in the awakening to *śūnyatā,* both good and evil are emptied and the duality is overcome.

From the Buddhist point of view, the weakness of Manichaeism does not lie in its dualistic view of good and evil as two independent principles but in the rigidity of that dualism, which takes the two independent principles as substantial realities. It is not a mistake for Manichaeism to take good and evil as two equally powerful principles rather than emphasizing the priority of good over evil. It is, however, a mistake for Manichaeism to end with this dualistic view without attempting to transcend it.

In the history of Christianity, St. Augustine strongly rejected the ultimate dualism of Manichaeism and insisted that only good has substantial being whereas evil is unreal—hence, his theory of evil as the privation of good. Given the belief that a good God is the sole ultimate reality, it is inevitable that evil be interpreted as privation. However, if the monotheistic God is unambiguously good, what is evil, and where does it come from? Theodicy thus becomes a serious problem.

As we say earlier, Augustine emphasized evil will, that is, the ill-use of human free will, as the origin of evil. Thereby God is freed from all responsibility. However, Genesis suggests an evil even before Adam's ill-use of his freedom in the form of the serpent's temptation. Since he was created free, Adam had the possibility of falling or not falling. Although the possibility of falling is not an evil in itself, Adam yielded to the temptation and actually fell. Why did God not turn the human will toward the good without doing violence to its nature, so that we can freely do good? To this Augustine replied, "simply because God did not wish to." Is there not a mystery here?

Recently, the Irenaean type of theodicy has been reformulated in John Hick's book *Evil and the God of Love.* The Irenaean theodicy, which regards the fall of Adam as a virtually inevitable incident in humanity's development, is more acceptable than the Augustinian one. However, I am afraid that in this type of theodicy the problem of the Fall is understood somewhat from the outside, objectively, as a problem of human development, while its existential meaning is more or less overlooked. I personally appreciate the Augustinian type of theodicy, which focuses on the problem of free will and thereby grasps the issue from within one's being more existentially than the Irenaean one. And, in this sense, I think the Augustinian approach is more appropriate and justifiable. Yet Augustinian theodicy ends with the mystery of evil. To speak of the mystery of evil is, however, nothing but to confess the insolubility of the problem of evil and God. For if God is conceived of as the creator of all the universe, all-good and all-powerful, the origin of evil is ultimately untraceable except to the "mystery of evil." This is at best a half-solution. To complete the solution one must go beyond mystery and radically reinterpret the notion of God. It is quite natural for Christianity to reject the Manichaean form of dualism because Christianity is fundamentally monotheistic. However, if Christianity is simply monotheistic and rejects any form of duality of good and evil, Christianity becomes abstracted from human actuality. Theodicy is an attempt to include the duality of good and evil within the monotheistic character of Christianity without destroying the character. However, there remains an essential tension between the duality of good and evil and the framework of monotheism. Thus, as we see in Augustine's theodicy, the origin of evil tends to be explained in terms of mystery.

In the history of Christian thought down to the present, there have been many variations of these two types of theodicy. In my view, neither dualism nor monotheism can solve the problem of evil satisfactorily. We must find a position which is neither dualistic nor monotheistic.

V

Buddhists try to go beyond the duality of good and evil and to awaken to *śūnyatā,* which transcends both good and evil. This is because, insofar as we remain in the duality, we are involved in and limited by it. In the realm of good and evil, an ethical imperative (Thou ought to do this) and the cry of desire (I want to do that) are always in constant conflict. Thus we become slaves to sin and guilt. There is no final rest in the realm of good and evil. To attain the abode of final rest, we must go beyond the dichotomy of good and evil and return to the root and source from which good and evil emerged. That root and source is grasped in Buddhism as "emptiness," or *śūnyatā,* because it is neither good nor evil. When the Six Patriarch, Hui-nêng, was asked by the monk Ming what the truth of Buddhism was, he said: "When your mind is not dwelling on the dualism of good and evil, what is your original face before you were born?" "Your original face before you were born" is simply a Zen term for *śūnyatā,* because only through the realization of *śūnyatā* do we awaken to our true self. Another important point raised by Hui-nêng's answer concerns the words "before you were born." This symbolic phrase does not necessarily indicate "before" in the temporal sense, but rather "before" in the ontological sense, that is, the ontological foundation, or root and source on which the duality of good and evil is established. Therefore, this "before" can and should be realized right now and right here in the depth of the absolute present.

We may translate Hui-nêng's question into the Christian context by asking, What is your original face before Adam committed sin? or even by asking, What is your original face before God created the world? Adam is not merely the first man in a remote past, nor is his fall an event apart from us, one which took place far distant from us in time. As Kierkegaard rightly said, we ourselves committed sin in Adam. Adam is none other than ourselves. Adam is the first one of mankind and at the same time is each of us. Thus the Zen question concerning "your original face" may be understood as a question concerning "your original face" before you ate the fruit of the knowledge of good and evil. It may also be understood as a more radical question; What is your original face before God created the world? For Zen persistently asks, "After all things are reduced to oneness; where would that One be reduced?"[20] God created everything out of nothing. God is the only creator. All things are reduced to one God. To what, however, would that one God be reduced? Everything comes from God. Where did God come from? This is a question which must be asked.

God created everything out of nothing. Therefore, it cannot be said that God came from something nor can it be said that God is reduced to something. Accordingly, the only answer to this question is that God came from nothingness. God is reduced to nothingness. However, this nothingness is different from the nothing out of which God created everything. The nothing out of which God created everything is nothing in a relative sense. On the other hand, the nothingness from which God may be said to emerge is nothingness in its non-relative sense. This nothingness in the absolute sense is exactly the same as Buddhism's *śūnyatā*. This absolute nothingness from which even God emerged is not unfamiliar to Christianity. Christian mystics talked about the Godhead from which the personal God emerged, and they described the Godhead in terms of nothingness, as seen, for instance, in St. John of the Cross and the anonymous author of *The Cloud of Unknowing*. However, in Buddhism, this absolute nothingness from which even God came to exist is precisely the "original face" of ourselves which is beyond good and evil. The Buddhist solution to the problem of evil can be found in the realization of absolute nothingness, or *śūnyatā*, as the awakening to true self. It is neither dualistic nor monotheistic.

VI

The final question is how ethics then can be established on the realization of *śūnyatā*. Having transcended the duality of good and evil, to what moral principles may one appeal that are in keeping with the spirit of this liberating experience?

First, in Buddhism, the realization of *śūnyatā* is not merely a goal to be reached, but the ground on which everything in life is established. It is, indeed, the point of departure from which we can properly and realistically begin our life and activity. In other words, it is the root and source from which the duality of good and evil and all other forms of duality have come to be realized.

Second, when we take the realization of *śūnyatā* as the point of departure as well as the goal of our life, the duality of good and evil is viewed in a new light, namely, from the viewpoint of *śūnyatā* or the awakening experience itself. In this light, the distinction between good and evil is thoroughly relativized by dropping away any and all sense of absolute good and absolute evil. Furthermore, the distinction between good and evil is not only relativized, but the two values are reversed. In this regard however, the relativization and the reversion of the distinction between good and evil does not destroy human ethics as is often believed. Of course, one may say that if the relativization and reversion of the good-evil distinction takes place within the context of an ethical life, it will necessarily entail a loss of the firmness and intensity of commitment to the ethical principles by which a person might give meaning and integrity to his life.

However, in Christianity as in Buddhism, which goes beyond mere ethics to a higher commitment to the will of God (consider Kierkegaard's "teleological suspension of the ethical" in his interpretation of the Abraham-Isaac story), some relativization and reversion of the good-evil distinction is necessitated. This fact is clearly seen in Jesus' words, "I came not to call the righteous but sinners," and "Why call ye me good: there is none good but the Father." Sinners, therefore, have priority over the righteous (i.e., those who obey the letter of the law, but neglect the spirit) in the light of salvation through Jesus Christ. However, in Christianity, where God is believed to be the highest good and the ruler of the world and history, the distinction between good and evil is not completely relativized nor reversed. Given the belief that God is both righteous and loving, the complete relativization and reversion of the good-evil distinction is not acceptable. In Buddhism, by contrast, the complete relativization and reversion of the good-evil distinction is totally realized without fear of destroying the basis of the ethical life. This is due to the fact that the "transvaluation of values" is realized not within a certain established framework of ethical life nor under the rule and judgment of the all-good and all-powerful God, but in and through the realization of the boundless openness of *śūnyatā* in which there is no one God.

Third, in the awakening to the boundless openness of *śūnyatā* and the relativization and reversion of the good-evil distinction, the basis of the ethical life is not destroyed but is rather preserved, clarified, and strengthened. This ultimate experience makes the distinction between good and evil clearer than before because the distinction is thoroughly realized without any limitation in the awakening to the boundless openness of *śūnyatā*. At the same time, the relativization and reversion of the good-evil distinction in this awakening leads us to the realization of the undifferentiated sameness of good and evil.

The first aspect, that is, the clearer realization of the good-evil distinction, indicates *prajña,* or Buddhist wisdom. The distinction of things or matters more clearly realized in enlightenment than before is well indicated in the following discourse of Ch'ing yuan Wei hsin, a Chinese Zen master of the T'ang Dynasty:

> Before I studied Zen, to me mountains were mountains and waters were waters. After I got an insight into the truth of Zen through the instruction of a good master, mountains to me were not mountains and waters were not waters. But after this, when I really attained the abode of rest, that is, enlightenment, mountains were really mountains, waters were really waters.[21]

The second aspect that is the realization of the sameness of good-evil through the relativization and reversion of its distinction entails *karuñā,* Buddhist compassion. This compassionate aspect is emphatically expressed both in Pure Land and Zen Buddhism as follows:

> Even the virtuous can attain rebirth in the Pure Land, how much more so the wicked![22]
> The immaculate practitioner takes three kalpas to enter nirvana, whereas the apostate *bhikkhu* (monk) does not fall into hell.[23]

This twofold realization of the clearer distinction between good and evil on the one hand and of the undifferentiated unity and reversion of good and evil on the other, is nothing but a *reappraisal* of the good-evil duality in the new light of *śūnyatā.* Herein, Buddhist ethical life is established in the light of *prajña* (wisdom) and *karuṇā* (compassion) where, without the distinction of good and evil, the distinction is clearly realized.

The distinction and unity, wisdom and compassion, are dynamically working together in Buddhist ethical life because the boundless openness of *śūnyatā* is taken as the ground of the ethical life. If, however, *śūnyatā* is taken as the goal or the objective of our life and not as the ground or the point of departure, then the Buddhist life falls into the indifference of good and evil and an apathetic attitude toward social evil. The risk and tendency of falling into ethical indifference is always latent in the Buddhist life. In no few instances, Buddhist history illustrates this. In this respect, it is important and significant for Buddhism to have a serious encounter with Christianity which is ethical as well as religious.

In conclusion, let me quote a Zen story as an example of the dynamism of Zen compassion.

One day a visitor asked Joshu, an outstanding Zen master of the T'ang dynasty: "Where will you go after death?"
"I will go straightforwardly to hell!" answered the master.
"How could it be that such a great Zen master as you would fall into hell?" retorted the visitor.
To this the master said:
"If I will not go to hell, who will save you at the bottom of hell?!"[24]

NOTES

1. Exod. 20.2-17; Deut. 5.6-21.
2. *The New Catholic Encyclopedia,* 13:239.
3. Ibid.
4. Rom. 5.17.
5. John Hick, *Evil and the God of Love* (London: Macmillan, 1966), p. 377.
6. *Dhammapada* 14. 5.
7. Masao Abe, "The Idea of Purity in Mahāyāna Buddhism," *Numen* 13, fasc. 3 (October 1966).
8. Gen. 1.31.
9. *The Encyclopedia of Philosophy,* 3:136.
10. Augustine, *Enchiridon* 4.
11. Augustine, *City of God* 12. 6.
12. Ibid.
13. Augustine, *On Free Will* 3. *xvii.* 49.
14. *New Catholic Encyclopedia,* 5:669.
15. *Encyclopedia of Philosophy,* 3:138.
16. Augustine, *Enchiridon* 4. 421.
17. Ibid.
18. Rom. 7.19.
19. Rom. 7.20.
20. *Pi-yen lu (Hekiganroku),* case 45, Taishō 48:181 c.
21. Abe, "Zen is not a Philosophy," but . . . ," *Theologische Zeitschrift* 33 (1977).
22. *Tannishō, A Tract Deploring the Heresies of Faith* (Higashi Honganji, 1961), p. 6.
23. *Zenmon nejushu,* copied by Seizan Yanagida, 2:120.
24. *Chao-chou lu (Joshuroku)* ed. Ryōmin Akizuki, Chikuma edition, p. 170.

CHAPTER 8

No-Self, No-Mind, and Emptiness Revisited

Winston L. King

Not the least of the many obstacles to appreciation and appropriation of the values and religious experiences of traditions other than one's own is the mutual misunderstanding of crucial terms. In the area of Buddhist and Christian misunderstandings, the terms that gather around the thought and experience-centers of "personal" in Christianity, and "impersonal" in Buddhism, are of particular significance. Christianity speaks continually in personalistic terms of self, soul, individual, and the like. Contrastingly, Buddhism is rich in such terms as no-self, no-soul, no-mind, and emptiness. The conceptions of those religiously ultimate destinies of heaven and nirvana have the same personal and impersonal quality, respectively. To many in both traditions, the two sets of terms and their related experiences seem to be mutually exclusive, or at the very least, at opposite ends of the religious spectrum.

THE TRADITIONAL STEREOTYPES

What has occurred in the Buddhist and Christian traditions, both with respect to adherents' understanding of their own and the other's tradition, is the progressive building up of a set of stereotyped interpretations of the "personal" and the "impersonal" polarities of the two vocabularies, so that the respective sets of terms expressive of these qualities become used in inter-religious dialogues as party slogans and fighting words. The consequence is that dialogue often becomes argument and confrontation. It is to be observed in passing that the use of the term "impersonal" for Buddhist conceptions of the nature of human individuality, is of course Western-Christian and imposes nuances in its usage which are not actually in the Buddhist viewpoint. It may be useful then to first briefly describe the Buddhist-impersonal and the Christian-personal stereotypes as they frequently appear in interfaith discussions.

The Theravāda Stereotype

Beginning with the Theravāda Buddhist stereotype, it can be summarized thus: What is mistakenly called a "self " or "soul" by the average person (and the Christian) is actually a compounded, nonintegral combination of elements in constant flux from moment to moment, and is part and parcel of a universe of continual change. The only constants are the component molecular elements and their more usual modes of relationship and change. To make the Theravāda stereotye more concrete, two models will be useful. The first of these, which purports to analyze the nature of a human being in a cross-sectional manner, is the famous chariot analogy used by the monk Nāgasena in *The Questions of King Milinda*. The monarch Milinda has just arrived to question Nāgasena concerning Buddhist statements about the self. He observes at length that Buddhists say that the term "self " or "ego" is "but a way of counting, a term, appellation, convenient designation and name" for the parts of a human being, namely "hair of the head, hair of the body, nails, teeth" all thirty-two of them, down to and including "saliva, snot, synovial fluid, urine, brain" which are combined into a body-shape or form characterized by sensation, perception, predispositions, and consciousness. But no one of these, nor all of them together, nor any additional factor can be termed a "self " or "ego." Hence "Nāgasena" and every other "self " are nullities fraudulently parading as "persons."

Nāgasena, in response, questions the king about the chariot in which he has just arrived, and by using the same logical analysis forces him to admit that there is actually no chariot either, in the sense of a substantial chariot-entity, or any "chariotness," but that "chariot," just as "self," is but "a way of counting, term, appellation, etc." of *its* parts.[1] Thus if one visualizes himself in terms of this model, he finds himself using a three-dimensional molecular model that is almost empty of substance and being tempted to poke a finger into himself to see if anything is truly there!

The other models, used by Nāgasena in the same work, are presented in linear-temporal terms. Taking the illustration of a candle flame, he asks whether it is the "same" (i.e., substantially identical) flame that burns throughout the night. Again he inquires whether it is the "very milk itself " which endures unchangingly through its successive transformations into sour cream, butter, and ghee, Nāgasena's answer is negative. Rather, he concludes that it is through "connection" with the first candle-flame moment, and with the fresh milk state, that the succeeding flame-moments and curd-cheese-ghee results appear. Hence we have the general principle that:

> The elements of being join one another in serial succession; one element perishes, another arises, succeeding each other instantaneously.

Applying this logic to a person, Nāgasena argues:

> Therefore neither as the same nor as a different person do you arrive
> [from a previous state or birth] at your latest aggregation of
> consciousness.[2]

In applying this model, one has a vision of himself as a stream of fireflies
flowing along through the dark of a summer's night.

Finally, to cap the negative climax: The goal of the Buddhist salvational
discipline is *nibbana (nirvana)*, the "going out" of the candle flame of self-
awareness, the absolute end of the succession of moments of body-mind
existence, the dissipation of the constituent parts of the "self" into the
universe, without remainder.

The Mahāyāna Buddhist Stereotype

The Mahāyāna stereotypical view of self is more difficult to neatly specify because of the varied words and images used to describe it. We might choose
the *ālaya-vijñāna* or storehouse consciousness of the Yogācāra school. This
entity appears to be an individual or superindividual depository and reservoir
of all of an individual's past-action effects, a kind of Buddhist collective
unconscious. Edward Conze interpreted it as a Mahāyānist grasping at some
device or other to stay the progressively complete destruction—by Buddhist
logical analysis—of even a functional selfhood.[3] We might also choose the
void, or emptiness *(śunyatā)* of all the forms given to us by thought and
sensibility, as well as the thinker and senser himself. In Nāgārjuna's terms:

> Form, sound, taste, touch, smell, and the *dharmas* (i.e., component
> elements);
> This sixfold substance *(vastu)* of desire, hate, and delusion is imagined.
> Form, sound, taste, touch, smell, and the *dharmas* are
> Merely the form of a fairy castle, like a mirage, a dream.[4]

For Nāgārjuna, even the Theravāda *nibbana*, sought as a refuge from and final
denial of selfhood, is no different from its opposite, samsara (the unending
round of birth-death existences). None of these terms, experiences, or sensa-
tions point to reality. They are all empty of substance and being.

Yet again one might choose the no-mind of Zen, thus described by Hui-
nêng, the Sixth Patriarch:

> There is no Bodhi-tree,
> Nor stand of mirror bright.
> Since all is void,
> Where can the dust alight? [5]

That is to say, Hui-nêng did not allow even the mirror of the bright, empty Wisdom-mind.

But I have chosen still another image or model to represent the Mahāyāna view of selfhood—that of Fa-tsang's hall of mirrors. This Hua-yen figure implicitly contains most of the elements of these three types of selfhood views, as well as including the distinctive Mahāyāna feature of the organic interconnectedness of all entities. Our description of Fa-tsang's illustrative device is as follows:

> In the ceiling and floor, on all four walls, and even in the four corners of the room were fixed huge mirrors—all facing one another.

Then Fa-tsang placed a Buddha image in the center and told the visiting empress, for whom he had prepared this visible parable, or model, of the relation of self and the world to each other:

> In each and every reflection of any [one] mirror you will find all the reflections of all the other mirrors, together with the specific Buddha image in each, without omission or misplacement. [6]

Thus the totality of mirrors and the Buddha image (the totality of all existents in the universe) is to be found entire and without distortion in each and every mirror (i.e., self, entity, or even dust mote in the universe). What makes this mutual interpenetration of all selves and entities in the total universe possible is the fact that "all is Mind," Mind only; and equally importantly, no self or entity has any self-inclosed, independent reality of its own. It is, so to speak, but a crossroads, a convergence point wherein all the universe comes together. It is a nexus of connections; no separate individual or self is to be found there.

In the end this picture seems, to the Western Christian, little different from that of Nāgasena's chariot and candle flame. *There*, to be sure, Nāgasena was at pains to prove that all seeming entities, especially human selves, are non-entities and have only external relations—in atomistic style—with other seeming entities. *Here*, in Hua-yen, the organic interconnectedness of all entities is stressed; they are internally related. But to non-Buddhists the end result of totally permeative interconnectedness seems completely destructive of selfhood, in the Western Christian sense at least. To repeat: Here in Mahāyāna we have crossroads, connection points, and in essence a total interdependence of each self with, and its constitution by, everything else. Or to put it differently: Universal (Buddha) Mind swallows up individual, personal mind completely. Consequently the best counsel of both the Theravāda and Mahāyāna Buddhist to the Christian world is that its illusory belief in selfhood, both human and divine, is what prevents Christianity from offering true salvation to humanity.

The Christian Stereotype

Though there is considerable variety in Christian doctrine on almost every other point, with respect to person, self, or soul there is a basic biblical model which generally pervades the various Christian conceptions of the self, no matter how much divergence there is in detail. For the most part Christian introspection has been an examination of the states of the self or soul, not an analysis of its nature, or speculation as to its existence. The following biblical passages (RSV) give us the distinctive Western Christian soul or self-image:

> So God created man in his own image, in the image of God he created him, male and female he created them . . . then the Lord God formed man of dust from the ground, and breathed into his nostrils the breath of life; and man became a living being . . . [And] the Lord God called to the man, and said to him, "Where are you?" (Gen. 1.27; 2.7; 3.9) And I saw the holy city, new Jerusalem, coming down out of heaven from God, prepared as a bride adorned for her husband; and I heard a great voice from the throne saying, "Behold, the dwelling of God is with men . . . God himself will dwell with them; he will wipe away every tear from their eyes, and death shall be no more, neither shall there be mourning nor crying nor pain any more. (Rev. 21.2-4)

The fundamental conception comes through quite clearly. In Christianity humanity is conceived to be a spiritual-mental-physical entity, created by God in his own spiritual-mental-image or nature. This personhood of divine quality is humanity's most distinctive and precious quality. As a self or person we can respond to our Maker, the God-Self, and look forward to eternal personal fellowship with him in heaven. In another passage (Rev. 20.14) we read that those who do not attain to this heavenly existence, will spend their eternity in suffering. The self or soul, once given, is indestructible: it is imbued with the eternity of its Giver.

Summary

Given these widely divergent views of the self or person, it requires no imagination to see them functioning as direct opposites and natural enemies of each other in all Christian-Buddhist interrelationships. To the Buddhist, the Christian seems ineradicably trapped in Christianity itself by an all pervasive, totally defeating illusion of a narrowly conceived and largely static self or soul. And to compound his hopeless, helpless situation he projects personhood onto his ultimate reality, God, and views his salvation as the eternal perpetuation of his selfhood in heaven! Conversely, the Christian sees Buddhism in any of its forms, Theravāda or Mahāyāna, as teaching the dissolution of all individuality, the destruction of selfhood and all of its personal and moral values which the Christian so greatly cherishes. They are to be swallowed up by no-mind, no-soul, the void, the Buddha-mind: they disappear in Buddhism into the great oneness of the nothingness of nirvana—and the Christian is asked to think of *this* as salvation! Thus in the end Buddhists find Christian salvation to be the eternalization of human bondage, disguised as heaven but in reality one of the higher hells, so to speak; and Christians find in nirvana nothing but annihilation.

CAN THE IMPASSE BE BROKEN?

To suggest some possibilities for meaningful interchange is the purpose of this essay. But it must be recognized that there are right and wrong ways of attempting to break the present impasse.

Stressing the Mystical and Impersonal Elements in Christianity

This attempt has been made in several different ways, four examples of which will be noted here.

First, there is what may be called the Christian incarnational divinity of man, stemming from human creation in the image of God and Christ's redemption of that sin-tarnished image by his quality of God-man. Pope John Paul II recently gave expression to this view in his *Redemptor Hominis* by the presence of God, not because of any religious affiliation, baptism, or whatever, but because God has already united the divine with the human" and that "the church's responsibility is . . . to struggle for the full actualization of each human person."[7] This might be taken, by rather freely interpreting it, as the Christian equivalent of the Mahāyāna doctrine of the Buddha-nature in every human being.

Second, we may observe some of the efforts of the late D. T. Suzuki in this direction, this time from the Buddhist side. He once said to me that Meister

Eckhart was "the leading Zen man in the West." And in his book *Mysticism: Christian and Buddhist* he expounds at some length what he regarded as the near identity, or at least essential likeness, of Eckhart's doctrine of the Godhead in its relation to humanity's inner spark, to Zen expression of the oneness of the human mind with thusness, emptiness, and the Buddha-mind, experienced in *satori*. He refuses to let himself be deterred from equating Eckhart's experience of oneness with the Godhead, with Zen *satori* in its experiential core, despite the "little point" of creatureliness to which Eckhart says the human being must always return.[8]

Third, and correlate with Eckhart's mystical Zen quality of statement and experience, is the general *via negativa* tradition of which Eckhart was a proponent or at least partial inheritor. Eckhart indeed often quotes from the masters of the negative way to knowledge, as in the following words:

> St. Dionysius says, God is naught. Meaning that God is as incomprehensible as naught. St. Bernard says, I know now what God is; but what I know not that he is, the same is he. . . . Dionysius and Gregory both teach that the divine being is not comprehensible in any sense, not to any wit nor understanding . . . . To know him really is to know him as unknowable.[9]

Many passages of this sort could be quoted from the medieval Christian mystics in which conceptual opposites are joined together (the blinding brightness of the divine light that is darkness to human understanding), and vivid phrases created ("the cloud of unknowing") to indicate the superintellectual nature of the divine knowledge of God and the inexpressibility of mystical experiences. To many Western and some Eastern observers, these have seemed deeply akin to the vocabulary and enlightenment experiences in Buddhism.

Fourth may be noted the efforts of Dr. Lynn A. de Silva, director of the Ecumenical Institute in Sri Lanka and editor of *Dialogue,* a periodical devoted to Buddhist-Christian interchange. In seeking to bypass difficulties or to transform the noncommunication between Christians and Buddhists in the subject of the Christian soul versus the Buddhist no-soul (*anatta*) into meaningful dialogue, he has on repeated occasions adopted and adapted the *anatta* terminology for Christian usage by pointing out that the Christian belief in self or soul is more radically *anatta* than the Buddhist non-belief. That is, the human soul as such does not exist before its creation at each birth. Here, then, not even that endless chain of births as no-selves or pseudo-selves recognized by Buddhism exists. Instead, there is sheer nullity brought into being by divine creativity!

What shall we say of these attempts to get over the self versus no-self, personal versus impersonal impasse between Buddhism and Christianity? Though I favored such approaches at one time, I have come to suspect them of having only limited use, and as perhaps having misleading implications and consequences. In this connection there are specific remarks to be made about the four examples just given, and two further basic considerations.

With respect to Pope John Paul's statement, which seems quite immanentalist and appears to abolish the traditional Christian abyss between holy God and sinful man, this must be said: It is not as immanentalist as it seems. It is only in Christ, the God-man, that the human and the divine are perfectly united, and even here "without confusion," that is, without an indiscriminate blending into oneness. No Roman Catholic pontiff has ever taught, or ever will teach, that man-soul as such is identical in essence with God, in the same way that ordinary mind is Buddha-mind, and our nature, just as it is, is Buddha-nature, as Mahāyāna Buddhism maintains.

With respect to Eckhart in particular, it is to be noted that his Zen-like statements about the unity of man-soul and Godhead were precisely what brought against him official charges of monistic heresy by the Church of his time. He died, opportunely for him perhaps, before his trial could take place, though he had already stoutly defended himself as fully Christian. And to extend judgment to Dionysian mysticism in general, one must say that it never comprised the mainstream of Christian theology or experience, and was viewed more or less cautiously, even negatively, by many in the Christian community. Therefore, to take as representatively Christian that which is somewhat atypical of Christianity, that which rather awkwardly joins its mystical-impersonal tendencies with the Christian personalist devotional mainstream, is itself rather an awkward juxtaposition. It is to say of that which is not typically Christian, "See how much Christians are like Buddhists; how much more Buddhist we are than we thought."

With respect to his Christian *anatta* emphasis, Dr. de Silva told me that it has been quite helpful in forwarding his conversations with Buddhists.[10] I cannot doubt this statement in view of the many years he has been engaged in such dialogue. But what is doubtful to me is whether this is the best or right way to promote Buddhist-Christian dialogue in the long run.

However, more fundamental to the matter of profitable dialogue over Christian personalism and Buddhist impersonalism are the two following considerations. First, it should be observed that Christian personalism as a theory has never been very well articulated, in sharp contrast to Buddhism, which abounds with exhaustive and subtle analyses of personality and personal experience, and has produced theories strikingly similar to some types of modern Western psychological theory. As a result, attempts to affirm the self or soul in Christian terms, over against the "nihilistic" Buddhist analyses thereof, have as a rule been little more then flat positive assertions. Hence, we can only conclude that this theoretically dubious but stubbornly held conviction of self, soul, or person in Western Christian cultures has its roots in something other than theoretical logic or penetrating analysis. This situation suggests that the Christian conviction of the reality and immense importance of the concretely observable, perpetually functioning thinking-feeling-acting individual — no matter what modern psychology and Buddhist negative analysis may say about its ontological reality — is rooted deeply in Western Christian life-consciousness. Hence, it is from this center of personal awareness that one must speak to Buddhists, not from the mystical-impersonal fringes of the Christian tradition.

Second, and correlate to the first, when Christians speak in personalistic terms and assert or take for granted the existence of an immortal soul or unique self, they are in actuality (and emotionally) expressing an experience rather than asserting an ontological theory. For even though the errors of positing an enduring personal essence or the impossibility of putting one's finger on an identical, unchanging soul or self be convincingly pointed out, the *experience* of being an *experiencer* remains the most real and vital fact of human existence. And Christian personalism is the assertion of this experiental reality.

Again, therefore, we are forced to the conclusion that, if genuine dialogue between Christians and Buddhists is to take place, the Christian must speak out of the depth and fullness of his personal life and experience, and from that center seek to understand and be understood. Next in order, then, is a fuller exploration of that personalism.

Western Christian Personalism
as the Experience of Transcendence

The Western experience (and conception) of selfhood, generally speaking, is the human inner-transcendence of physical and social limitation. Several types may be noted.

1. *Transcendence of inanimateness and mere awareness.* Westerners are very much aware of their aliveness in contrast to inanimate beings. And they are proudly conscious of their own *self*-consciousness which makes them unique individuals.

2. *Transcendence of animality.* The sense of human uniqueness, growing in considerable part out of the Judeo-Christian tradition of being made in the image of God, has been a major component of Western Christian consciousness. Westerners have continuously asserted their uniqueness in order to raise and maintain themselves above animal-physical base action and

motivation, being keenly aware of the danger of coming under the dominance of mere physical animality.

3. *Transcendence of time and space.* Westerners have gloried in the power of rational thought to escape the bounds of small physical size and strength, and by philosophy and science to penetrate the order of nature and in a considerable measure assert power over that nature, both by theory and physical contrivance.

4. *Transcendence of limited values.* In art and morality Westerners have experienced the lure of the infinite and ideal, creating new forms of beauty and aiming for perfection of their inner being.

It scarcely needs saying that in actual practice this hope and sense of transcendence, mediated and expressed by Western self-consciousness, has demonstrated many weaknesses and produced many evils. The strong emphasis upon human uniqueness has cut us off from fellow feeling for our natural environment and made us into its destructive exploiter. It often makes us haughty and assertive of our humanity rather than humble in its possession. And the strong Western assertiveness of rational, self-conscious individualism has often fashioned a prison for the Western psyche within its own self-image. Thus experiencing life, persons find themselves isolated both from nature and fellow humans by the very strength of that sense of selfhood which has been so assiduously built up. Indeed it often divides a person within himself. He is fearful of Eastern immanence and its organic inclusion in other being, of the loss of his individual mind in the cosmic Buddha-mind, of emptiness and no-self because they threaten to swallow up his treasured selfhood without remainder. Yet on the other hand he deeply and unceasingly yearns for some way to transcend his "self-"imposed limits and to lose that very self itself in someone or something greater—or even to be able to reach out of his self-constructed confinement and make genuine contact with another human being.

It is to this condition that the Christian self-ideal has sought to speak, but not altogether successfully, because the Christian ideal and experience of self has been strongly affected by the Greek rationalist component of Western culture. Indeed the Christian and Greek-Western self-ideals often seem to be in an almost symbiotic relation to each other. But in any case, what the fully Christian vision of ideal selfhood intends to present to the world is a mode of *self*-transcendence, even *Western-self*-transcendence. A person is not to conceive of himself as self-created, made in his own image, but in the image of the Supreme Self, God, whose Selfhood provides humanity with both the substance and the goal of true selfhood.

Obviously such an assertion is more the expression of a hope or aspiration than of a visible, effectual reality. For though humanity may be made in the image of God-Self, all Christian sects without exception agree that somehow, somewhere, the brightness of that image has been tarnished and its powers diminished. Therefore, when Pope John Paul asserts that humanity is "suffused by the presence of God," this is essentially a statement of faith and hope rather than one of realization or present factuality. It is the expression of the continuing need of the grace of God to enable humanity to possibly, just possibly, attain to something of true divine-human selfhood in the future, a plea for the prodigal son to return to his Father.

Yet this hopeful plea and assertion is not mere unfounded hope. There is the witness of some actual lives—that of Jesus preeminently, and those of some others in observable measure—in which human beings have transcended the confine of narrow selfhood into larger selfhood. In truth many ordinary people, at least fitfully and infrequently, have, under the inspiration of Christ, been able to experience unselfish compassion, to extend and receive forgiveness for wrongs done each other, and to experience an enlarging, empowering communion with the living God. In other words, the hopefully asserted divine sonship of mankind occasionally enables the Western self to escape from its prison of static, closely confined individualism into the immensities of the unlimited and unlimiting love of God and persons; to lose its narrowness and tightness by being crucified with Christ and raised into a new and larger selfhood.

THE LATENT AND FUNCTIONAL SELF IN BUDDHISM

Turning to Buddhism we shall find, under its impersonal formulations, a latent but basic and functional selfhood. In considering the functional actualities beneath the Buddhist impersonal, immanental, and negative statements about self, three principles will be viewed as conjointly applying:

1. The impersonal, monistic-immanental, and negative qualities of Buddhist language about the self are not the same functionally as they appear to be literally. That is, there is in all statements about the self, even the non-self ones, a latent but functional personalism. It is latent, that is, frequently understated and denied, but it is also genuine and central to Buddhism as an operative religion. The Buddhist monism, so frequently asserted in Mahāyāna writings (all is Mind), is not Western substantialist monism, but a kind of organic unity among diversities which allows of interindividual action. And the negative statements are only negative in a positive sense, like those of Western negative theology. This is especially the case for statements about *experience*.

2. The *goal* of all these negativistic statements—no-soul, no-mind, emptiness—is the liberation of the individual selfhood from the trammels of narrow, static formulations and experiences of self-identity into the larger selfhood of self's denial.

3. The ostensibly ontological-metaphysical statements of Buddhism, especially Mahāyāna Buddhism, such as the void, thusness, Buddha-mind,
the Great Mind, and the Dharmakāya (absolute-reality essence of the
Buddha) are essentially *methodological* and *experiential*. The original
definition of religion by the Buddha to Māluṅkyaputta *(Middle Length
Sayings, sutta* 63) was that it had nothing to do with philosophical-
theological statements about the universe or final being-states, but only
with psychic release from human bondage. Relunctantly, with the passing years and the need to defend itself against articulate philosophies,
Buddhism coined various seemingly metaphysical terms such as the
above. But we must be prepared to think of them as essentially existential and experiential, especially when they relate to the self.

From this triple-based viewpoint then, let us observe some of the facets of
Buddhist statements that have given the Western Christian the most difficulty because of their "impersonal," "monistic-immanental," and "negative"
qualities.

The No-self of Theravāda Buddhism

One of the outstanding features of Theravāda Buddhism is its rigid insistence
upon the unreality of the human self, and its conviction that the illusion of
the reality of the self is the root of human bondage and suffering in this present life, as well as the source of infinite rebirths into the same sort of
bondage. But within this no-self citadel itself, there are several elements of
what the West would call the "personal."

In the Pali Canon, Gotama Buddha, even after, or should we say, especially
after his enlightenment experience—which made of his "self " a "gone-out
no-self " that had achieved *nibbana* in this life—*functionally* speaking was
more of a "person" rather than less. In terms of responsiveness to others, the
penetrating perception of their natures, his own expanded mental and spiritual powers, and total inward control, Gotama had become a type of
"superperson."

In popular Buddhism today, that is, Buddhism as a functioning religion,
even though technically the Buddha in his final and absolute gone-outness in
nibbana is totally beyond all personalistic communications, there remains a
vital religious heritage of the Buddha as a living spiritual force which (who?)
responds directly to individual human needs. I once asked a Burmese Buddhist layman if there were still available—even after the Buddha's *nibbana*—a
response to the Buddhist who sent out a spiritual SOS. His instantaneous
reply was, "Yes, of course."

The unreal self, or no-self, of Theravāda Buddhism, this mere collection of the thirty-two components listed by Nāgasena plus the mental and feeling factors, is, in the words of the Venerable U Thittila, "a very special," probably unique "combination of elements."

In further expansion of this point: Though theoretically there is no continuingly identical self or soul which persists through the infinitely long chain of rebirths that each living individual embodies, but only ages-long "karmic energy," this "energy" is also of a very special sort. It contains quite personalized characteristics such as abilities, cast of character, and moral proclivities which are passed on intact from one birth to another.

In a still further, and very important, extension of the special qualities of the human being, there is a kind of hidden but supremely significant functional selfhood which is intrinsic to the no-self. This hidden self comes into sharp focus and essential activity in the meditative discipline.

> As to the ultimate purpose of Satipaṭṭhana [mindfulness techniques], Mindfulness on Postures will bring an initial awareness of the impersonal nature of the body, and will be conductive to an inner alienation from it. In the course of the practice one will come to view the postures [of one's own body] just as unconcernedly as one views the automatic movements of a life-sized puppet. . . . By looking at the postures with such a detached objectivity, the habitual identification with the body will begin to dissolve.

And a few pages later in the same book the author notes, in keeping with the Pali Canon tradition, that this same detached introspective attention can and should be given to one's own feelings, mind states, and mental processes, in order to discover *their* impersonal nature also:

> Here too, mind is placed in front of the clear mirror of Bare Attention. The object of observation is here the condition and the level of mind, or consciousness, as it presents itself in a given moment.[11]

By definition a Theravāda Buddhist would, of course, never use the term "self " for this power of "Bare Attention" and we need not dispute over that. But there it is; a center of consciousness, an awareness which by its inherent nature operates from a point of vantage which is somehow outside and above the ordinary thinking-feeling process of the inner activities of the no-self. In fact, it can observe the inmost structure and functioning of the no-self itself, that no-self which only seems to be a self. And most important of all: This capacity for Bare Attention is the innermost kernel, the *sine qua non* of the salvational (enlightenment) process. This point will be returned to later.

In a very interesting passage in the Pali Canon (*Middle Length Sayings* 1.137-40) the Buddha asks this question of his disciples: "But is it fitting to regard that which is impermanent, painful, liable to change as 'This is mind, this is I, this is my self,'? " And they reply in the negative. The immediate application of this negative response (to which the Buddha agrees) was to the five components (*khandhas*) that make up a human being or "person." Such elements as these, especially because they cannot be controlled by the mind or will, are in no way worthy to be called a self.

It is then the more interesting to read the description of an individual (or mind? or self?) that has gained enlightenment:

> Just as a rock of one solid mass remains unshaken by the wind, even so neither visible forms, nor sounds, nor odours, nor tastes, nor bodily impressions, neither the desired nor the undesired, can cause such a one to waver. Steadfast is his mind, gained is deliverance.[12]

Here surely is some sort of mental entity—a power of Bare Attention, a "mind" or "state of mind" or "person" or "self " that has attained to complete freedom from "that which is impermanent, painful, liable to change" and is therefore, it would seem, by the implied definition, a true "self."

The Empty, Formless Self of Mahāyāna Buddhism

It is true that in Mahāyāna Buddhism the term "self " is not forbidden to use in connection with the faith; indeed the "true" or "original" self is much spoken of in some circles. But certainly ordinary selfhood, as the prime embodiment of selfishness and samsaric attachment, is as much warred against as in Theravāda Buddhism; and the terms in which "true" selfhood, Buddha-selfhood one might say, are spoken of are fully as daunting to the Western Christian mind. But here we shall be examining the key Mahāyāna terms indicating true or real selfhood for their existential and experiential implications. This is in keeping with the earlier suggestion that most Buddhist terms of this sort should properly be viewed as experiential rather than ontological in their import.

No-mind. We are often told in Zen texts that the calculating, conceptualizing mind must be destroyed—at least as an avenue to enlightenment. Indeed this is the prime purpose of meditation on the koan *mu*. D. T. Suzuki graphically describes, in *Zen Buddhism and Psychoanalysis*, the "destruction" of all *self*-consciousness, or awareness of "I," by the continuous thinking and saying of *"mu, mu, mu."* There results a climactic moment of total immanence, when all subjective awareness as such is annihilated and replaced by *mu*-awareness. The meditator has himself "become" *mu* (or nothingness).[13]

But this is different, as Suzuki notes, from mere mental vacuity. It is at least mind-filled-with-nothingness. The Sixth Patriarch, Hui-nêng, told his disciples that it was a mistake to attempt to blank out thought; an individual with blanked-out thought was no different, no more enlightened than a stump or stone. Rather he was to "think as not thinking," that is, with nonconceptual awareness. And D. T. Suzuki appended a significant comment to the above description:

> For Zen this [moment of immanental unity of consciousness] is not enough; there must be a certain awakening which breaks up the equilibrium and brings one back to the relative level of consciousness [i.e., of duality of subject-object, person-to-person awareness] when a *satori* takes place....[14]

In the Zen view then, a trancelike sense of unity with some ultimate is not the fullness of *satori*, but only its precondition. One must go on through it, modified by it, to a new sort of absolute-relative awareness of the world of multiplicity which he is now reentering.

> But this so called relative level is not [any longer] really relative—this is the moment when the finite mind realizes that it is rooted in the infinite. In terms of Christianity, this is the time when the soul hears directly or inwardly the voice of the living God.[15]

Such a breakthrough into a new mode of consciousness is of course not to be mechanically produced by psychosomatic discipline; it comes to some, and not to others; it is a gift of grace. Yet there *is* a non-*satori* analogue to post-*satori* no-mind, in "secular" life. D. T. Suzuki liked to illustrate this type of no-mind, or mindless, action by pointing to one of his cats and saying: "When that cat jumps down from the table to the floor to eat, it does not think, like a human being 'I am hungry and want to eat that food, and will now jump down,' no, it just jumps." The implication was that human beings at their highest and best should be able to thus act in nearly all, if not all, life situations.

He further defined no-mind in terms of Japanese swordsmanship, which is the practice of the art of "thinking as though not thinking."

> It is a state of mind known as *munen* or *muso*, 'no thought' or 'no-reflection.' This does not mean just to be without thoughts, ideas, feelings, etc. . . . It means letting your natural faculties act in a consciousness free from thoughts, reflections, or affections of any kind. . . . However well a man may be trained in the art, the swordsman can never be the master of his technical knowledge unless all his psychic hindrances are removed and he can keep the mind in the state of emptiness, even purged of whatever technique he has obtained. The entire body together with the four limbs will then be capable of displaying for the first time and to its full extent, all the art acquired by the training of several years. They will move as if automatically. *Emptiness is one-mind-ness, one-mind-ness is no-mind-ness.*[16]

While this is on the lower plane of swordsmanship, the special quality of no-mind is much the same both in good swordsmanship and in good Zen living. Zen-*satori* living is no-mindedness permeating the *total* consciousness and *all* of one's awareness and actions; it is living in perpetually flexible harmony and interaction between all of the inner realities of one's own body-mind; rather than being a description of the ontological nature of the human mind, it is a description of the saved, or enlightened mode of life.

Emptiness (śūnyatā). This term is frequently used in Zen writings. It is used as a meditational subject *(koan)*, to describe the meditationally achieved state of mind, the nature of phenomena, or even the universe itself. When used on the personal, experiential level it is roughly the same as no-mind. In a Hui-nêng-like statement Suzuki Shosan (1579-1655, samurai turned Soto Zen monk) protested against a meditative interpretation and experience of emptiness and no-mind that made the meditator dull and blank:

> Therefore they work at a form of zazen that is like an empty insect case. They think that the real no-thought, no-mind is to be completely dull and silent, thinking of nothing at all. This is a great mistake. This sort of practice will diminish one's capacities; one may become ill, even insane. The Buddha Dharma of no-thought, no-mind is a no-thought no-mind *that can be used in every circumstance.* No-thought, no-mind is to be used when one is sad, when one is joyful, indeed on every occasion. Nowadays there are many who, falling into 'nothingness views,' do harm to people. Saying, 'We have the Original Emptiness,' they maintain impassive faces.[17]

When *śunyatā* is taken as cosmic in character and, accordingly, the Dharmakāya (Absolute Buddha-reality) is said to be empty (devoid) of all distinguishing characteristics, and in turn all phenomena to be empty of true reality, then it appears to have become a kind of ultimate reality. (Should it be called the Buddhist equivalent of God?) But whatever its true nature, we must not be led astray on two points. First, its negative form of designation is not mere nullity, but rather a kind of Buddhist *via negativa* term, whose negative character is a witness to the indescribable fullness of *śunyatā*. Thus it is the fountainhead of all experienceable phenomena; it is "revealed" in them. And again it is not a cold abstraction; it has a compassionate "personal" quality that pours out its richness inexhaustibly, and is the essence of the true self. As Professor Masao Abe has written:

> True Śūnyatā, being the negation of sheer emptiness as well as sheer fullness, is an active and creative emptiness which, just because of being itself empty, lets everything and everyone be and work respectively in their particularity. Each [individual entity] is not simply something with a particular form, but *equally* and *respectively,* the self-expression through the taking form, of the true Śūnyatā, that is, *the True Self which is beyong every form.*[18]

All is Mind. This statement forms an important part of Fa-tsang's mirror analogy. And as observed above, though it is mentalistic-spiritual in quality, contrasted to the Western Christian view of the importance and integrity of individual minds, this phrasing suggests a great overmind (the Buddha-mind) which reduces these individual minds to mere wavelets on the surface of its oceanic depths and widths. It seems to be an impersonal mental substance rather than a true mind. Or, to use the former figure, the individual and his mind are but a crossroads of connections with no real individuality or personality at the junction.

But this is to misjudge such statements. We must remember here again that such seeming ontological-metaphysical statements must be viewed as primarily human-existential, experiential. And so it is here. This "All is Mind" assertion is not intended to destroy mental individuality (selfness) but to enhance it on two scores: (1) Individual minds are not to be thought of as atoms, only externally related to other minds and the rest of the world; but they are to be understood as organically, internally connected with other minds and the world, to have an identity of essential nature with their environment, though differentiated in particulars. All minds are essentially the Buddha-mind; as *minds* they are the Buddha-mind. (2) The statement that "All is Mind" gives our little individual minds the assurance that we, as spiritual-mental beings, are not orphaned in the universe, but are integral to it, part and parcel of a spiritual whole. And thus, though this relationship may seem a little too close for the comfort of the individualistic Westerner, who fondly treasures his independent standing room as a self or soul, it is not a remainderless engulfment.

In conclusion, and as illustrative both of the latent personalism of the most impersonal no-self terms to be found in Buddhism, and of the experiential component of the most metaphysical sounding words in the Buddhist vocabulary, two passages may be quoted, one having to do with nirvana, and the other with the Dharmakāya (Absolute Buddha-reality). The first is a famous passage from Rudolf Otto's *The Idea of the Holy*:

> I recall vividly a conversation I had with a Buddhist monk. He had been putting before me methodically and pertinaciously the arguments for the Buddhist 'theology of negation,' the doctrine of Anātman and 'entire emptiness.' When he made an end, I asked him then what Nirvana itself is; and after a long pause came at last the single answer, low and restrained: 'Bliss unspeakable.' And the hushed restraint of that answer, the solemnity of his voice, demeanor, and gesture, made more than clear what was meant than the words themselves.[19]

The second is the account of the enlightenment experience of a thirteenth-century Zen monk:

> One night sitting far into the night I kept my eyes open and was aware of my sitting in my seat. All of a sudden the sound of striking the board in front of the head monk's room reached my ear, which at once revealed to me the 'original man' in full. . . . Hastily I came down from the seat and ran out into the moonlit night . . . where looking up to the sky I laughed loudly, 'Oh, how great is the Dharmakāya! The Absolute Reality! Oh, how great and immense for evermore.'
>
> Thence my joy knew no bounds . . . I went about with no special purpose in the mountains, walking this way and that. I thought of the sun and the moon traversing in a day through a space 4,000,000,000 miles wide . . . 'They say the district of Yang is the center of the earth. If so, this place must be 2,000,000,000 miles away from where the sun rises; and how is it that as soon as it comes up, its rays lose no time in striking my face?' I reflected again, 'The rays of my own eye travel just as instantaneously as those of the sun . . . ; *my eyes, my mind, are they not the Dharma-*

kāya itself?' Thinking thus, I felt all the bonds snapped and broken in pieces that had been tying me for so many ages. How many numberless years I had been sitting in the hole of ants! *Today even in every pore of my skin there lie all the Buddha lands in the ten quarters.*[20]

REASSESSMENT OF BUDDHIST IMPERSONALISM AND CHRISTIAN PERSONALISM

Four points have now been made. First, the stereotype versions of Christian self and Buddhist non-self, which pit them against each other and make genuine dialogue impossible, have been described. Second, it has been suggested that Christianity should relate to Buddhism in this area out of the *fullness,* and not the mystical semi-denial, of its personalism. Third, an interpretation of Christian selfhood in terms of experience rather than soul-theory has been given; and the goal of that experience has been described as opening ordinary selfhood up to a Christ-like dimension. Fourth, Theravāda and Mahāyāna (Zen) Buddhist *im*personal language has been analyzed to contain a latent but central personalism, and its ontological-impersonal categories to be primarily experiential. It is now time to draw these strands together.

Because it is foundational for a meaningful dialogue about "self," it must again be emphasized that such Buddhist terms as no-self, no-mind, Universal Buddha-mind, emptiness, and Absolute Buddha-reality (Dharmakāya) should in this connection be taken as existential and experiential, rather than as metaphysical. Their ontological significance must be set aside for the moment. And on such a basis the following principles relative to Buddhist impersonalism can be utilized:

1. The Buddhist "impersonal" terms just noted all express and describe a liberating, enlarging experience of a greater-than-ordinary-individual wholeness.
2. They indicate an experience of freedom and flexibility in terms of the concepts and experiences of selfhood. Zen writings are full of the sound of the breaking of the shackles of narrowly conceived and experienced selfhood.
3. They contain a sense of the possiblity of radically restructuring the given, inherited, limited, static versions of selfhood that society and tradition impose upon each of us.
4. The negative, that is, "impersonal," form given to Buddhist statements about the self, is an important, even essential, means for gaining that freedom, at least as Buddhism views it.

On the Christian side the theological, ontological questions relating to selfhood are taken more seriously than in Buddhism. But for the purposes of dialogue and possible shared experiences of a larger, freer selfhood, Christian ontology must also be bracketed out of the conversation. Then it can be clearly observed that *Christian* selfhood (not Western) has aims remarkably similar to those of Buddhism, though stated differently. Christianity too seeks freedom for the self from the narrowness of inherited patterns, even from some of its own. And such is the direction indicated by its basic terms. For example it seeks a new and greater selfhood in Christ: the old man of sin, selfishness, and static limitations is to be "buried with Christ in baptism" and raised with him into newness of life. To use another figure: the old (ordinary, traditional) self is to be "crucified with Christ," to be "lost" for Christ's sake. The new self which replaces it is to be such a self that it is "no longer I who live, but Christ who lives in me." When Christian selfhood is thought of in such experiential terms it is surely not too unlike the true formless *śūnyatā* self of Buddhism, that "selfless interiority which the Japanese have often rendered by such emotionally pregnant words as Emptiness and Nothingness."[21]

On such a basis, then, it is possible to say: the self, here interpreted as the essence of experienceable and experienced selfhood, in both Buddhism and Christianity, is precisely the human capacity to transcend self by becoming true self. Even with strictly no-self Theravāda Buddhism this is the case. To return to a former example: we are told that there is within the human psyche the power of Bare Attention, the ability to become clearly and dispassionately aware of what goes on within one's own no-self, be it bodily, sensory, emotional, or mental. That is to say, intrinsic to this psyche, even though the name "self" be refused it, is the power of *self*-transcendence. And Mahāyāna Buddhism, in a differing way but with the same essential meaning, speaks of the transcendent psychical power with which to break through ordinary consciousness into a direct knowledge of the original or true self, the Buddha-mind in our minds.

It may be said, as the existentialists have, that self-transcendence is the distinguishing mark of any and every human psyche, even the ordinary one. And so it is. Every person has had the experience of becoming so engrossed in something or other that his total attention is immersed in the object of his concern. Temporarily he forgets where he is in time and space, has no "idea" of what he is doing, is unaware of bodily feelings or of special emotions, and is without consciousness of personal identity. Awareness has transcended its physical and narrowly personal boundaries, and become *im*partial and *im*personal. But this power of the human mind to thus become *im*personal and detached is the very essence and acme of its personalism.

It is precisely this ordinary power of the mind to transcend itself—but not self—that both Buddhism and Christianity seek to maximize and transform. They both seek a religious, that is, a *total* self-transcendence. They summon the human self to transcend the narrowness of exclusive self-concern—concern for self-aggrandizement, for only personal gains and losses, joys and sorrows, or an angry existentialist defiance of God and the universe in terms of self-assertion—into an awareness of others, a concern for their concern, sorrow in their sorrow, and joy in their joy. There is the call here, especially for the Christian, to a more self-forgetful, joyous acceptance of the universe that evirons him. Buddhism and Christianity, as religious faiths, try to "save" men, to elevate them from the casual, accidental, and episodic experience of selflessness, to a daily, habitual, instinctive embodiment of it. And they both say, though in different terms—"It is not I that live, but Christ in me," or "My eyes, my mind, are they not the Dharma-kāya itself? "—that when total self-transcendence *has* become habitual and spontaneous, then "salvation" has indeed come to pass; the Buddha-mind has been attained, the prodigal has returned to the Father.

The moral of all this is that such terms as "self " and "no-self," "personal" and "impersonal," "fullness" and "emptiness," should cease to be mere party slogans, and become avenues for the mutual exploration of each other's dearest self-freeing experiences. Perhaps we should speak of the "impersonal," that is, selflessly compassionate, personalism of the Christ-self, and of the "personal," in other words, self-transcending, impersonalism of Buddha-mindedness. And perhaps too we may speak without contradiction of the "transcendent immanence" of each of us in each other, in the universe, in the Dharmakāya or God, and equally appropriately of the "immanent transcendence" that is possible to each of us as innately superpersonal persons.

Notes

1. Quoted in H. C. Warren, *Buddhism in Translations* (New York: Atheneum, 1963), pp. 130-133.
2. Ibid., pp. 149-150.
3. Edward Conze, *Buddhism* (New York: Philosophical Library, n.d.), pp. 168-171.
4. Frederick J. Streng, *Emptiness* (Nashville: Abingdon, 1967), p. 211.
5. D. T. Suzuki, *The Zen Doctrine of No-Mind* (London: Rider, 1949), p. 22.
6. Garma C. C. Chang, *The Buddhist Teaching of Totality* (University Park: Penn State Press, 1971), p. 24.
7. Harvey Cox, "Perspective," *Harvard Divinity Bulletin,* October-November 1979, p. 179.
8. D. T. Suzuki, *Mysticism: Christian and Buddhist* (New York: Macmillan, 1957), Sec. 1, Chap. 3.
9. *Meister Eckhart,* trans. C. de B. Evans (New York: Lucis Publishing, n.d.), p. 82.
10. In conversation at Buddhist-Christian Conference, Honolulu, June 1980.

11. Nyanaponika Thera, *The Heart of Buddhist Meditation* (Colombo: Word of the Buddha Publishing Committee, 1953), pp. 74, 81.

12. Quoted from *The Book of Gradual Sayings* 4.55, in Nyanatiloka, ed., *Buddhist Dictionary* (Colombo: Frewin and Company, 1972), p. 106.

13. D. T. Suzuki, Erich Fromm, and Richard De Martino, *Zen Buddhism and Psychoanalysis* (New York: Harper and Brothers, 1960), p. 46.

14. Ibid., pp. 46-47.

15. Ibid.

16. D. T. Suzuki, *Zen and Japanese Culture* (Princeton: Princeton University Press, 1959), pp. 127, 152.

17. Tesshin Suzuki, ed., *Complete Collected Works of Suzuki Shōsan (Suzuki Shōsan dōnin senshū)* (Tokyo: Sankibo Busshorin, 1962), "Roankyō" 1, 70, 112.

18. Masao Abe, review of *Christianity and the Encounter of the World Religions,* by Paul Tillich, *Eastern Buddhist,* N.S. 1, No. 1 (1965): 119. Last italics added.

19. Rudolf Otto, *The Idea of the Holy* (New York: Oxford University Press, 1958), p. 39.

20. D. T. Suzuki, *Essays in Zen Buddhism, First Series* (New York: Harper and Brothers, 1949), p. 265. Italics added.

21. Joseph J. Spae, *Buddhist-Christian Empathy* (Chicago: Chicago Institute of Theology and Culture, 1980), p. 16.

CHAPTER 9

Selfhood Without Selfishness: Buddhist and Christian Approaches to Authentic Living

Frederick J. Streng

Our first reaction to the word "religions" in the conference title "East-West Religions in Encounter" might be to feel that we are clear about the term "religion," and define the religions simply as "Christianity" and "Buddhism." The discussion, then, is an encounter of two religious traditions (in the abstract) or two communities committed to certain beliefs, rituals, spiritual practices, and ethics. Or, we may say that communities in general cannot encounter each other, only individual people encounter other people. This poses the questions: What is the encounter of religions? and Where does the encounter take place?

I think that there are various kinds of encounters which take place in different forms and situations. One sort of encounter is that which takes place within each person as he or she becomes aware of the differences in assumptions that people have about the nature and purpose of religion itself. To recognize that another intelligent, ethical, and religiously sensitive person may believe something different from what one cherishes as a superlative value oneself, and even that another entire orientation to authentic living is quite different from one's own, raises a profound question about the validity of one's own views. To engage in this sort of internal encounter is, I think, most appropriate for moral and religiously sensitive people who are aware of the religiously plural world in which we now live. Part of the encounter of "East-West religions," then, is that found within oneself between alternative definitions of the nature and the internal dynamic of religious life itself.

To explore this encounter I want to use as a springboard the thoughts of two well-known philosophers of religion on the question, What is religion? They are Paul Tillich[1] and Keiji Nishitani.[2] Their writings are especially useful because each philosopher speaks out of his religious and cultural background, but raises the question about the nature of religion in light of the contemporary sensitivity to human self-alienation, cynicism regarding any ultimate values, and anxiety about sudden or creeping world catastrophe. Both men recognize that each age must reformulate its truths and reassert its core orientation to authentic living in light of contemporary issues and concerns. Both see the predominant issue of the twentieth century to be a loss of human centeredness in the ultimate reality whereby one can transcend self-centeredness. The experience of this loss might be termed "psychological nihilism." It is the existential awareness that a self-centered or selfish effort to "be somebody" leads to despair and exhaustion.

In a basic way this consideration of what religion is, within the context of the contemporary experience of psychological nihilism, is a continuation of the Buddhist-Christian dialogue that has taken place during the past three decades. It is an attempt both to take seriously the differences within and be-tween Buddhism and Christianity, and to recognize the need to reformulate issues, reconceive ideas, and reassert deep commitments in the effort to foster understanding and an enhancement of life. I recognize with gratitude the efforts of many scholars and religious leaders who have worked toward communication; they include Masao Abe, Bhikkhu Buddhadasa, John Cobb, Tomas Merton, Winston King, Joseph Spae, Lynn de Silva, and Hans Waldenfals. My goal here is in line with that stated by Professor Abe when he called for "opening up a new spiritual horizon for the coming one world—by breaking through the bondaries of the patterns of thought and belief of the two religions."[3]

Both Paul Tillich and Keiji Nishitani feel the urgency of defining and defending religion in light of their own sensitivities to the limitations of traditional religious forms. Nevertheless they want to show the vitality and inherent dynamic of religious faith and insight for readers living in cultures dominated by a cynicism juxtaposed with a yearning for national identity, a despair often overlaid with revolutionary and utopian idealism, and a sense of rootedness in an imperial nationalism contradicted by a need to respond to a convulsively changing worldwide community. With a clear perception of the existential concerns prominent in the literature and philosophy of the twentieth century, they speak to the sense of the control that technology has on the lives of all people today, and the experience of discovering or creating new values different from those of their ancestors. What is it that holds together the past, present, and future? How can a person express freedom and still participate in significant relationships that limit one's freedom? How does one know when one is living authentically? When is an awareness of oneself merely superficial in contrast to a depth perception of the real self? These questions, say both of these philosophers, can be considered as as-pects of the larger question, What is religion?, for this question focuses on the nature of the self-in-existence in relation to the true nature of things.

In defining the nature of religion in the context of the problematic and ful-fillment of the self-in-existence, Tillich and Nishitani intend to speak to a human condition and possibility that is universal, that extends beyond the teaching and practices of a single historical religious tradition. At the same time their answers to the problem of a contemporary deep despair are derived from their experience within Christian and Buddhist traditions. By showing several elements in the alternate definitions of religion, both of which address a basic problematic of modern life, we hope to gain some insight into the axi-ological structures that provide alternate strategies for quality living; that is, by looking at some basic concepts of the self, such as modes of consciousness, the nature of the trans-ego ultimate reality, and the radical condition of evil in life we can perceive different structures of value formation which result in alternate emphases in experiencing the self. We want to see how the value-giving structures that define what is better or worse in life also provide the basic character of what is considered authentic. Then, in the final section, we want to raise the possibility of adjusting some of the elements for possible new alternatives in the self-understanding of each tradition.

MODES OF CONSCIOUSNESS IN THE DISCOVERY OF SELF

Paul Tillich, speaking out of a Christian context, and Keiji Nishitani, speak-ing out of a Buddhist background, affirm the mainline position of each tradi-tion when they say that in order to know the deepest reality of the self a person must transcend the concerns of the psycho-physical self, or the ego. There is a recognition that the habitual perception of selfhood that most people have is intrinsically related to the deepest reality of life, but at the same time habitual perception gives a false perspective for knowing the nature of selfhood. The correction to this false experience of selfhood is found in religious faith, insight, and practice. In subsequent sections I want to analyze the differences in the notions of the ultimate reality and of the radical condition of evil in existence; however, first I want to look at the way each of these philosophers understands the role and nature of consciousness, because for each of them whatever is real in existence depends radically on being conscious of the nature of things. The actualization of the true self begins with full awareness of one's nature.

For Tillich, human existence is that sort of reality whose fulfillment is in or through *meaning*. He makes this clear when he defends his analytic-intuitive philosophical method—which he calls "metalogic"—for under-standing the core of religious life; this method, he says, "must assume that the principles of meaning to which consciousness submits itself in the spiritu-al act are at the same time the principles of meaning to which being is subjected. It must assume that the meaning of being comes to expression in the consciousness informed by meaning."[4] In this way Tillich justifies his contention that it is possible to know something at all; the self can truly be aware of the nature of existence in which it already is ensconsed. Human consciousness strives for a fulfillment of meaning; to be human means that one tries to unify all the elements of one's consciousness, both the ideal or theoretical aspects and the material or practical aspects of one's experience. Reality is not exterior to the act of the human spirit that seeks to either receive or bestow a unifying awareness to all facets of life. He makes clear that meaning is the core of conscious existence when he states:

> Meaning is the common characteristic of the ultimate unity of the theoretical and the practicial sphere of spirit, of scientific and aesthetic, of legal and social structures. The spiritual reality in which the spirit-bearing forces (Gestalt) lives and creates, is a meaning-reality (Sinnwirklichkeit).[5]

There are three elements in every expression of meaning: (1) an awareness of the interconnection of the separate aspects of meaning, (2) the awareness that every particular meaning is related to an unconditioned and ultimate meaningfulness, and (3) that while there is no complete unity of meaning in any existing (and, thus, conditioned) meaning, there is "the demand to fulfill the unconditioned meaning."[6] Here is the basis for Tillich's claim that every cultural form has as its basis an ontological character; any cultural form can be a medium for the spirit-bearing forces. Indeed, not every cultural expression has an intention to express the unconditioned meaning; in fact, there are demonic expressions when the unconditional meaning is denied. However, it is the *demand* for the attempt to present the unity of all meaning that makes the unconditional meaning actual in form.[7]

The consciousness of meaning, then, is the place where the spirit takes form. The role of the personality in exposing both the, at least partially, unified cultural meaning and the unconditional ground for all meaning is made clear when Tillich states:

> The real meaning-fulfillment is one in which bestowal of meaning takes place in the sphere of individual reality bound to nature; an ideal fulfillment is one in which the giving of meaning involves no transformation in the material sphere, but rather a fulfillment of the existent thing in its immediate formation. . . . Personality is the place of meaning-fulfillment, both real and ideal.[8]

At the same time, Tillich makes clear that there is a distinction between the expression of (partially) unified meaning in culture and the self-conscious awareness of the unconditioned meaning of religious life. In this context of interpretation, religion is the attempt to grasp the unity of meaning which is directed toward what exists unconditionally *(das unbedingt Seiende)*.[9] The definition of religion is, then, "the sum total of all spiritual acts directed toward grasping the unconditional import of meaning through the fulfillment of the unity of meaning."[10]

The basic mode for the synthesis of form, content, and the Unconditional is a symbol. This symbol of unity can never be regarded as absolute, otherwise, it is demonic. It is, rather, "a symbol of the plumb line by which all [syntheses] are measured and found wanting it; it is the plumb line that symbolizes authentic fulfillment of meaning."[11] In sum, the spiritual consciousness for Tillich is the creation of a reality through meaning which stands under the demand of unconditional reality; the purest form of this is a symbol which paradoxically unites and judges all symbols.

Like Tillich, Keiji Nishitani sees the self in its conventional cultural expression as an expression of the nature of things, while at the same time pointing out that without a deeper awareness than is commonly experienced, a person will be caught in the overwhelming sense of transcience and meaninglessness. However, for Nishitani, the key to gaining a fulfilling perspective is not to create a symbolic meaning that stands under the demand of the Unconditional; rather, it is to become fully aware of the manner of our existence. Full awareness requires a breakthrough in the field of consciousness so that one no longer is aware of a separate ego which is presumably to be fulfilled. For him, religion is defined as "an existential exposure of the problematical which is contained in the usual mode of self-being."[12] While all of life is transcient, and human beings encounter the reality of non-being at each step, it is only in religion that human beings reach a deepening of the perception of their transcience so that they see nothingness manifest in their own being. In Zen awareness this is called "coming to oneself." Nishitani explains such a moment of awareness when he writes:

> The opening up of the horizon of nothingness out of the ground of our life is the occasion of the radical about-face in our life itself. This turn-about is no other than the transformation from the self-centered (or man-centered) attitude which asks concerning all things, what is their use to us (or to man), to that of asking for what purpose do we ourselves exist.[13]

This awareness must be more than an intellectual comprehension of reality; it has to be a total realization in spirit, soul, and body. As Tillich spoke of "meaning-reality"—that is, of the reality of our being known through meaning—Nishitani says that placing our self in the "horizon of nothingness" is the moment when "reality itself comes to its own realization."[14] He elaborates this notion by commenting:

> This real awareness of Reality is our real being itself and constitutes the true reality of our existence. And this is because that awareness actualizes itself as one with the self-realization of Reality itself.[15]

In this context he proposes to answer the question of What is religion? by "tracing the path through which the quest for what is truly real is *really* pursued."[16]

The key activity in this quest is the shift out of everyday consciousness to an intuitive identity with the nothingness that is at the root of the field of being. In the everyday consciousness of thinking and objectifying our experience, we are rarely in contact with ourselves, only with images of ourselves. Similarly we are not in contact with things in the world, but with our ego-based response to them. While all things, self, and feelings, are relatively real, he continues, "it cannot be said that they are present in their true reality in the field of consciousness, while they are always present only in the form of representation."[17]

To see the world in representations, or through a subject-object awareness, is only one—and a limited—way of being-in-existence. It is a self-centered way of being. Nishitani explains the peculiarity of this way of being by commenting: "What is called the 'ego' consists of the procedure that the self-consciousness endlessly reflects only itself."[18] To recognize that we participate in different modes of becoming by means of different modes of consciousness is a basic step in seeing the self within the horizon of fundamental nothingness. Thus, Nishitani's brief but revealing statement on the power of knowing is not surprising: "Knowing always contains a sort of transcendence over what is known."[19]

As Tillich recognizes that the meanings found in culture are distinguishable from the religious grasp of the unconditional import of meaning, so Nishitani affirms that the general awareness of the transcience and uncertainty of existence experienced by everyone is distinguishable from "Great Doubt," which presents itself as the nothingness at the root of self-awareness. The nature of "Great Doubt" is different from a relative doubt as a phenomenon of consciousness. Nishitani describes the uncovering of the nothingness as the foundation of oneself and all things as the Great Doubt, which is also a self-awareness more fundamental than ego-consciousness:

> When the self breaks-through the field of 'being' only, that is, the field
> of consciousness, and reaches the nothingness lying at the base, it is able
> for the first time to attain a subjectivity that can not be objectified in any
> way. This is a self-awareness more basic than self-consciousness.[20]

Such an awareness of nothingness appears as inevitable; and the person becomes a mass of doubt. Here Nishitani is careful to admonish the reader that this realization of the nothingness at the foundation of both subjectivity and objectivity is not their annihilation; it is, however, the death of the ego understood as the illusory, self-centered attachment to the self-image.

ONTOLOGICAL FOUNDATIONS OF TRUE SELFHOOD

In the above discussion of Tillich's and Nishitani's understandings of authentic selfhood in the context of universal human experience I have already referred to the fact that for each philosopher true selfhood is rooted in the ultimate nature of things. For Tillich the reality of being through meaning resides finally in the Unconditional, or divine, ground of meaning which is also ultimate being. For Nishitani, the reality known in Great Doubt is nothingness, or the "field of emptiness," which is at the root of all awareness of being. I cannot develop in much detail here the ontological descriptions in Tillich's and Nishitani's work;[21] I can only point to some of the implications of their respective ontologies for an understanding of authentic selfhood. In continuation of Nishitani's concern with becoming fully aware of the emptiness at the root of all being, I will first discuss his notion of the "field of emptiness," and then turn to Tillich's notion of unconditional being.

Nishitani summarizes his position when he states: "It is only in a field where the 'being' of all things is a being at one with emptiness that it is possible for all things to gather into One, even while each is a reality as an absolutely unique being."[22] This notion of emptiness is not a negative principle that calls into question the reality of life. Rather, it is the root, or basic, field in which the affirmative and negative aspects of life are at all possible. At the same time, as suggested before, it is a state of awareness, instead of a substantive reality, which gives a certain quality or character to the arising and dissipation of existence.

The interplay between the affirmative and negative aspects in emptiness is perceived, however, only when one realizes that the perception requires a complete negation of any abstraction or representation of either emptiness or being-itself. This is a radical kind of negativity which seeks to plumb the very depths of a notion of emptiness by negating even emptiness as a notion. Only by negating the particular forms of one's experience can a person get beyond the negation itself to a sense that there is an intrinsic relatedness between all things. Once one "passes through" the claim of absolute negativity as the opposite to a universal essence (being-itself), then one does not perceive life as absurd; nor need a person develop his or her ego-strength as a superman or wonder woman; rather there is a new mode of being, namely, non-attachment to being-itself; this a person perceives as he or she moves through the experience of Great Doubt.

The implication of this ontological experience of negativity is that a thing is "itself " when it is "not-itself " (without ceasing to be itself). When one perceives emptiness, one recognizes that the character of a particular form is intrinsically related to other forms; thus, there is no need to preserve that form's own identity independently. Nishitani describes the nature of identity and relationship in the field of emptiness as follows:

> [E]ach thing is itself while not being itself, is not itself while being itself; its 'being' is unreal in its truth and true in its unreality. This may sound queer at first but, in fact, through such a view, we are enabled for the first time to conceive a *'force'* by virtue of which all things are gathered and brought into relationship to one another—a 'force' which,
> since ancient times, has been called nature *(physis, natura).* [23]

This perspective contrasts with a definition of reality as the substance of a thing, which assumes that there is something wholly external to us, something which maintains itself in an unchanging way and is external to our subjective apprehension.

The direct awareness of emptiness as the most profound mode of being indicates that the field of emptiness is at the root of even the most conventional perception of existence. Nishitani states this explicitly when he says that the field of emptiness "opens up, as it were, still nearer to ourselves than the ourselves we are ordinarily thinking of. In other words by converting what is ordinarily called "self " to the field of emptiness, we became truly ourselves." [24] The field of emptiness ultimately appears as a field of wisdom which is called "knowing of unknowing." [25] When the self has a field of emptiness as its home ground, it is free from the attachment to things-in-themselves or to abstract principles.

For Tillich, in contrast, human anxiety is not the expression of the radical field of emptiness at the root of being-in-existence; rather, this fundamental anxiety is rooted in the very structure of being. [26] It is a dialectical form of non-being—expressed in the Greek phrase *me on*—that is intrinsically related to being. In the dialectical relationship between non-being *(me on)* and being *(to on)* the abyss of non-being is found in all existence. For Tillich, the threat of non-being is the ontological ground for causality in the world, since it shows the inability of anything to rest on itself and its need for other things as a condition for its own survival.[27] Even more importantly for the existential experience of change and transcience of life, change is seen to result automatically in anxiety. He claims that the recognition of any change has two implications: (1) that there should be an unchanging being, and (2) change is the threat to that basic reality.

According to Tillich, while in existence there is a dialectical relation between being and non-being, non-being is entirely dependent on being for any ontological value. He insists that "nonbeing is literally nothing except in relation to being."[28] Even in the direct experience of human finitude people must look at themselves and experience non-being from the viewpoint of "a potential infinity." The power of being as being-itself cannot have a beginning or an end; it is simply the basic presupposition for anything to be. This power of being as experienced in the individual is the power of infinite self-transcendence. He states this as follows: "The power of infinite self-transcendence is an expression of man belonging to that which is beyond nonbeing, namely, to being-itself."[29] We should note, however, that infinity is not being-itself; because being-itself lies beyond "the polarity of finitude and infinite self-transcendence."[30]

The power of infinite self-transcendence as the dynamic through which being-itself is expressed is a very important notion for Tillich since, for him, a person's reality is manifested by an activity of self-transcendence. As we saw before, Tillich holds that one's being is expressed through meaning, and all meaning finally is an expression to some degree of the drive to unconditional meaning. Being-itself precedes both finitude and the partial synthesis of meaning, as well as the implicit drive for infinite self-transcendence. At the same time the drive for infinite self-transcendence is a negation of finitude (and thus some balm for the pain of existential anxiety) because it is the expression of being-itself within finitude.

In Tillich's perspective, then, the highest quality of human life is a positive and ultimately meaningful action. In this way human beings manifest infinite self-transcendence, which expresses the ontological negation of non-being. The highest quality of human life depends on being-itself while at the same time it is a positive action within finite existence. While Tillich holds that "being is essentially related to nonbeing,"[31] being-itself is not essentially in a state of disruption or chaos. This is not a bipolar view between being and non-being (as is found, for example, in the yin-yang notion of Taoism). Being-itself is the primal *a priori.* Continuity in life is therefore credited to the presence of being, and any change is understood to be real where it is identified substantially as a causal force which arises from being or "what is" from one moment to another. The "courage to be" is an act of a finite self-transcendence through dependence on being-itself; it is also the infinite drive for "what is" to seek self-transcendence.

The act of self-transcendence through meaning has an ontological implication for another aspect of human experience. Humanity, claims Tillich, is a kind of being in which a person is intuitively aware of the subject-object bipolar structure in awareness of being.[32] To ask the question about being presupposes two actualities: an asking subject, and an object about which the question is asked. The experience of self-centeredness in an objective world is the basic dialectical ontological structure of life. This structure is something which, according to Tillich, cannot be derived; it must be accepted.[33] While "self " and "the environment in which the self exists" determine each other, selfhood "is an original phenomenon which logically precedes all questions of existence."[34] Human beings have an immediate experience of the polar structure of vitality and intentionality. Human vitality requires intentionality in order to relate meaningful structures to the dynamic that is inherent in the nature of being. This becomes crucial in Tillich's understanding of human selfhood since it is through the shaping of reality in meaningful structures that human beings can formulate their sense of selfhood.

THE RADICAL CONDITION OF EVIL IN EXISTENCE

If the unconditional ground of being is the drive of every cultural form for Tillich, and emptiness is the fundamental condition for all existence, why is there evil in the world? Both Tillich and Nishitani contend that evil is not simply non-perfection of the actualization of the nature of things, but intrinsic to being-in-existence. To say this, of course, does not mean that any given evil act is inevitable; rather, evil is a condition which resists the expression of the ultimate nature of things in existence.

Tillich states his understanding of sin as follows: "In the sphere of the spiritual fulfillment through meaning the resistance of the material (i.e., specificity, conditioning limitations of meaning) becomes a positive hostility to meaning; it becomes 'sin.' . . . The immediate resistance of matter to form becomes in the sphere of the spirit guilt."[35] For him, the term "matter" does not express physical material seen in common experience; it "expresses the basic originative creative principle found in everything real, and reaches even into the sphere of the spirit-bearing *Gestalten*."[36] Or, he explains: "*Matter* is the expression for the import of meaning viewed as detached from its unconditionedness and making possible particular contents of meaning."[37] Because all being-through-meaning drives toward unconditional meaning (as discussed previously), the resistance of the limitation inherent in specific meanings works against the unconditional demand of the spirit to be free.

In light of this basic resistance to allow the unconditional meaning to take form, any *form* that claims to bear the inexhaustible import of unconditional meaning is seen to be demonic. The demonic has no unity of form; however, it can be mistaken for the Holy since it has an ecstatic breakthrough quality as does the Holy. While both the Holy and the demonic burst through form, the former does this in a creative way, while the latter does this with a destructive intention. Tillich explains:

> [G]race breaks through the form while both acknowledging the form and affirming the unconditional form, whereas the demonic does not submit to the unconditional form. The demonic has all the forms of expression that obtain for the sacred, but it has them with the mark of opposition to the unconditional form, and with the intention of destruction. The holy negativity of the abyss becomes demonic negativity through the loss of unconditional form.[38]

The total loss of form, then, indicates the loss of meaning, and the creative power of being is turned to self-destruction. Here Tillich opposes a position that tries to transcend forms by destruction of all forms. He makes this clear in reference to religious experience whose goal is to eliminate all forms, when he says: "The nearer a religion stands to the undifferentiated attitude, the less it achieves authentic representations of God. Things in their immediate appearance are bearers of the Holy."[39] Evil, then, can either be the force which denies the importance of all form, or forms which presume to fully bear the import of unconditional meaning.

In contrast, Nishitani, who calls for a radical shift in awareness about the self in the context of Great Doubt, says: "Sin or evil comes to present itself in its true reality only on a field which transcends the field of the conscious self. . . . The fundamental awareness of evil occurs when, on the occasion of particular evils within time, their origin is traced down to the foundation of the very existence of the self."[40] For him, any analytic description of evil is an understanding that is based on ego awareness; rather, a person must get to the boundary of self-consciousness, and experience directly the radical sin, which Buddhists have called "*karma* from before the time infinite," and "*avidyā* (basic blindness)."[41] To reach "the *real* experience of our sin and evil," he continues, ". . . is possible in religion alone."[42]

It is not a discussion of original sin or in looking for the sources of crime in social causes—it is not even in a consideration of individual decisions—that one can really know the radical sinful condition of being-in-existence. Only when the whole being is thrown into Great Doubt and

knows the ego as a projection in the field of emptiness that one grasps evil as
the condition of personal existence. Nishitani articulates this when he says:

> The ground of the subject itself is the place where radical evil
> originates; and so, in the awareness of that evil, the subject is aware of
> itself, in its own ground, as the real realization of that evil — of that evil
> as reality.[43]

When a person recognizes sin and doubt as constituent with being-
in-existence he or she experiences a turnabout of reality. In the field of
emptiness the self is nothing. It cannot be regarded as pure or impure, as
good over against bad. The field of emptiness, comments Nishitani, should
not be thought of as "innate in human beings," but as "the formal aspect of
the united whole of contents and form (in existence), the totality of which is
said to be corrupted."[44] At the same time, when one is fully aware of this radical sin, the "self" becomes a "place to receive." At that moment, he
continues, "the place where the hope of the self was exhausted and the self
became nothing. . . . Itself is opened from beyond, by the love of God, but
even then it is opened as the place to receive — as the receptacle of — that
very love."[45]

BREAKING TRADITIONAL BOUNDARIES

By comparing the positions of Tillich and Nishitani concerning three areas
in the religious transformation of selfhood we can note similarities and differences that make an encounter between these two orientations significant
for dealing with the psychological nihilism of the contemporary scene. The
basic similarities include the recognition that a deep understanding of the
nature of selfhood requires placing the self within a context of the nature of
existence. When this is done, both philosophers claim, the psychosocial self,
in other words, the ego, must be understood to have its basic resources for
meaning and insight in an ultimate (e.g., unconditional or radically empty)
order of reality-awareness. Also, while evil is a fundamental condition of
being-in-existence, the ensnaring ignorance and self-destroying meaninglessness of life can be overcome so that a person can live authentically in the
world.

There are also some important differences:

1. Tillich affirms that authentic being is found in the drive for (symbolic)
   meaning, which includes a clear distinction between subject and object.

Nishitani claims that authentic being is the full awareness that nothingness (emptiness) is the ground of life, which is known in the Great
Doubt, whereby a person turns from attachment to a subject-object
dualism.

2. For Tillich, ultimate reality is the Unconditional, or being-itself, which
   is basic to, but distinct from, existence which is defined by the threat of
   non-being. For Nishitani, the field of emptiness (nothingness) is the
   final nature of all being, and a nondualistic awareness of the emptiness
   of all things is a perfect mode of being-in-existence.

3. Evil in the world is a self-destructive mode of the drive for unconditional meaning, according to Tillich's perspective; and while the necessarily
   limited meaning in existence prevents the perfect unity of meaning
   within existence, divine grace is always actualized in some particular
   form that bears witness to the Unconditional. For Nishitani evil is the
   ego-centered manner of being-in-existence, which can be avoided by
   becoming fully aware of the egoless nature of existence, and the self is
   open to receive all things in their empty nature.

If we were to leave these positions side by side as two quite different orientations to actualizing authentic existence, the nature of the encounter may
appear to be a stand off of two mutually exclusive positions. Indeed, these
two contemporary philosophers could be studied to show how differently
they deal with the issue of authentic selfhood because the basic metaphysics
and root metaphors in the Christian and Buddhist *traditions* are quite
divergent. However, we have another concern in mind; for, as indicated in
the introduction, an exposure to significant differences of religious value formation may permit an internal encounter within a person who is ready for a
new spiritual horizon. This requires breaking through the boundaries of
traditional patterns of thought and practice. It goes without saying that the
following suggestions for dropping some traditional positions in Christianity
and Buddhism, and integrating alternate positions from the other religion are
more probes for future thinking than comprehensive analyses of the issues
involved.

To the Christian community I would suggest that the understanding of the
ground of one's being-in-existence as the field of emptiness is a viable alternative to the notions of God as being-itself, and of selfhood as an inviolable
base for personal significance and moral choice. I should note that several
Christian theologians have sympathetically examined some aspects of this
issue, for example, John Cobb and Lynn de Silva.[46] To push beyond the
notion of being-itself as the perfectly completed and unconditional ground
for all limited and conditioned things in existence would allow for a much
more positive awareness of change and the transcience of life. In the con-

temporary period, where adjusting to rapidly changing forms and structures of life is nearly a condition for survival, the recognition that change is a fundamental condition of life would encourage the development of humane skills for dealing with change. Change would not be seen only in negative terms such as the non-being that threatens the expression of being. Nor would changing existence itself be labeled as the basic cause of human anxiety about life. Rather, change would be seen as neutral; and the attachment to false expectations of unchanging objects of feelings would be regarded as the root cause of anxiety about life.

Also by probing the depth of contradiction, doubt, and despair—that is, opening up oneself to absolute negation—the inconsistencies, disappointments, and unfulfilled needs of life will be placed in a deeper (or higher) frame of awareness. They will be placed in the experience of insoluble difficulty that can psychologically break open blocks to experiencing life anew. As Nishitani describes the field of emptiness, it is not another realm or state of mind, but the "formal aspect of the united whole of contents and form: which includes being and non-being, self and other, this and not-this, conditioned and unconditioned. All of this is not some static whole but the process of interdependent forms that are subjective and objective, the act of knowing and what-is-known.[47] To affirm the interdependent co-arising of existence as a continuing creation suggests that value is not found in the world's being dependent on a primordial eternal creator, but in the quality of the interrelatedness found in any moment. This quality, however, is not found primarily in the unity of meaning, but in the openness, or freedom for interrelationship at a deep level of awareness. While many standard Christian doctrines would have to be reconsidered by affirming the field of emptiness, I want to call attention to the sort of Christology that would center on the image of Christ given in Phillipians 2.7, in which the paradigm of divine action in the world is that Christ "emptied himself " and became a human being.

To the Buddhist community I suggest that the insight into the emptiness of everything can be understood as a positive act of consciousness. This is a viable alternative to the usual stress placed on simply avoiding the illusory barriers of the subject-object dualism or self-centered choice of some limited intended goal. The recognition that the insight (*prajñā*) of the fundamental emptiness of all existing things participates in the depending co-arising of any form would stress the ontological significance of friendliness (*maitrī*) and compassion (*karuna*), as necessary and constituent factors of the bodhisattva path. The process of being-in-existence as experienced in "enlightenment-being" (bodhisattva) could then fully recognize the unconscious and non-conscious psycho-social-physical structures which inform the actual expression of being-in-existence-in an-enlightened-manner. Then the compassion for other suffering sentient beings would not be seen only as an internal "feeling with others," it would be a positive creative act that is as much in the field of emptiness as any form. To think along these lines would allow affirming the importance of the quality of creating form—in distinction to the common stress on formless awareness—in the particular act of enlightenment-being, while still recognizing that form is empty, that is, interrelated, and not existing-in-itself. This would provide an ontological imperative for Buddhists to actively engage in developing psychological (interpersonal) skills and social ethics; it would counter the judgment sometimes made that Buddhist insight results in social passivity and acceptance of the status quo.

The Buddhist tradition, also, will have to adjust some of its thinking if the realization of insight (*prajñā*) is seen as an act of consciousness which is paradoxically involved in both the limitations of existence and is free from the attachment to those limitations. However, such a basic text as the *Perfection of Wisdom in Eight Thousand Lines* suggests something of the act of consciousness, as a skill-in-means, which combines wisdom (insight, *prajñā*) to avoid reaching the limit of reality (*bhūta-koṭi*) midway. In this text the Lord Buddha says:

> [A bodhisattva who contemplates emptiness does not realize emptiness] because a Bodhisattva contemplates that emptiness which is possessed of the best of all modes [i.e., of the six perfections]. He does, however, not contemplate that 'I shall realize,' or 'I should realize,' but he contemplates that 'this is the time for complete conquest, and not for realization.' Without losing himself in his concentration, he ties his thought to an objective support (for his compassion) and he determines that he will take hold of perfect wisdom [which is essentially skill-in-means], and he will not realize [emptiness, because its realization is not the final goal]. Meanwhile, however, the Bodhisattva does not lose
> the dharmas which act as the wings to enlightenment.[48]

By recognizing the conscious—albeit empty—act of skill-in-means, the bodhisattva realizes the *"ultimate* reality-limit" (*param-bhūta-koṭi*). In Chapter 20 of this same work the Buddha explains that skillful means is the key to realizing the ultimate reality-limit:

> Since [the bodhisattva] has not abandoned all beings, he is thus able to win full enlightenment, safely and securely. At the time when a Bodhisattva has made all beings into an objective support for his thought of friendliness, and with the highest friendliness ties himself to them, at

that time he rises above the factiousness of the defilements and of Mara
[i.e., death, evil], he rises above the level of Disciple and
Pratyekabuddha, and he abides in that concentration [on friendliness].[49]

Here we see that the *Perfection of Wisdom Sutra* recognizes the value of skill-
fully creating an object of consciousness to express great compassion, and by
doing this without anxiety and attachment expresses an enlightened manner
of being-in-existence.

Within these few suggestions of how Christians can learn from a Buddhist
orientation and Buddhists from a Christian orientation we may glimpse the
new spiritual horizon that awaits a sensitive encounter of these religious
perspectives. It is a horizon in which religious faith and insight are seen
neither as simply the act of meaning-fulfillment that depends on being-itself
or on a unique personal self, nor as simply a trans-conscious mode of perceiving an illusory world. Rather it is a process of ultimate transformation that is
at once an action which participates in the particularity and non-conscious
forces of life, and a mode of perceiving the changing forms of life such that
there is both meaning and freedom without attachment to the forms. Such a
vision does not look for an expression of an ideal or eternal pattern which is
to be duplicated indefinitely, but is a sensitivity to a variety of possibilities
that arise from different dimensions of experience, for example, physical,
social, aesthetic, logical, or symbolic. To move from one dimension to another requires agility and care to recognize the needs of all people at different
levels of fulfillment. By such encounter Christians and Buddhists may develop new vocabularies that can communicate enriching experiences and deep-
ened sensitivities for unselfish selfhood in an everchanging world.

NOTES

1. Paul Tillich, *What is Religion?* ed. J. L. Adams (New York: Harper and Row, 1969).

2. Keiji Nishitani, *Shūkyō to wa Nanika* (What is Religion?) (Tokyo: Sōbunsha, 1961).
Chap. 1 is translated in "What is Religion?" in Vol. 2 of *Philosophical Studies of Japan* (Tokyo:
Japan Society for the Promotion of Science, 1960); Chap. 2 is translated in "The Personal and
the Impersonal in Religion," *Eastern Buddhist*, n.s. 3, No. 1 (June 1970) and 3, No. 2 (October
1970); Chap. 3 is translated in "Nihilism and Śūnyatā," *Eastern Buddhist*, n.s. 4, No. 2 (October
1971) and 5, No. 1 (May 1972); Chap. 4 is translated in "The Standpoint of Śūnyatā," *Eastern
Buddhist* 6, No. 1 (May 1973) and 6, No. 2 (October 1973).

3. Masao Abe, "The Crucial Points: An Introduction to the Symposium on Christianity and
Buddhism," *Japanese Religions* 8, No. 4 (October 1975): 3.

4. Tillich, *What Is Religion?*, p. 42.

5. Ibid., 56-57.

6. Ibid., p. 57.

7. Ibid., p. 59.

8. Ibid., p. 64.

9. Ibid., p. 66.

10. Ibid., p. 60

11. Ibid., p. 22. This is a formulation of James Luther Adams, who wrote the introduction to Tillich's *What Is Religion?*

12. Nishitani, "What is Religion?" p. 35.

13. Ibid., p. 24.

14. Ibid., p. 25.

15. Ibid., p. 25.

16. Ibid., p. 26.

17. Ibid., p. 30.

18. Ibid., p. 34.

19. Ibid., p. 33.

20. Ibid., p. 36.

21. See some of the ontological issues discussed in Masao Abe, "Non-Being and *Mu:* The Metaphysical Nature of Negativity in the East and the West," *Religious Studies* 11, No. 2 (June 1975): 181-192; and in Yoshinori Takeuchi, "Buddhism and Existentialism: The Dialogue between Oriental and Occidental Thought," in W. Leibrecht, ed., *Religion and Culture: Essays in Honor of Paul Tillich* (New York: Harper and Brothers, 1959).

22. Nishitani, "The Standpoint of Śūnyatā," *Eastern Buddhist* 6, No. 2 (October 1973): 66.

23. Ibid.

24. Ibid., p. 68.

25. Nishitani, "Standpoint of Śūnyatā," *Eastern Buddhist* 6, No. 1 (May 1973): 70.

26. Tillich, *Systematic Theology* (Chicago: University of Chicago Press, 1952), 1: 191.

27. Ibid., p. 196.

28. Ibid., p. 189.

29. Ibid., p. 191.

30. Ibid.

31. Ibid., p. 202.

32. Ibid., p. 164.

33. Ibid., p. 174.

34. Ibid., p. 169.

35. Tillich, *What Is Religion?* p. 85.

36. Ibid., p. 64.

37. Ibid., p. 63.

38. Ibid., p. 86.

39. Ibid., pp. 94, 95.

40. Nishitani, "What is Religion?" pp. 41, 42.

41. Ibid., p. 43.

42. Ibid.

43. Ibid., p. 42.

44. Ibid., p. 45.

45. Ibid.

46. John Cobb, "Can a Christian Be a Buddhist, Too?" *Japanese Religions* 10, No. 3 (December 1978): 1-20; and Lynn de Silva, *The Problem of the Self in Buddhism and Christianity* (New York: Barnes and Noble, 1979) see especially Chaps. 9 and 12.

47. For a comparison of different procedures for knowing reality as found in the twentieth-century British-American philosopher A. N. Whitehead and the second-century Buddhist seer Nāgārjuna, see F. J. Streng, "Metaphysics, Negative Dialectic, and the Expression of the Inexpressible," *Philosophy East and West* 25, No. 4: 429-447.

48. *Perfection of Wisdom in Eight Thousand Lines and Its Verse Summary (Aṣṭasāhasrikā-prajñā pāramitā-ratna-guṇa-saṃcaya-gāthā)*, trans. Edward Conze (Berkeley: Four Seasons Foundation, 1973), p. 222.

49. Ibid., p. 224.

PART IV

CHRISTIAN RENEWAL IN JAPANESE CULTURE

CHAPTER 10

Paul and Shinran; Jesus and Zen: What Lies at the Ground of Human Existence?

Seiichi Yagi

When we compare Christianity with Buddhism, for instance Paul with Shinran, we find remarkable similarities, especially in their concept of grace and faith. We see also sharp differences between them. For Shinran, for example, there is no retribution of God, nor death of the Son of God for the justification of sinners.[1] Where such similarities and differences originate is a very interesting problem. To solve this, we must consider the epistemological axes on which thinking moves. But another way of comparison is also possible; we can set Paul and Shinran side by side over against Jesus and Zen. It is possible because the depth of the self from which their utterances were made, and the depth of the transcendent on which they stood, are the same in Paul and Shinran on the one hand, in Jesus and Zen on the other. Through these comparisons, I think we can not only see the structure of religious existence more clearly, but we can compare Christianity and Buddhism in a more accurate way.

I

In the following we shall see what is meant by an "axis" on which thinking moves. In the New Testament there are three types of theology.[2] The reason why there is not one but three different types of theology is explained by the fact that there are three interrelated axes of thinking: the communal, the individual, and the interpersonal. Thus in the first place, there is theological thinking which moves on the axis of communality. This theology is usually called "salvation-history," and is comprised of several interrelated themes. God made the Covenant with the people of Israel and gave them the Law. On the basis of the Covenant humanity should observe the Law, and by doing so be justified before God. But humanity did not observe it and, having transgressed the Law, became guilty before God, so that we must be punished with death. God has overlooked the sins of the past in his forebearance, but now in order to show his justice and faithfulness to the Covenant, he made Christ the means of expiating sin by his sacrificial death. On account of the Atonement by Christ, humanity is justified before God without complying with the Law. Christ was raised to life, and on the basis of this event, a New Covenant has been made between God and humanity, and this event is the fulfillment of the prophecy of the Old Testament, that is to say, the fulfillment of the will of God. Now the new people of God are gathered, namely the Church, and a new ethics is given to it. But Christian ethics no longer brings despair because, having been justified, Christians are liberated from God's retribution. Christians expect the end of the world, in which Jesus Christ will come again and judge the living and the dead, but the people who belong to him have already entered the Kingdom of God.

This theology had been shaped in its essential form in primitive Christianity before Paul.[3] The center of this theology lies in the justification of sinners on account of the Atonement by Christ, through which God showed himself to be just.[4] Its conceptions are Jewish. But what concerns us is that all conceptions in this theology are communal. The people of God, Covenant, Law, sin as the transgression of the Law, prophecy about the destiny of the people, atonement, the establishment of the new people of God—that is, the Church—the end of the history of mankind and the world, the judgment of the living and the dead by Christ, the Kingdom of God . . . all these conceptions have their home in the relationship of God with his people. In short, not individual persons as such, but individuals who belong to a special community of persons as a whole are related to God. We can say that the locus of this theology is the communality of people over against God. This communality is what I call the axis on which this type of theological thinking moves. This becomes clearer when we compare this type of theology (I name it theology A) with the second type of theology (theology B), for the axis of theology B is the individuality of persons.

The archetype of theology B we find in the Christ hymn which Paul quotes in Philippians 2.6-11:[5] "Christ was of divine nature from the first; yet he did not think to snatch at equality with God, but made himself nothing, assuming the nature of a slave. Bearing the human likeness, revealed in human shape, he humbled himself, and in obedience accepted even death. Therefore God raised him to the heights and bestowed on him the name above all names, that at the name of Jesus every knee should bow—in heaven, on earth, and in the depths—and every tongue confess, 'Jesus Christ is Lord,' to the glory of God the Father." In theology B both the salvation-history of the people of God before the Incarnation of Christ and the prospect of the coming end of the world are lacking.

It is easy to see that the theology of the Fourth Gospel agrees in its essential structure with this Christ hymn.[6] Without discussing the theology of John in detail I would like to point out one thing: the central conception of the theology of John is not the justification of sinners, but the eternal life given to persons through faith (John 5.24 and passim). In the Fourth Gospel the meaning of the cross of Jesus does not involve atonement for sins.[7] The central conceptions of faith and eternal life show that the basic problem here lies in the existence of persons. We ask for the ground of our being and find the answer in the message of eternal life given to the believer. The Jewish character of theology A has disappeared in the Hellenistic world of the gentile, so that the cross and resurrection of Jesus Christ are now understood in terms of victory over the power of sin and death. Through faith the believer participates in Christ who is life itself, so that eternal life is given to him or her. Consequently, the axis on which theological thinking of this type moves is the individuality of persons, because its question and answer centers around the problem of the being of the individual. The forensic conceptions which have their locus in communality do not appear here at all, or if they appear, their meanings are changed so that they are no longer forensic.[8]

There is a third type of theology in the New Testament, the theology of love, which I would call theology C. Its basic thesis is that the person who loves, knows God, because God is love and love comes from him.[9] The event of salvation by Christ is here understood as the expression of the love of God for persons, and the axis on which theological thinking moves is in this case the interpersonal relationship of "I and Thou."[10]

These three types of theology are seldom present in the New Testament in their pure forms. In the writings of Paul, for example, theology A and theology B are combined. We can easily ascertain this when we see how the Law had both communal and individual meaning for Paul, for the Law determines not only the duty of the people of Israel as a matter of course, but it is the way of life for the individual person (Rom. 7.10).[11]

If we compare Paul with Shinran, it is obvious that they agree in their understanding of grace and faith. It is also well known that in Shinran's thought forensic conceptions such as atonement are lacking. We can now see the reason why. The axis of thinking is for Shinran only individual, hence, forensic conceptions have no room in his thought, whereas Paul's theology embraces the two axes of communality and individuality. Insofar as Paul thinks in communal terms his thinking is different from that of Shinran. Shinran knows no salvation-history such as is found in the New Testament. The thinking of Shinran is eminently individual. He says, for example, that he has never called the name of Amida Buddha for other persons, not even his parents,[12] and that the salvation-event made possible by Amida Buddha has occurred for Shinran himself alone.[13] Of course every believer can say that for himself, otherwise Shinran would not have preached Amida to others. It is interesting to compare this with Galatians 2.20b: "The life I now live in my fleshy existence I live by faith in the son of God who . . . sacrificed himself for me." Here the word "faith" appears in combination with "life," both being the motifs of theology B. Through a more precise analysis we can show how in Paul two basic theses are combined: namely, "justification on account of the Atonement" (objective event) and "eternal life given through faith" (existential decision), so that the peculiar Pauline thesis is formed, "justification by faith alone."[14]

If what I have said is correct, we should compare Shinran primarily with John, not Paul. This comparison is indeed fruitful. Not only does the Seventeenth Vow of Amida Buddha remind us of Philippians 2.10 ("every tongue shall confess, 'Jesus Christ is Lord.'"), and not only is the Savior both in Shinran's writings and John called "life and light,"[15] but also the whole structure of theological thinking is similar (see Fig. 1). In Shinran the formless Dharmakaya took the form of a man called Hozo, who having finished his saving deeds to prepare the Pure Land, became the Sambhogakaya who is now called Amida Buddha, and who is continually working for the salvation of persons by means of his saving power (ekō).* This process of salvation work is comparable with that of the theology of John, in which the Logos became flesh in the man Jesus, who, having finished his saving deeds (revelation of the Father), was raised up to heaven to become the heavenly Lord, whence he works for the salvation of persons through the work of the Holy Spirit (John 14.15-20; 16.12-15).

Further, we find a parallel to Johannine Christology in Shinran's thought. For Shinran Sambhogakaya comes from Dharmakaya and reveals the former,[16] just as the case of John, where Christ is called the Son of God and reveals God (John 1.18; 14.9). Of course we can ask here whether the form-

---

*According to traditional Mahāyāna Buddhist thought, all Buddhas are manifestations of the interrelated forms or "bodies" (Trikāya). Dharmakāya usually refers to the "suchness" of enlightenment itself, i.e., that which all buddhas embody which makes a buddha a buddha. In this sense, Dharmakāya is "ultimate reality." Sambhogakāya refers to the "reward body" or "body of bliss" which all buddhas produce for themselves as the result of obtaining enlightenment. The third "body," Nirmāṇakāya, refers to the form or the "body" of a buddha existing under the conditions of historical existence, for example, Gautama the Buddha. In Pure Land Buddhism, Amida Buddha is a buddha existing on the level of Sambhogakāya as the residing buddha of the Pure Land. Ekō (Skt., pariṇāma) or "merit transference," in Pure Land faith, means the transfer of Amida's merits to persons, which in turn causes their rebirth (ōjō) into the Pure Land at the time of their deaths.— Ed.

less Dharmakāya corresponds in John to the Logos, or rather to God, an important problem which, regrettably, I cannot treat here.

II

The second problem which I shall discuss concerns the depth of the self from which religious language originates. This problem also has to do with the objectivity of God. When utterance is made from the standpoint of the usual self speaking public, objectifying language, God is spoken of in the third person.[17] However, the transcendent is the ultimate subject of the self when utterance is made from the standpoint of the ultimate depth of the self, so that it is even possible that the transcendent seems to speak in the first person through the mouth of a human being. Furthermore, God is objective to the usual self when the usual self is communal and God is the ground of the community, whereas God is "over against" the self when the usual self stands before God as an individual. Here also we must consider the axis of thinking, and this will involve examining the depths of the self in connection with the objectivity of God. We shall begin by reflecting on the axis of communality, because in the Judeo-Christian tradition, God is eminently the God of a people in community. The individual person is not understood as an individual in the sense of modern individualism, but as a member of the people of God.

In the time of the Old Testament the Covenant was the basis on which Israel became the people of God, and the Covenant was the ground of the Law through which the people encountered the will of God. Even in our situation, law and morality are something objective and normative from the standpoint of the usual self. So God is also objective and normative in the Judeo-Christian tradition because he is the ground of the historical community. That is to say, because a person speaks of God from the standpoint of the usual self, he speaks of God with a language common to all participants of the Judeo-Christian tradition. Therefore, to speak of God cannot be separated from speaking of the history of the people of God, and in the interrelation between God and his people God has been encountered as personal.

In opposition to this, Buddhist thinking in general centers around the problem of the individual self, that is to say, around the existential problems inherent in being a self. This is especially clear in Shinran's thought.[18] In Zen Buddhism the central problem is expressed by the motto, "To clarify the matter of being a self." Zen Buddhists often feel suspicious about the objectivity and personality of God because the communal character of Judeo-

Christian thought is alien to them. There is also another reason — Zen Buddhists can stand on the deeper level of the self, deeper than the usual self, namely, the activity of *mu* in them.* They speak directly from this reality, so that the ultimate reality is understood neither as object nor as "over against," but as the ultimate self that transcends the "I."[19] The result is that their language sounds to Christian ears as if they absolutized themselves and as if they had no sense of historical reality. This means that to understand Zen Buddhists, we Christians must regard the axis of thinking and the depth of the self from which Zen utterances are made. But it is also true that there is a serious problem in the Christian tradition. Insofar as God is merely objective and normative, he is simply transcendent and the scriptures which reveal his will become heteronomous. God then becomes a transcendent entity that reveals his will only through special mediators whom man must legalistically obey. This was especially the case in Judaism in the time of Jesus and Paul. But in Christianity an essential change occurred. The transcendent became immanent, so that God was not experienced merely as a totally transcendent reality.

By immanence I do not only mean the incarnation of the Logos as Jesus. In the words of St. Paul, "For through the law I died to law, I have been crucified with Christ, the life I now live is not my life, but Christ lives in me" (Gal. 2.20). Christ lives not only in Paul, but in all Christians (Rom. 8:10). The words "Christ in me" denote that Christ is the ultimate subject of the self. At the ground of the self-identity that I am I, there is the fact that I have died and Christ lives in me. So "Christ in me" is the ultimate agent, the ultimate subject of my subjectivity. This does not mean, of course, that I am possessed by an alien power so that my usual self disappears in a state of ecstasy. On the contrary, by the immanence of Christ in me the authentic existence of myself is realized, in other words, the usual self is not destroyed but established in Christian existence, as is shown by the case of Paul. On the other hand, "Christ in me" does not mean the deification of human nature. This misunderstanding derives from the confusion of the usual self with the transcendent-immanent in the self (Christ in me), so that the usual self seems to be deified.

Mu literally means "no" or "none," and is the response to a question once asked of the Chinese Zen master Chao-Chou (Jap., Jōshu), "does a dog have the Buddha-nature?" (see Zenkei Shibayama, *Zen Comments on the Mumonkan* [New York: Harper and Row, 1974], pp. 19-31). In koan meditation, Zen students are often given the task of meditating on Chao-Chou's *"mu."* That is, they are given the task of discovering for themselves why Chao-Chou responded no to the question, does a dog have the Buddha Nature? The point is that *mu* is not mere negation, but the expression and the activity of the Buddha-nature itself. — Ed.

In the foregoing we observed two things: the paradoxical relation between the subjectivity and objectivity of the transcendent, and the relation of "Christ in me" to the usual self. In the religious language of communality, the transcendent is, being objective to the usual self, at the same time the ultimate subject of the self. The relation of both aspects is as follows (see fig. 2): Paul, in whom Christ abides, can even say that Christ is the activity of life itself ("To live is Christ," [Phil. 1.21]). The fruits, that is, the expressions of the immanent Christ, are to him freedom and love (Gal. 5.1, 22). And when he says that love is the fulfillment of the Law (Rom. 13.10),[20] the Law ceases to be heteronomous since it becomes the outer expression of an inner love. This is so because the Law now describes the form love takes when it expresses itself. God speaks to us through the Law with a "Thou shalt." But now the "I will" of love becomes resonant with the "Thou shalt" of the Law. Inner love is in sympathy with outer law, and this is the whole foundation of Christian ethics. And when we inquire into the ground of this resonance, we find the paradox that the transcendent, which speaks to us through the Law and demands our obedience with its authoritative "Thou shalt," is at the same time the ultimate subject of the self, the deepest ground of "I will." We thus discover the first paradox that the ultimate object of selfhood is at the same time the ultimate subject of selfhood.

The second paradox is that the transcendent is spoken of both in the first person and in the third person. Directly after the quoted sentence about the immanence of Christ, Paul says, "Now the life I live in my fleshly existence, I live by faith in the Son of God who loved me and sacrificed himself for me" (Gal. 2.20b). "I" in this sentence is the self in its fleshly existence, namely the usual self, which Paul discriminates from "Christ in me." He also discriminates it from "Christ" as the object of his faith, "Christ" in both cases being identical. The matter is somewhat confusing. The "Christ in me" is the ultimate subject of the usual self. It can be the subject of human utterance, and in this case a human being can speak in the name of the transcendent. But the usual self can be, and should be, discriminated from this transcendent reality. Then, from the standpoint of the usual self, "Christ in me" is spoken of in the third person. Not only the transcendent as objective to the self, but the transcendent as the subject of the self, as at the same time the object of faith from the standpoint of the usual self, "Christ in me" is spoken of in the third person. Not only the transcendent as objective to the self, but the transcendent as the subject of the self, is at the same time the object of faith from the standpoint of the usual self. For surely Christ, who not only accomplished his saving work, but lives in "me," is now the object of faith. (Gal. 2.20b). In short, in the relation of the usual self which believes and Christ as the ultimate subject of selfhood, we ascertain two levels of the "I," that is, the usual self and its ultimate ground. "Christ in me" is the ultimate subject of the usual self. He is the "I" of the usual "I." But this ultimate subject, namely, "Christ in me," is spoken of at the same time in the third person from the standpoint of the usual self.

Here is the second paradox. The transcendent is spoken of both in the first person and in the third person. That the transcendent is spoken of in the third person is evident and needs no explanation. That the transcendent is spoken of in the first person seems to be a dangerous thesis. But this possibility is implied in Paul's words. The mission he carried out is surely his own work. But of his mission Paul says that it is Christ who carried it out (Rom. 15.18). His own work is ultimately the work done by Christ. Therefore, when Paul says "I have done it," this "I" is Christ himself in the deepest level of subjectivity. Thus we must discriminate between levels of subjectivity. When Paul speaks from the standpoint of the usual self, or as the usual self, he speaks of Christ in the third (or second) person and understands himself as Christ's slave and apostle (Rom. 1.1 passim). But when Paul speaks from the deepest ground of his existence, he is conscious that it is Christ who speaks when he speaks: "I order, not I, but the Lord orders" (1 Cor. 7.10). The Lord is here not simply the Jesus of history (Mark 10.8-9), but Jesus and the heavenly Lord as one. I think, therefore, that we must take this word in its duplexity: it is Christ who speaks when Paul speaks.[21] In the religious language of Paul, the ground of authentic existence is expressed both in the first and in the third person.

When Shinran is compared with John, or with the theology B in Pauline thinking, we easily find these two paradoxes (see Fig. 3). In both Shinran and John, the transcendent (the Saviour) speaks to us, calls us, through the event in which he created the ground of our salvation, and demands our response. When we respond to this call in the decision of faith, the Saviour who calls us becomes the object of our faith. But the believer becomes in his faith conscious that it is the Saviour who gave him the very faith, that it is the Saviour who acts when he, the believer, believes.[22] In this sense the object of faith is at the same time the subject of faith. This is our first paradox. At the same time, in this structure, the second paradox is also implied; the Saviour who is objective-subjective is spoken of in the third person from the viewpoint of the usual self, though his activity constitutes the ultimate subjectivity of man at the ground of self-being. In fact we find that Shinran speaks regularly as the usual self. He speaks of Amida mainly in the third person, as did Paul.

III

We now come to the third point: the depths of the transcendent in which our religious thinkers are grounded. We shall begin with a consideration of

Jesus' thinking. The words of Jesus have all three axes: communality, individuality, and interpersonality. Consequently, his words can be classified into three groups: his words on the Law, on life, and on love. The first group concerns freedom from legalism; the second group, freedom from eager care for one's self; and the third group, unconditional love. These three groups correspond in their essential content to theology A, theology B, and theology C in primitive Christianity.

Let us begin by considering Jesus' words on the Law. In this context it is interesting to study the parable of the good Samaritan (Luke 10.30-37). In Luke this parable is combined with a debate about eternal life between Jesus and a lawyer (10.25-29). This combination may have been made by Luke because the debate itself seems to have been an independent tradition (Mark 12.28-34; Matthew 22.34-40). Yet this combination shows Jesus' way of thinking. To the lawyer the Law is the ground of his act. He acts so-and-so because these are written commandments in the books of the Law. Therefore it is quite natural that he asked Jesus who his neighbour was. If he should love his neighbour on the ground of the commandment of the Law, he must know who his neighbour is, otherwise he is not able to love his neighbour, for he does not know whom he should love. Here we see how he depends on words, concepts, and definitions. To the lawyer the Law is primary, love is secondary. The Law is the primary reality for him and the basis from which love is called into existence. The definition of "neighbour" comes first, and then the act of love as its consequence. In other words, to the lawyer love is a matter of the usual self separated from the work of the transcendent self in him.

The thinking of Jesus makes the clearest contrast to that of the lawyer. The parable of the good Samaritan shows that for Jesus love is primary, that love constitutes another person as a neighbour. The good Samaritan helped the wounded man not because the Law ordered him to do so, but because he was moved to pity (Luke 10.83), so that he could love even his enemy. It is not unjust to say, though it is not said explicitly, that the good Samaritan acted from the work of God in him, which expressed itself as pity to the wounded. It is also clear that the Samaritan thus fulfilled the will of God, according to the understanding of Jesus. All legalistic thinking is here broken and overcome. Jesus' thought and action did not depend on the Law, word, or definition, and it is here that we can see a point of contact between Jesus and Zen.

As social beings we have language. It is indispensable. By our language we transmit information, formulate our consensus, and define common measures of values. The language which is thus indispensable in our daily life must be understood by all members of our society in the same way. Otherwise it cannot function as the common, public language which transmits information, expresses our consensus, or defines common measures of value. Accordingly, the sentences we build must observe the principles of formal logic, the principle of identity, the principle of contradiction, and the principle of excluded middle. These principles exclude the ambiguity of meaning that is so destructive of community. If we do not observe these principles, the sentences we build lose their clarity and distinctness so that they become ambiguous. These principles are principles of the *sentences* we build in our daily, social life, *not* the principles of reality itself. Only in the world of our language is the object not the subject, an enemy one whom we hate and cannot love, the neighbour one whom we love and should not hate. But these sentences do not necessarily express the structure of reality itself, in which there is no object apart from the subject, no enemy apart from neighbour, and no neighbour apart from enemy. Nevertheless, because we are born and brought up in a linguistically constructed world, we confuse the concepts of language with reality itself. Thus we lose sight of reality as it is before it is conceptualized, and with it we lose the immediacy of life. We then know ourselves only through conceptualized abstractions. What is most important to note in this regard is that the subject of the common language is the usual self, which is not necessarily combined with the transcendent, and indeed is usually separated from the transcendent.

The awakening of Zen is possible when the closed system of our daily life language is broken and overcome, as in the case of Jesus, for whom true love becomes possible only when legalistic thinking is broken and overcome. There is, however, a difference. Zen is primarily concerned with thinking, whereas Jesus was primarily concerned with doing. But it is also evident that there are parallels between Jesus' teachings and Zen. In both the insight that conceptualization is something secondary, not primary, is emphasized. In this regard Paul does not seem to have been so radical as Jesus. Paul's thinking is still based on the premise of legalism, though he attained the insight into the error of legalism through his understanding of the faith.[23] The correspondence between Jesus and Zen is not confined to this parallel alone. To see this, we must survey the whole structure of Jesus' thinking (see Fig. 5). As was said, the words of Jesus are classified into three groups: the words about the Law, life, and love. The first group of his words preaches freedom from legalism; the second, freedom from eager care for one's own life; the third, freedom from closed love, or conditional love. The ground of this freedom for Jesus was "the rule of God," for it is the presence of the "rule of God" in a person that creates the ground for the expression of love in action to one's neighbour, which is the point of the parable of the good Samaritan.

The state in which the rule of God has found its fullest realization is the Kingdom of God. The Kingdom of God is an eschatological state which is realized at the expected end of the world. The thinking of Jesus is in this respect eschatological. He preached and expected the coming Kingdom of God. The "rule of God" was for Jesus the ground of his ethics, on the one hand, and the ground of his eschatology on the other. But there is one thing which we should not overlook. New Testament scholarship is seldom aware of the fact that some of the sayings of Jesus are not eschatological when he speaks of God. Consider, for example, the saying "God makes his sun rise on good and evil alike, and sends the rain on the just and the unjust" (Matt. 5.45). This saying is uneschatological because eschatology is a teaching which speaks of the opposition of good and evil and expects the final victory of good over evil. Therefore, where this opposition itself is overcome, as in the words just quoted, eschatology is impossible. There are other sayings of Jesus which are also uneschatological, for example, the sayings which tell us to put away anxious care about food and clothes, for the lilies of the field which are there today and thrown into the stove tomorrow are dressed up with a splendour which even Solomon could not attain (Matt. 6.25ff.). The understanding of time implied in this saying is that the world continues as it has been. There is no expectation of the coming end of the world. And in the process of events, not only life, but death is in the hands of God. God is the ultimate depth, in which the opposition of good and evil and life and death becomes relativized.

We should not understand this ontologically, as if God were the ground of both good and evil. The meaning is existential, that is, our eager care for the final victory of good over evil, along with our anxious will to destroy the "enemies of God," is simply irrelevant. It tells us that there is a depth in the religious life to which we can be awakened, a depth which is the ultimate ground of both subjectivity and objectivity, a depth which is deeper than the "rule of God." When we live out of and from this depth we are finally delivered from the existential suffering which arises when we are torn in two by the unreconciled oppositions of life and death, value and non-value, meaning and meaninglessness, or good and evil. This is not a simple denial of ethics. To the quesion of what we should do, the eschatological prospect of the "rule of God" gives us the necessary answer. But to the question, Who am I? "God" gives the final answer. The God of Jesus opens a horizon for us, in which our quest, or request, of ultimate meaning loses its meaning, the quest of meaning being a concern of the usual self.

We can compare this distinction and connection with the Buddhist view of the transcendent (see Fig. 7). Sambhogakāya or Amida Buddha is the ground of life and meaning, whereas Dharmakāya is the ultimate and formless reality (nothingness), and we become aware of its activities in our life *and* death, in being *and* non-being. Jesus speaks, when he speaks of God, from this ultimate depth of reality which corresponds to Dharmakāya, whereas his idea of the "rule of God" corresponds to Sambhogakāya

It is not possible to discuss Jesus' sayings about the Son of Man in detail at this point. The Son of Man is the eschatological divine figure who comes down from heaven to destroy the enemies of God and to save the people of God.[24] Suffice it to say at this juncture that the sayings of Jesus about the Son of Man can be classified into three groups. The first groups predicts the future advent of the Son of Man in divine glory (Mark 8.38, etc.). Here, he is spoken of in the third person. The second group describes the present work of the Son of Man on the earth (Mark 2.10, etc.). Here, it seems, Jesus identified himself with the Son of Man. The third group prophesies the suffering, death and resurrection of Jesus who calls himself the Son of Man (Mark 8.31, etc.). The third group is rightly held to be *vaticinium ex eventu,* and therefore as inauthentic as Jesus' sayings. Some scholars hold that the second group was formed through the mistranslation of the original Aramaic "Man" as the "Son of Man."[25] But this view is doubtful to me.

In the first group of sayings, Jesus discriminates himself from the Son of Man on the one hand, while at the same time uniting himself with him. He says: "If anyone is ashamed of me and my words in this wicked and godless age, the Son of Man will be ashamed of him, when he comes in the glory of his Father and of the holy angels" (Mark 8.38). Jesus is conscious of himself as the representative of the Son of Man in the first group of Son of Man sayings, and I find no reason for not understanding the second group in the same way. When Jesus says, for example, "The Son of Man is sovereign even over the Sabbath" (Mark 2.28), he seems to be referring to himself. But the situation is similar to Paul's experience of his words as the words of the heavenly Lord Christ, that Christ who spoke through Paul when Paul spoke.

We can see the same relation in the sayings of Jesus (see fig. 9). Jesus was conscious that the Son of Man acted when he acted. The relation of Jesus to the Son of Man is the same as the relation of Paul to Christ in him. To Jesus, the Son of Man is at the same time the transcendent which abides in Jesus and acts through him. The Son of Man acts when Jesus acts. The former is the ultimate subject of the latter. But Jesus as the usual self spoke of the Son of Man in the third person when he uttered the sayings of Mark 2.10 and 2.28. He did not directly identify himself with the Son of Man. But people of his time did not understand this relation. Hearing the words of Jesus about the present activities of the Son of Man through him, they thought that Jesus called himself the Son of Man, so that some deified Jesus while others were offended by him. At this stage we can compare Jesus with Paul, that is, with the "Son of Man" in Jesus and "Christ in me" with Paul. And we can understand Jesus' words about the Son of Man best, I think, when we see in the Son of Man the personification of "the rule of God." If so, we are led to the conclusion that the reality which Jesus called "the rule of God" or the "Son of Man" is the same as the reality which Paul, or primitive Christianity as a whole, called the resurrected Lord Christ. They are only different names for the same reality. Indeed we can ascertain this view through careful study of the New Testament, as I have done previously (cf. Fig. 6 with 5).[26]

But we must go a step further. We must ask who did speak when Jesus said in his Antitheses, "You have learned that our forefathers were told. . . . But I say to you" (Matt. 5.21ff.). In these words Jesus stood sovereign over the Mosiac Law which was given to the people of Israel by God. Therefore, he who can be sovereign over the Mosiac Law must be equal to God. New Testament scholars rightly see in these words that Jesus had a consciousness of divine authority.[27] But it is seldom asked who spoke in these words of Jesus. Is Jesus God? Did God speak through Jesus? Who was Jesus then? These christological problems seem to be asked without understanding the depths of the transcendent from which Jesus spoke and acted. It has not been clarified that the objective God as absolute otherness is at the same time the ultimate subject of the usual self, the subject, which is even deeper than the subjectivity which we have just seen as "Christ in me" or the "Son of Man" in Jesus. God is the ultimate subject of this reality. Jesus stood on it. The insight that the ultimate reality is at the same time objective and subjective is held most clearly in Zen, especially in the thought of Shin'ichi Hisamatsu, though objectivity was not stressed by him.[28] Jesus was also a man who could speak from this ultimate depth. When we understand this, we understand his sayings. This event was singular in Christian tradition. Yet it is a possibility for every person. While this conclusion might seem to imply a deification of human nature, this is not what is intended. Human existence becomes authentic when it stands on this ultimate level where it is decisively freed from the sin of wanting to be like God.

The antitheses of Jesus is not ethics because ethics is the concern of the usual self. His sayings are rooted in the depth where sinful care is exterminated and where love even of the enemy is present. On this depth all human beings, East and West, North and South, Christians and non-Christians, are united as one. This is the depth at the ground of every person. The usual self, when aware of this depth at the ground of every person. The usual self, when aware of this depth, begins to live and die according to its activities. Surely every person is a sinner, seen at the level of the usual self. It is true even of religious existence that it is deeply conscious of the reality of sin. Nevertheless, there is a depth where all oppositions are overcome, every sinful care is annihilated, a depth which is deeper than the Son of Man, the rule of God, "Christ" or "Amida Buddha" as Sambhogakāya. Jesus called it "God," Zen calls it "the formless." Both Jesus and Zen, it seems to me, know this depth and live it out.

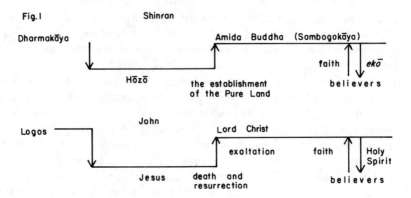

Fig.1

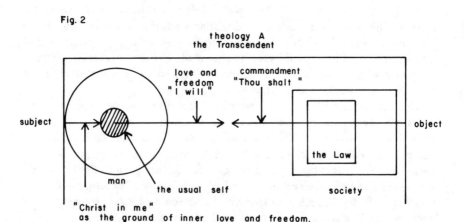

Fig. 2

Fig. 3

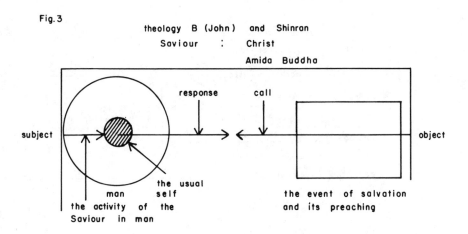

theology B (John) and Shinran
Saviour : Christ
Amida Buddha

response call

subject object

man the usual self

the activity of the
Saviour in man

the event of salvation
and its preaching

Fig. 4

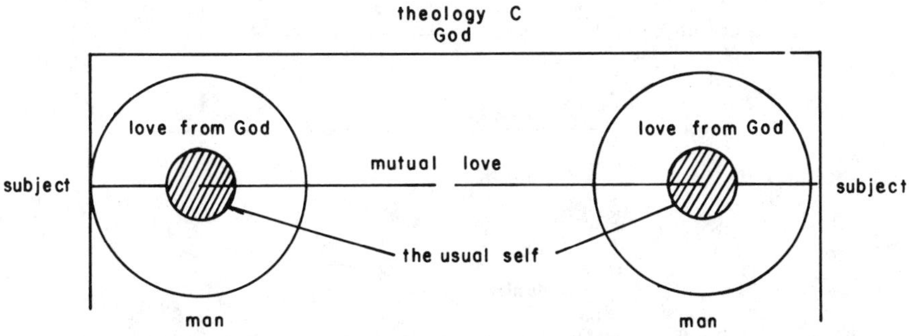

theology C
God

love from God mutual love love from God

subject subject

the usual self

man man

Fig. 5

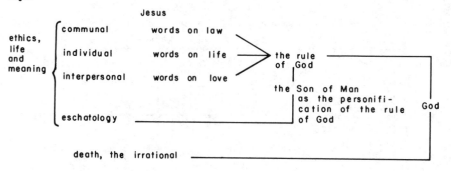

Fig. 6

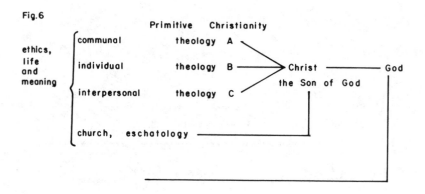

Fig. 7

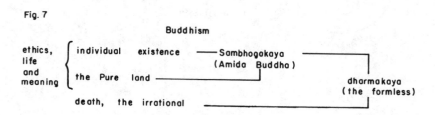

Fig. 8

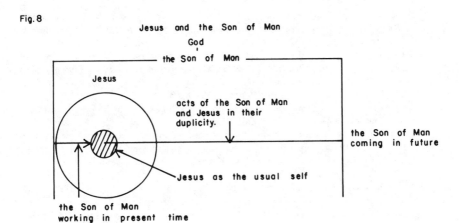

Jesus and the Son of Man

Fig. 9

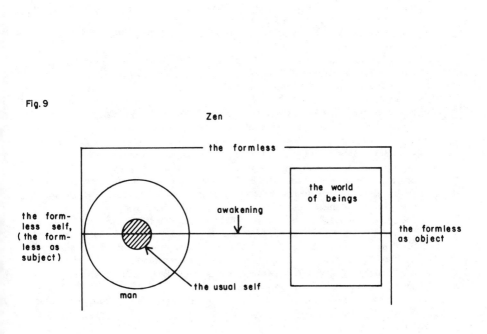

Zen

NOTES

1. These similarities and differences are widely known. To mention one instance, see Karl Barth, *Die Kirchliche Dogmatik, I: Die Lehre von Worte Gottes,* 2 (Zurich: Evangelischer Verlag A.G., 1945-70), p. 372ff.

2. See Seiichi Yagi, *Shinyaku Shisō no Seiritsu* (The Formation of New Testament Thinking) (Tokyo: Shinkyō Shuppansha, 1963), Chap. 2; and *Kiristo to Iesu* (Christ and Jesus) (Tokyo: Kodanshya, 1969), Chap. 3.

3. 1 Cor. 15.3-5 had been formed before Paul joined the primitive Christian church, for he received the kerygma from it (1 Cor. 15.3). The priority of this saying to Pauline literature is widely accepted in modern NT scholarship. For example, see Joachim Jeremias, *The Parables of Jesus* (London: Ruckworth, 1939), p. 95ff.

4. It is noteworthy that in pre-Pauline kerygma the death of Christ took place to show the righteousness of God (Rom. 3.25-26). Paul added "grace" and "faith" to this tradition, in which faith and justification by faith had not been mentioned originally. See Rudolf Bultmann, *Theology of the New Testament,* trans. Kendrick Grobel (New York: Charles Scribner's Sons, 1951), 1:47; and E. Kasemann, "Zum Verstandnis von Rom. 3, 24-26," *Exegetische Versuche und Besinnungen* 1 (1960):96ff.

5. Since the classical study on this hymn by E. Lohmeyer, "Kyrios Christos" (1928), it is widely accepted that Paul was citing here an old Christ hymn of the primitive church and that he added to it his comment, "death of the cross," in Vol. 8. It is therefore omitted in the following quotation.

6. Quotation from John and comparison with our hymn may be omitted. The theology of John is not quite the same as the theology of our Christ hymn. See Kasemann, *Jesu letzter Wille nach John 17* (1971), Chap. 2.

7. C. H. Dodd, *The Interpretation of the Fourth Gospel* (Cambridge: At the University Press, 1965), pp. 239ff.

8. E.g., "judgment" *(kriris)* is in John the separation of those who believe in Christ from those who do not (John 3.19). John 5.24-30 is an inauthentic gloss. See Bultmann, *Das Evangelium des Johannes* (Gottingen: Vandenhoeck, 1941).

9. 1 John 4.7-10.

10. See Martin Buber, *I and Thou* (New York: Charles Scribner's Sons, 1958).

11. As was mentioned in No. 4, it was Paul who added the motifs of faith and grace to Rom. 3.25-26. The earliest kerygma of primitive Christianity (type A) preached the objective event of the Atonement for the sake of the righteousness of God. But the acceptance of this kerygma implied an existential decision of faith which abandons any attempt to set up human righteousness before God by the works of the Law, i.e., any attempt to justify the human self by oneself. Paul developed this very motif, so that he came to the insight that not only the transgressions of the Law, but legalism itself, is the sin (Rom. 10.1-4; 14.23). Therefore Pauline theology includes the themes of (1) the transgression of the Law is sin which must be punished (motif of theology A, Rom. 1.18; 3.20); and (2) unbelief itself is sin (Rom. 14.23), so that even those who have fulfilled the commandments of the Law completely cannot attain righteousness before God (the motif of theology B, Gal. 3.5-7; Phil. 3.6-9). Many incongruences in Paul can be explained from the combination of two different types of theology.

12. See Ryosetsu Fujiwara, trans. *The Tanni Shō* (Kyoto: Ryukoku University Translation Series, 1962), Chap. 5.

13. Ibid., epilogue.

14. See No. 11. Righteousness means to fulfill what is required in the Covenant relation between God and his people. In this relation, God required faith from Abraham, and there-

fore his faith was counted as his righteousness (Gen. 15.6; Rom. 4.3). In the situation of the New Covenant between God and man (1 Cor. 11.25), it is faith that God requires from man, so that faith is counted as the righteousness of the man (Rom. 4; Gal. 3).

15. Ian Gillman, "Motifs of 'Light' and 'Life' in Eastern Christianity and Mahāyāna Buddhism" (Paper read at the Conference on East-West Religions in Encounter, Honolulu, June 18, 1980).

16. See "Shinshū Seikyō Zenshō Hensanjo," in *Shinshū Shogyō Zenshō* (Kyoto: Oyogi Kōbendo and Kōkyō Shōin, 1958), 2:168ff.

17. By "usual self" we understand the subject of objectifying language common to all members of a society. It is conscious of being a constituent of society and of standing in commonly shared traditions. When it makes a decision, it is conscious of being responsible for the decision. In other words, the usual self is the subject of the consciousness of responsibility, sinfulness, and guilt.

18. Both Paul and Shinran speak mainly as the usual self united with the transcendent. It is interesting to see that they experienced guilt-consciousness and that they argue on the basis of authoritative tradition. Paul supports his arguments with quotations from the Old Testament, Shinran from sutras. It is seldom the case with Jesus and Zen. To both Paul and Shinran the Saviour has the character of being "over against" the believer, whereas Zen rejects this aspect. All these facts are signs that Paul and Shinran speak as the usual self in religious life.

19. Shin'ichi Hisamatsu said that he had no *bonno* (sinful passions, evil care for oneself), and that he did not die ("Kaku no shukyō" [Religion of Awakening], in *Dialogue with S. Hisamatsu and S. Yagi* [1980], 4ff, 257). R. Akizuki, who was a disciple of D. T. Suzuki's, told me this anecdote: At an international congress of the science of religion Suzuki asked the audience, "In Genesis is told the story of creation. Now who was there at the event of creation?" Since there was no answer Suzuki replied himself and said, "It was 'I.'" If we should give a Christian interpretation of his saying, "I" corresponds to "Christ in me" (Gal. 2.20), i.e., the Logos, through which all things came to be (John 1.3). That is, Suzuki spoke from the reality which Christians call "Christ in me."

20. In Paul we see some confusion between communality and interpersonality. Love is in Paul the principle of the former. In our emperical situation communality overlaps with interpersonality.

21. See also 1 Cor. 14.37; 2 Cor. 13.3. On the contrary, the otherness of Christ is evident (1 Cor. 7.12). Then Christ is spoken of in the third person.

22. 1 Cor. 12.3; John 5.65. In Shinran's teachings the ultimate subject of human faith in Amida is the saving power of Amida's vows. It comes from the power of Amida. See Fujiwara, *Tanni Shō,* Chap. 8.

23. See No. 11.

24. The history of the investigation is described in Bultmann, *Theology of the New Testament,* pp. 31ff.

25. Ibid.

26. See Yagi, *Shinyaku Shisō no Seiritsu; Kiristo to Iesu, Bukkyō to Kiristokyō no Setten* (Ten Points of Contact between Buddhism and Christianity) (Kyoto: Hōzōkan, 1975).

27. Kasemann, "Das Problem des historischen Jesus," in *Exegetische Versuche und Besinnungen.*

28. See No. 1 and Fig. 9. The formless is the ground of both subjectivity and objective beings. Since it is spoken of in the first person, the line which denotes awakening has no discontinuity, as in the other figures.

CHAPTER 11

The Encounter of Christianity with the Buddhist Logic of *Soku*: an Essay in Topological Theology

Masaaki Honda

The universality of religious faith obviates the distinction of East or West. But faith must be incarnated in history according to different cultural and spiritual contexts. That is why a Japanese theology for Japanese Christians is necessary. In order to proclaim and develop the mystery of the Incarnation and the death and resurrection of Jesus Christ, it is the task of Japanese Christians to formulate a new theology in dialogical encounter with Buddhist thought in Asia in general and Japan in particular.

THE SECOND VATICAN COUNCIL

The Catholic Church, as it proclaimed and interpreted the mysteries of Christ's death and resurrection, placed too much emphasis on establishing a fixed doctrinal system. The main thrust of Catholic theology before the Second Vatican Council (1962-65) was toward formulating and defending an official system of doctrine which Christians were to apply *a priori* to the conditions of life in the world. The presuppositions of this theology were overwhelmingly Greek-rationalistic, and it displayed little interest in the philosophy of nothingness *śūnyatā* which undergirds most of the spirituality of East Asia.

Sarvepalli Radhakrishnan pointed to this problem in his description of the activities of Christian missionaries in India during the period of British rule.

> The Christian missionaries of that day did not recognize anything vital or valuable in the Indian religions. For them, the native faiths were a mass of unredeemed darkness and error. They had supreme contempt for the heathen religions and wished to root them out, lock, stock, and barrel. It is a natural tendency of the human mind to suppose that its own god is God of all the earth, while all other gods are "mumbo

jumbo" made with human hands. That Christianity is the one true religion and all other religions are utterly false has been the belief, not only
of the rank and file in the Christian Church, but also of many Christian
men and women of high intellectual standing. This aggressive propagan-
da lacked the one thing needful — charity.[1]

This sort of religious imperialism is a reflex reaction rooted in the monarchist
God of traditional Christian thought, which in turn is based on Aristotelian
epistemology. God is thus conceived of as a primal substance whose nature is
to be a subject without predicates, and who is therefore an irreversible being
whose only relationship with the world is an utter transcendence that leaves
little room for his loving involvement with the world, especially as this is affirmed by the New Testament. In short, God becomes a deity who sits alone
in heaven and judges the world without incarnating himself into it.

But the Second Vatican Council vigorously declared an end to this long-
established European-centered theology by affirming a "more dynamic, evolutionary concept of the reality" *(notionem magis dynamicam atque evolutivam)*
of the Church.[2] For example, "The Church is not bound exclusively and in-
dissolubly to any race or nation";[3] thus "the Catholic Church rejects nothing
which is true and holy in these religions. She looks with sincere respect upon
those ways of conduct and of life, those rules and teachings which, though
differing in many particulars from what she holds and sets forth, nevertheless
often reflect a ray of that Truth which enlightens all men."[4] In this manner
the council recognized the possibility of valid revelation apart from Christian
tradition, and the following policy for the education of seminarians was
promulgated: "In their philosophical and theological studies, let them consider the points of contact between the traditions and religion of their homeland
and the Christian religion."[5] Finally, the council especially encouraged lay
persons to "prepare for dialogue with non-Christians."[6]

There are historical precedents for the council's decisions. The Fathers of
the Greek and Latin churches responded to the historical necessity of creating
a theology that could speak to the concerns of Hellenistic culture by articulat-
ing Christian faith through the categories of the Greek philosophers, especially Plato. St. Thomas utilized the philosophy of Aristotle as the foundation of
European Catholic philosophy and theology. Since then, however, European
Christianity has been confronted with the necessity of expressing itself more
concretely through the spiritual inheritance of Asia, especially as it is found
in Buddhism. It is within this context that I wish to explore the Buddhist philosophy of Kitarō Nishida as a medium for rethinking Christian theology.

I. Onodera evaluated Nishida as "a unique philosopher who established
the logic of realization that expresses Japanese spirituality." But at the same

time, Onodera observed that "there lies concealed in Nishida's thought the philosophical foundation for opening up a new, broader theology of the Holy Spirit,"[7] an element of theological reflection long ignored in the West. The core of this proposal lies in Nishida's conception of a topological logic, and the main purpose of this essay is to formulate a Christian view of the world and of human experience in terms of this concept. In so doing, I shall endeavor to establish a logical foundation for a new theological vision that is expressive of the religious experience of Asian Christians.

THERE IS THE WORLD BECAUSE THERE IS GOD: THERE IS GOD BECAUSE THERE IS THE WORLD

A major problem that became evident in my encounter with Nishida's philosophy was a sense of incongruity as I tried to reexamine the relation between God and the world by means of a proposition of topological logic which I shall call "the principle of reversibility." Nishida's wording of this principle is: "There are sentient beings because there is the Buddha; there is the Buddha because there are sentient beings. There is the world of creatures because there is God the creator; there is God because there is the world of creatures."[8] Setting aside the first line for the moment, the second statement concerning the relationship between God and the world is unconvincing to most Christians, who are trained to affirm the absolute irreversibility—that is, the absolute ontological difference—between God as creator and the world of creatures he creates. This has, in fact, long been part of the doctrinal core of Christian faith. This difficulty, however, may perhaps stem from an attempt to understand the principle of reversibility by means of the habitual, dualistic mode of thought through which we affirm a split in the relationship between subject and object.

I first understood this point upon reconsidering my own experience of conversion to Christianity during my youth. In that experience I was at first filled only with the sense of irreversibility between myself and God. I experienced God as an absolutely objective, transcendent, and impersonal reality totally unaffected by the existence of the world he created and the finite creatures dwelling within the world. Later, I gradually became aware that irreversibility was compatible with, because it required, reversibility. In other words, I became aware that the irreversible reality of God is not so one-sided as to be able only to arouse the feeling of awe in one's encounter with God. God's irreversible nature—what God's reality is in itself—is simultaneously the reversible source of the human experience of love, freedom, and trust as deriving ultimately from God. I experienced God as a caring and loving personal reality that is concerned for the quality of life of the creatures existing in the world. Consequently, love, freedom, and trust are flowers that bloom in the ground of reversibility in such a way that irreversibility is understood as the source of reversibility. This, it seems to me, was an experience of what Nishida meant by reversibility united with absolute irreversibility, and it is in this sense that Christian conversion or Buddhist enlightenment—what Nishida called the "spiritual fact" in both traditions—is essentially self-awareness of some form of this relationship.

If it is true that the awareness of irreversibility is the source of the experience of reversibility, and if it is equally true that it is impossible to be aware of irreversibility (the absolute ontological separation between God and the world) apart from an awareness of reversibility (the unity of God and the world experienced in faith), then it can only be concluded that reversibility and irreversibility are the mutual, simultaneous, interdependent "spiritual facts" of religious faith. And even though one might be more strongly emphasized than the other—reversibility in Buddhism and irreversibility in Christianity, for example—neither can in fact be separated from the other.

Therefore, Nishida's proposition "There is the world because there is God; there is God because there is the world" should not be interpreted in a monistic or pantheistic sense, but rather in terms of a unity of opposites in which each term maintains its unique reality precisely because of its relationship with its opposite. Or, in Nishida's language, the principle of reversibility involves the identity of opposites in the sense of "not one, not two."

To illustrate, consider the proposition There is B because of A; there is A because of B. Topological logic does not imply the separation of A from B in such a way that one term is understood as a reality distinct from the other. This is dualistic, abstract thinking. At the same time, the reduction of A to B or of B to A is a monism that is equally dualistic in its assumptions. The history of Western philosophy seems to have swung like a pendulum between dualistic and monistic modes of thought. To Nishida, however, monistic understandings of the world are forms of abstract conceptualization projected onto the world from the side of our felt separation of subject and object. As such, monistic philosophies are as much linguistic contrivances as are philosophical dualisms. Nishida's point was that philosophical monisms are nothing but linguistically transformed dualisms, and as such no monistic philosophy can provide a logic that accurately expresses the concrete facts of human existence in the world.

Let us reconsider now A and B and their relation. "If there is no relation, there cannot be any relational terms. If there are no relational terms, there can be no relation." Neither A nor B preexists independently of their relation, nor does their relation preexist independently of A and B. Both the relation and the two terms related, as well as the interdependence and independence of each term, are formed simultaneously in their mutual causation.

The independent reality of the individual depends upon its relation to an opposing reality, which at the same time determines that relation. "The self has something which cannot be easily dissolved in the relation, but involves the relation. . . . The individual has the significance of the general."[9]

The identity of the former proposition, "there is B because there is A," with the latter proposition, "there is A because there is B," can be understood in this sense. "There is the world because there is God" and "There is God because there is the world" are not two different propositions. They are interdependent. That is, the presence of God's irreversibility and the simultaneous reversibility of God and the world are two moments integrated by the "not one, not two" character of the "spiritual fact" of our faith.

Whether A is God or the Buddha, the logical form of the relation between A and B does not differ for Nishida. Needless to say, this never meant for him that there are no differences between Christian and Buddhist religious experience. Still, the "spiritual facts" of Christian faith and Buddhist experience possess the same logical form and, as S. Ueda points out, Nishida was even of the opinion that "the relation of the identity of opposites is itself the very reality and the very fact as it is."[10] Does this mean that the true reality is the "relation" and not the "absolute"? It seems to me that this question is based on false dualistic assumptions. For in topological logic no relation is prior to the terms of the relation, nor does A have ontological priority over B, or B over A. Priority rather lies in the simultaneous causality inherent in both the terms in relation and the relation itself. This is the basis of Nishida's notion that when the Absolute, whether it is named God or the Buddha, incarnates itself into the finite world, the Absolute becomes a nothing constituting the self-negating ground (no-thing-ness) of the finite individuals comprising the world. This Absolute Nishida identified with God, the "true whole One," who is "in this world by his self-negation to the end."[11]

Thus the reversible relation between the absolute and the relative in Nishida's logic is grounded in the Buddhist notion of the identity of opposites, which he once expressed rather poetically as "absolute charity boundlessly embracing even those who stand against it."[12] In this sense, we can understand reversibility as the reversibility which contains irreversibility within itself. Although irreversibility denies reversibility, the latter contains the former in itself as its denier. To affirm otherwise means that reversibility cannot become what Nishida called "the logic of absolute charity," for absolute charity, in the sense of God's love for the world as revealed through Christ, can only be understood as the irreversible response of God to the finite, reversible world. That is, God's love for the world and what love there is in the world for God are united in the absolute charity of the "not one, not two" nature of the relationship. In this way, the principle of reversibility becomes the logic of absolute charity in the relation of reversibility-*soku*-irreversiblity and irreversibility-*soku*-reversibility.* As such, it is a form of logic that expresses or presupposes a nonsubstantial ontology, and only when it is so understood can it function as "the logic of the New Testament" guiding the faith and practice of Asian Christians.

THE WORLD OF COSMIC REVELATION

The revelations of the Old and New Testaments form the proper ground of historical Christian faith. However, there is also an aspect of revelation which Christianity can share with Buddhism in its encounter with the Absolute, which I shall call "cosmic revelation." By cosmic revelation I refer to the common revelatory ground shared by both Buddhism and Christianity.

Zen Buddhist masters have answered the question What is the Buddha? in many different ways. For example, Master Fuketsu once asked, "Where can non-Buddha exist?" Joshu answered, "An oak tree in the garden"; and to the same question Dozan responded, "Three pounds of flax." Each answer to this koan expresses the fact that everything is the self-negating manifestation of the Absolute, which Buddhism generally names Buddha-nature. Therefore, enlightenment is the realization of one's own identity as grounded in the *soku* relation of the part (an oak tree) to the whole (Buddha-nature).

Father Thomas Merton clearly understood this when he suggested that the logic of Zen insight "is not a pantheistic submersion or a loss of self in 'Nature' or 'the One.' It is not a withdrawal into one's spiritual essence and a denial of matter and the world."[13] On the contrary, Merton interpreted the Zen experience of enlightenment (satori) as an event quite different from the sort of monistic union in which the subject is absorbed in its object or the object dissolved in the subject. This is clearly indicated in his interpretation of the well-known passage from the *Genjōkōan* (Koan in Daily Life) chapter of Dōgen's *Shōbōgenzo* (The Eye and Treasure of the True Dharma): "Zen insight is Being's awareness of itself in us." Merton took this statement

---

Soku literally means "identity." In the Tendai (Ch., T'ien-t'ai) school of Buddhism, *soku* is explained in terms of six degrees: (1) identity at the level of suchness or underlying principle; (2) identity through hearing that all dharmas are the Buddha's Dharma; (3) identity through the effort of religious practice; (4) identity in one's life through the practice of contemplation and wisdom; (5) identity through partial realization of the truth; and (6) ultimate identity when the practitioner enters Buddhahood. (T'ien-t'ai Chih-i, *Mo-ho chih-kuan*, Taishō Shinshu Daizokyzōkyō [Tokyo: Daizō Shuppan, 1924-32], 46:10b-c) — —.Ed.

to mean that Buddhist insight as understood in Zen is "a recognition that the whole world is aware of itself in me, and that 'I' am no longer an individual and limited self, still less a disembodied soul, but that my 'identity' is to be sought not in that separation from all that is, but in oneness (indeed 'convergence') with all that is. This identity is not the denial of my own personal reality but its highest affirmation."[14] It seems to me that not a few Christian mystics have groped for expressions of their own experience by means of similar forms of topological logic.

Other sorts of propositions suggest the same idea. Nishida states, for example, that "God is quite absent and yet quite present at the same time in any part of the world."[15] St. Francis of Assisi in the *Canticle of the Sun* seems to have expressed a similar experience. It can also be seen in Pseudo-Dionysius the Areopagite's statement that "God is the sun, the stars, the fire, the water, the wind, the dewdrops, the clouds, the rocks; that is, God is all that exists."[16] This same perception is part of Buddhist teaching and experience, the clearest example of which is Dōgen's interpretation of the doctrine that all sentient beings possess the Buddha-nature. In both traditions it is possible to see what Buddhists call *soku hi*, or "identity with difference," at work. The experience of it is embodied in the words of the Old Testament psalmist who affirmed, "The heavens declare the glory of God, and the firmament proclaims the work of his hands" (Ps. 19.1). In short, all of these propositions are expressions of the one-*soku*-the man, the part-*soku*-the whole.[17]

It is also worth noting in this regard that St. Thomas believed the resurrection to be a state in which a "unity of opposites" between the soul and the body is completely achieved. For example, in the following passage from the *Summa contra Gentiles,* Thomas states:

> . . . the soul is naturally united with the body, because of its being essentially the form of the body. Therefore it is against the nature of the soul to be without the body. But nothing that is against nature can be lasting. Therefore the soul will not be forever without the body. Thus the immortality of the soul seems to require the resurrection of the body.[18]

While Thomas appears to be dualistically separating soul and body as two ontologically distinct entities, in fact he believed that as soon as human nature is perfected in heaven after the resurrection of the body, the irreversibility between soul and body is completely abolished, and the relation of "not one, not two" finally realized. This is possible because—even in this world—where there is body there is soul, where there is soul there is body, in a sort of natural unity. The resurrection is simply the final completion of an already existent state of affairs involving the unity of opposition between soul and body. In other words, Thomas like St. Paul taught what Christian tradition usually understands as a "realized eschatology."[19] It may also be justly called a topological eschatology.

Previously I made reference to trees and flax as self-negating forms or expressions of Buddha-nature. But obviously trees and flax cannot negate themselves, because they are unconscious entities. Entities not aware of their own finitude, their own death, cannot experience selfhood in any form. The topological world is therefore a world of human experience.[20] Humanity is humanity for God, and God is God for humanity expressing himself through creation. We are able to encounter God through any of his creatures. The absolute ontological separation between God and humanity is simultaneously a unity. From this viewpoint it is possible to comprehend the meaning of the faltering language of such Christian mystics as Johannes Eriugena, Meister Eckhart, Ruysbroeck, Nicolaus Cusanus, and the author of *The Cloud of Unknowing*. But at the same time, since the mystery and works of God can only be encountered by human beings within the conditions of historical existence, the logic of this world is the logic not just of cosmic revelation but of historical revelation in general.

A RE-EXAMINATION OF BASIC CHRISTIAN CONCEPTS

The God of the Trinity

In the Old Testament, faith in *'el* (the masculine singular name for God) is identical with faith in *'elohim* (the masculine plural name for God, literally, "gods"). On the other hand, the New Testament reveals the nature of God as a Trinity which transcends the grammatical categories of singular and plural. Once more, the Trinity as a doctrine affirming that God's nature is one essence *(una essentia)* possessing three persons *(tres personas)* was never intended as a proposition to which we must assent merely intellectually. In fact, the doctrine of the Trinity is nothing but a symbolic pointer to the immeasurable mystery of God, and as such it is the central truth of Christian faith around which everything else revolves. This is so because the Trinity expresses the perfect interdependency of the One and the Three Persons under the comprehensive dominion of the One.[21] The eternal simultaneity of Three Persons possessing one essence is, of course, a transcategorical relation which cannot be understood or even expressed in terms of Aristotle's concepts of substance and accident. On the other hand, it is possible to understand the Trinity as a Christian   counterpart   of   the   doctrine   of   the   one   and   the   many (one-*soku*-many) of the Kegon school of Buddhism.* In Nishida's words, "This world of historical reality where we are born, where we work, and where we will die, logically speaking, must be the identity of contradiction between the one and the many."[22] The world of historical reality is the "place" where the Trinity exists. But as such, the world is not a container of the Trinity, like a paper wrapper containings its package. The Trinity is not "in" any particular place, but rather the place is "in" the Trinity. In short, the Trinity's place is the work of the Holy Spirit, whose main function is to confront the Father and the Son with one another in their distinctive relationships. Needless to say, the work of the Holy Spirit is not something external to the Father and the Son, as a container is external to its contents, for the Holy Spirit works through the interdependent relationship of the Father with the Son. Consequently, the *topos* of the Trinity is the existential place where persons are confronted by the Holy Spirit.

The implication of this understanding is that the Father is Father only in interrelationship with the Son, and the Son is only Son in interrelationship with the Father by means of the activity of the Holy Spirit. Or as St. Augustine once said, the Trinity is a truth established "not by substance" but "by relation." However, "this relation is not accidental, for it is unchangeable."[23] Of course, so far as the Father is the source of the Son's reality, their relationship must be irreversible. "The Son can do nothing of himself, but only what he sees the Father doing" (John 5.19). But at the same time, "the Father and the Son are one" (John 10.30; 17.11), so that the Son is the source of the Father's reality as well, since the Father can only be "Father" in relation to the Son. Here the irreversibility reverses itself because the Father and the Son are in an interdependent relationship of mutual simultaneous causality.

It is at this point that we are able to grasp the relativity of the absolute and the absoluteness of the relative in the divine reality. The God of the Trinity is a God of interrelationship expressing itself through love *(agape)*. This in turn means that the highest mode of reality is nothing but pure interdependent relation. In fact, it is even possible to conceive of this relation as the original mode of existence of God as absolute nothing-*soku*-absolute being. If we do so, it also becomes possible to conceive of humanity as being created

---

*The Kegon (Chin, Hua-yen) bases its distinctive interpretation of Buddhist philosophy on the *Avatamsaka-sutra*. This school is noted for its teaching that all things possess Buddha-nature and that each of the constituting elements of existence *(dharmas)* at any moment of space-time is interpenetrated by and interdependent with every other constituting element of existence. — — -Ed.

by God as a copy *(imago Dei)* of the Trinity. Understood thusly, personhood is also relative to itself, for humanity originates as a form of interdependent relationship between father, mother, and child. And just as the psychic health of the individual depends on the integration within himself of the paternal principle and the maternal principle,[24] so Christian faith teaches that authentic human existence means the realization of the relationship of the Father and the Son without one's life through the unifying work of the Holy Spirit.

The Divine-Human Nature of Jesus Christ

It is also possible to think of the divine-human nature of Jesus Christ in terms of the relation of "not one, not two." If we emphasize only the side of "not one" and then identify Christ's divine nature (the Logos) with the Buddhist idea of Dharma, thereby separating the divinity of Christ from the humanity of Jesus, it will not be possible to express the meaning of the divine-human nature of Jesus Christ in any authentically Christian or Buddhist way. This is so because in the Buddhist notion of Dharma, *kū* (emptiness) is never separate from *shiki* (form); that is, it is possible to affirm that Christ is for Christian faith none other than the personification of the principle *shikisoku-zeku* (form is not different from emptiness). For just as there is no *kū* without *shiki,* so the divinity of Christ can only be manifested through his humanity. "He who sees me sees also the Father" (John 14.9). Therefore he who cannot apprehend the humanity of Jesus cannot apprehend the divinity of Christ, just as his divinity cannot be apprehended apart from his humanity, for both natures are utterly interdependent.

The Creation Out of Nothing

It is further possible to reinterpret the doctrine of creation by means of a topological exegesis of Genesis 1.1, "In the beginning God created heaven and earth." If we understand this "beginning" as the *topos* of absolute nothingness, the "creation out of nothing" *(creatio ex nihilo)* becomes the self-determination of absolute nothingness, resulting in the polarity of heaven and earth. "Out of nothing" *(ex nihilo)* does not only mean the nonexistence of a preexistent matter out of which God made the world; it also denies a dualistic split between God and his creatures, so that their identity in absolute contradiction is revealed. That is, the *topos* of "place" or God's creation lies in the "not one, not two" character of his nature as absolute nothingness.

According to the Thomistic view, however, creation out of nothing implies creation by the free will of God. Such creation is incidental and secondary to the nature of God, for it is nothing but the *habitus* (accident) of God.[25] We cannot think in any other way if we want to emphasize the transcendence of God according to the categories of Aristotle. God's creative action upon nothingness by *habitus*, however, can never be understood as the expression of selfless love through the medium of absolute nothingness, for the distinction between *natura* (substance) and *habitus* is, properly speaking, only a "linguistic distinction" *(modus loquendi)*. It is not a distinction of "the mode of being" *(modus essendi)*.

Modus loquendi statements are not statements of ontology in Thomas's theology, however, for Thomas recognized that the freedom of God is the freedom of his absolute self-negation. It is not a relative freedom by which God decides to create or not to create, as if creativity were not part of his very nature as God. Rather, God's creativity is freedom-*soku*-necessity, so that God cannot help but create by the diffusion of *agapé*. His freedom *is* necessity. Once more, God's necessity is not mere determinism, but necessity-*soku*-freedom, freedom-*soku*-necessity, as revealed by the love of God for his creation as manifested on the cross. Creation in Christian faith therefore cannot be understood as an accidental, secondary work of God, especially if creativity is understood in terms of a logic grounded in the experience that "he who has died to himself completely, completely lives" *(Hekigan-Roku,* 41). Thus the logic of absolute nothingness can become the logic of the Incarnation and of death and resurrection. Understood in this way, "creation out of nothing" becomes an expression of God's work of selfless love in the form of his absolute self-negation-*soku* his absolute self-affirmation.

THE CONCEPT OF GOD IN OBJECT LOGIC:
THE DOUBLE-EDGED SWORD

Our sense of sight is physiologically the sensation of brightness which is aroused when the retina is stimulated by rays of light or electromagnetic waves of a certain wavelength. Where we actually perceive color, however, is not "in" the retina but "in" the visual center of the cerebrum (the *topos* where inside and outside exist as the identity of opposites). For example, when we see the stars twinkling at night, we are conscious of them only in the distant sky, only in the external, objective, transcendent night sky, even though the shapes and colors of the stars have been formed in fact in the visual center of the cerebrum. This phenomenon is called projection, and in visual experience the perceived objective world "out there" derives from the internal place located "in" the cerebrum.

I think something similar occurs in the human encounter with God. When we are confronted by God, namely when "God is in our presence as a spiritual fact,"[26] God is experienced as the identity of immanence-

soku-transcendence in the *topos* of human history. But simultaneously, God is projected outward through the objectifications of reason, and he is thereby made into an external, transcendent, eternal, and infinite being. Here is the source of objectified concepts of God in traditional theology. But theological concepts are not the reality we experience in the encounter with God, and to this degree, religious experience of God's presence is similar to experiences of certain physiological data.

Even though Nishida wrote about the "many misunderstandings which arise from the view of object logic about the relation between God and man," he did not deny object logic itself. Rather he believed that "object logic is contained in concrete or topological logic as a moment of its self-determination."[27] The concept of God in object logic points to a concrete experiential reality which we cannot disregard as a mere abstract concept. At the same time, we must not confuse objective concepts *about* God with the experienced reality *of* God. As St. Augustine once said, "Wondrous is Your depth, my God, wondrous is your depth. It is awesome to look into that depth: an awe owed to honor, and a trembling arising from love."[28] St. Augustine had realized that the relation between himself and the mystery of God absolutely transcends intellectual discrimination. But at the same time, he never denied the *concept* of a transcendent God whom he regarded as an eternal, immutable being. In short, it is simply not possible to experience God merely through the abstract, one-sided projections of object logic. Ever since Plato, contemplation of an abstract doctrine of God has been used as a path toward experiencing the concrete reality of God. So even Greek philosophy urged the fusion of intellectual life and spiritual life, since abstract notions of God are only half the truth. Western emphasis on this half-truth, however, has produced the vain and dangerous illusion of belief in the possibility of encountering God, the highest being, at the height of intellectual abstraction from the world.[29]

The source of this illusion is the human propensity to "consider the thing thought of objectively as a substance which determines itself." Only when the true basis of *topos* becomes hidden through an overemphasis on object logic does the concept of God become "a sword that cuts off our life."[30]

The notion of God in Western rationalistic theology, thus, is a kind of double-edged sword. It possesses concrete meaning only insofar as it is understood as a moment of self-determination in topological logic. But as soon as this moment is doctrinally formulated in an abstract way, it becomes the irreversible, transcendent concept of the God of object logic. Although it may be "God for some philosophers," it is not "the God of Abraham, Isaac, Jacob." The living God of Jacob dwells in "the inner *topos*." Of course this inner *topos* is not merely immanent, but the place where the transcendence and the immanence, the irreversibility and the reversibility of God interpenetrate. It is the place of the real world, "the great heaven and the great earth," where the creativity of God expresses itself as his activity through the Holy Spirit.

NOTES

1. Sarvepalli Radhakrishnan, *East and West in Religion* (London: George Allen and Unwin, 1949), pp. 22-23.
2. Second Vatican Council, "Pastoral Constitution on the Church in the Modern World" (*Constitutio pastoralis de Eclesia in mundo hujos temporis*), No. 5.
3. Ibid., No. 8.
4. Second Vatican Council, "Declaration on the Relationship of the Church to Non-Christian Religions" (*Declaratio de Ecclesial habitudine ad religiones non-christianos*), No. 16.
5. "Degree on the Missionary Activity of the Church" (*Decretum de Activitate Missionali Ecclesial*), No. 16.
6. Ibid., No. 41.
7. I. Onodera, "The Critic of the Absolute Dialectic," *The Seishinin Women's University Bulletin* 24 (1976):48.
8. Kitarō Nishida, "Topological Logic and the Religious View of the World," in *Collected Philosophical Essays*, (Tokyo: Iwanami, 1946), 6:110. Even in the fourth chapter of *The Study of the Good*, we have the reversible proposition: "There is not God if there is not the world, just as there is not the world if there is not God" (Nishida, *The Study of Good* [Tokyo: Iwanami, 1924].
9. Nishida, "Topological Logic," p. 25.
10. S. Ueda, "Topological Logic and the Religious View of the World," in Vol. 22 of Nishida, *Gendai Nihon Shisō Taikei* (Tokyo: Hyakkaen, 1974).
11. Ibid., p. 110.
12. Nishida, *The Collection of Philosophical Theses*, 8:14.
13. Thomas Merton, *Mystics and Zen Masters* (New York: Delta Books, 1961), p. 17.
14. Ibid., pp. 17-18.
15. Nishida, "Topological Logic," p. 110.
16. Aquinas, *In De Divinis Nominibus* (Dionysii) c. 1, 6, 25.
17. The following statements from the writings of St. Paul and St. Augustine express similar experiences of the interdependent transcendence and immanence of God: "God is above everything . . . is in everything" (Ephes. 4.5); and "deeper than the deepest recesses of my soul . . . higher than the highest aspirations of my soul" (*Confessions* 3. 6, 11). These are topological propositions in the notion *analogia secundum esse* (*analogia entis*) of St. Thomas Aquinas: for example, "as the soul is total in any part of the body, so God is total in all things and in a single thing" (*Summa Theologiae* 1. a. 8, a. 2, ad 3).
18. Aquinas, *Summa contra Gentiles*, Lib. 4, e. 79.
19. *A New Catholic Commentary on Holy Scripture* (London: Thomas Nelson and Sons, 1969), pp. 1199, 1202.
20. Nishida, "Topological Logic," p. 145.
21. J. Ratzinger, *Einfuhrung in das Christentum*, (Munich: Kösel-Verlag GmgH and Co., 1970), Vol. 1, Chap. 5.
22. Nishida, *The Problems of Culture in Japan* (Tokyo: Iwanami, 1940), p. 16.

23. Augustine, *De Trintate* 5. 5, 6.
24. Erich Fromm, *The Art of Loving* (New York: Harper and Row, 1956), p. 44.
25. M. Matsumoto, "Essay on the Creation out of Nothing," in his *The Problems of Ontology* (Tokyo: Iwanami, 1956), p. 163.
26. Nishida, "Topological Logic," p. 84.
27. Ibid., p. 128.
28. Augustine, *Confessions* 12. 14, 17.
29. Cf. E. I. Watkin, "The Mysticism of St. Augustine," in *A Monument to St. Augustine* (London, 1930), p. 115.
30. Nishida, "Topological Logic," p. 136.

Taken as a whole these essays demonstrate that reflection about the relation of Buddhism and Christianity has broken out of the impasse in which it long seemed fixed. In doing so, it may well have pointed the way for fresh reflection about the relations among other living traditions as well. Most of the papers are written from the Christian side of this relation, and most of the comments which follow discuss what these Christian contributions signify with respect to the meaning for Christians of the encounter with Buddhism. At the end, however, I will offer some remarks on the stance of the Buddhist contributors.

Through most of Christian history there seemed to be a limited number of options for considering other traditions. They could be rejected as idolatrous, with the result that Christians would seek to eradicate them through the conversion of their followers. Hellenistic paganism was viewed in this way. They could be seen as embodying some goodness and truth which is fulfilled and perfected in Christianity. The Christian response to Neoplatonism illustrates this possibility. In this case, too, Christians seek the conversion of others, but the attainments of the other tradition are to be preserved. A third possibility is that the other tradition be viewed as nonreligious, in which case it could be allowed to continue alongside Christianity. The Jesuit missionaries in China received the authority of the pope to treat Confucianism in this way.

In the twentieth century many liberal Christians recognized the multiple religious ways as each valid in its own right. Tolerance became the major virtue, leading easily to indifference. Much of the energy of Christendom's scholarship in the field of religion went into the effort to attain a neutral methodology for the comparative study of religions. Partly in reaction to this, other Christians, such as Karl Barth, proposed that Christians cease thinking of Christianity chiefly as one religion alongside others. For them religion, including the Christian religion, is a human activity, whereas what is crucial to Christianity is God's decisive act in Jesus Christ. In the years after World War II the two fields of Christian theology and of history of religions developed quite separately and exercised little influence upon one another.

The papers in this collection, however, testify that this age of separate development is at an end. Christian theology is deeply affected by the encounter with Buddhism, and the comparative study of these two traditions is deeply informed by theological categories and concerns. But there is no return to the earlier Christian arrogance. All the Christian writers profoundly respect

Buddhism in its differences from Christianity. None of them treat it as an error to be extirpated or as a partial truth to be perfected and fulfilled in Christianity. The question for Christians is how to proceed now that we can no longer doubt the existence of another religious tradition which commands from us full respect precisely in its profound difference and opposition to our inherited faith.

Most of the papers provide substantial comparative study, but only two of them limit themselves largely to it. That of Buri is devoted to pointing out the historical-theological parallels between the two traditions and their shared predicament in the contemporary world. Maraldo shows us the importance of practice in both traditions and provides a comparative study of Dōgen and Francis of Assisi to illustrate the fruitfulness of a hermeneutics of practice.

There is little disposition in any of the papers in this collection to minimize the profound and extensive differences between Christianity and Buddhism, but two of them nevertheless seek a level at which these differences can be overcome. Augustine shows that a new form of sociology of religion is emerging which clarifies positively the role of faith. Both Buddhism and Christianity can be affirmed from this point of view as embodiments of this faith. Corless sees the divergences between the two traditions as inseparable at the level of ordinary consciousness. But he believes that both point to a level of superconsciousness at which all such diversity is transcended. From the perspective of that superconsciousness Corless is able to be a full participant in the practices of both communities.

Winston King's paper on the self does not seek a point of identity or commonality as do Augustine and Corless. He urges that Christians enter the discussion not from the side of the mystical element of our tradition, which seems to approximate Buddhism, but from the full emphasis on the personal self. Yet he argues persuasively that when the deepest meanings of Buddhists and of Christians are understood, they do not have the flatly contradictory character attributed to them in traditional stereotypes. A fruitful dialogue is possible, and one senses in reading King that in this dialogue each may learn from the other.

This mutual learning, or at least the Christian's learning from Buddhists, points to the concern of the largest group of contributors. These seek the transformation of Christianity through its encounter with Buddhism. This approach is set out programmatically by Paul Ingram. He points to process theology as a movement within Christianity which shows both the need and the possibility of such creative transformation of Christianity. Frederick Streng makes specific proposals as to how Christians can transform their doctrines by learning from Buddhists. For example, he proposes that we recognize that deeper than Tillich's "Being-Itself" is the Buddhist field of emptiness and that, in the light of the early Christian hymn in Phillipians 2, we can reformulate our Christology in terms of this field.

Whereas the American proponents of the transformation of Christianity write programmatically and suggestively, the Japanese Christians are already far advanced in the process of transformation. Honda stands in that small group of Japanese Christians who share with many Japanese Buddhists in their indebtedness to the Buddhist philosophy of Kitarō Nishida. He not only calls for a new theology based on this philosophy, replacing that of the Greeks, he also embodies and expresses important elements of the results that follow from such a program. Surely it is a profound transformation of Christianity.

Yagi writes more in the guise of a comparative study. But it would be misleading to classify him under that heading. Clearly his interest is theological. By identifying the three axes of the communal, the individual, and the interpersonal, he achieves a perspective for comparative study. But his understanding of these arises from a deep theological grappling both with the New Testament and the Buddhist texts, and it is at these depths that he finds points of identity between Jesus and Zen and between Paul and Shinran. His understanding of Jesus and of Paul is transformed in the process.

Ingram notes that whereas Christians have been the doctrinally more intolerant community, it is they who are now opening themselves to creative transformation by Buddhism. He sees an equal need for Buddhists to open themselves to such transformation by Christianity, but he does not see this happening. I believe he is correct that this is not occurring in a comparable way, certainly not in the Buddhist contributions to this volume. But rather than suggest that Buddhists are slow in taking the appropriate action, it would be well to consider whether from the Buddhist point of view creative transformation would represent an authentic response to Christianity.

To answer this requires clarification of the level at which creative transformation operates. If it is understood to operate at a superficial level, or even at any level short of the ultimate one, change or transformation is eminently appropriate for Buddhists. Buddhism is highly adaptable to diverse cultural settings and historical circumstances, and it can adopt and adapt practices and modes of organization from Christianity without particular difficulties. But for most Buddhists it does not seem appropriate to think of a creative transformation of the basic Buddhist experience of reality as empty. This is the indispensable and timeless essence of Buddhism.

Of course, many Christians seek a comparable essence of Christianity. Recognizing the incessant changes that surround us and carry the Church with them, theologians and ordinary believers alike seek to identify what remains constant through all change. But this effort has not been successful. One can now study the history of the attempts to identify once and for all the essence, or kernel, of Christianity. When one has realized how historically conditioned such efforts are, one is more ready to acknowledge the inappropriateness of such an approach. Christianity is a historical movement, and as long as it is a living movement it will be in process of change. When it responds healthily to new situations out of its heritage, it is transformed creatively. When it uncritically capitulates to the pressure of fashion or tries to protect itself from criticism or to defend what is no longer defensible, it decays. Creative transformation rather than replication of a once-and-for-all-established essence is the norm of its vitality and faithfulness. To call for Christians to be transformed in the encounter with Buddhism is to project into the new situation of the present and future a pattern which has characterized Christianity at its best throughout its history.

The difference between the Buddhist response to Christianity and the Christian response to Buddhism is hence bound up with fundamental differences in the two traditions. Buddhism points to a salvific condition that is deeper than all history and accessible always and everywhere. Christianity witnesses to the everchanging activity of God in the course of events. The new historical situation in which Christians encounter Buddhism individually and collectively calls for new responses from Christians at the deepest level. But all historical encounters are occasions for Buddhists to point again to the eternal Dharma.

It is important, therefore, that as Christians are creatively transformed in the encounter with Buddhism we not assume that such transformation is the measure of health and vitality also of Buddhists. Nor does the lack of interest in such transformation of themselves on the part of the Buddhist dialogue partners imply any failure on their part to take Christianity seriously. As Christians we must attend in real openness to learn how the Buddhist proposes to deal with the situation in our pluralistic age.

Ichimura declares 'śunyatā to be the basis for dialogue in a situation of religious pluralism. That is, we can understand one another and work together as we jointly free ourselves from the bondage and illusion by which our linguistic systems bind us. That includes, of course, freedom from bondage to the linguistic systems employed by Buddhists as well as those employed by Christians. In this sense relativity and pluralism are accepted. But the Buddhist way of accepting these and dealing with them is through the realization of 'śunyatā.

Abe's paper goes further than any other in this collection to argue for the superiority of one of the religious traditions, in this case Buddhism. Judging from this argument it is not clear that Buddhists would have anything to gain from dialogue with Christians, although clearly they are willing to share their deeper understanding with us. However, Abe modifies this impression at the end. Like Ichimura he grounds his thought in 'śunyatā (emptiness). But he recognizes that there is danger that Buddhists will see this as the goal of life rather than as the point of departure. When this happens Buddhists are in danger of being indifferent to good and evil. The dialogue with Christians can remind Buddhists of this danger and steer them away from it.

It is important that Christian participants in the dialogue with Buddhists recognize that the transformation to which we open ourselves in faithfulness to our heritage does not seem appropriate to most Buddhists in relation to theirs. But this need not deter us from proposing to Buddhists what appears to us as their need for transformation. Such proposals are implicit in Yagi's essay and explicit in Streng's. In the past, Christian criticisms of Buddhism have been readily acknowledged by Buddhists when they pointed to superficial levels. But Christian criticism has been experienced as lacking in understanding of the true depths of Buddhism. Hence the Christian-Buddhist dialogue has rarely raised for Buddhists such fundamental questions as it has raised for Christians. However, Streng and Yagi represent a new generation of criticism which Buddhists will have to take more seriously. Whether such criticism will evoke a recognition of the need for transformation at a deeper level is not yet clear.

John B. Cobb, Jr.

MASAO ABE is Gest Professor at Haverford College, Pennsylvania. He is a graduate of Kyoto University and taught philosophy at Nara University until his arrival at Claremont in 1978. Over the past fifteen years he has lectured widely in the United States along with serving as Visiting Professor of Religion on the faculties of Columbia University, the University of Chicago, Princeton University, and Carleton College. He is an eminent Zen Buddhist teacher, philosopher, and scholar. A major focus of his publications has been comparative studies of Buddhism and Christianity. His articles and essays have appeared in numerous Japanese and English journals, including, *International Philosophical Quarterly, Philosophy East and West,* and the *Eastern Buddhist,* which he not only serves as an editor, but which is also in the process of publishing a collection of his essays under the title *Zen and Philosophy.*

MORRIS J. AUGUSTINE holds the position of professor on the Faculty of Letters at Kansai University, Japan. Prior to his association with Kansai University, he taught for eight years in American universities and seven years in Japanese universities. He received his S.T.D. degree in Catholic Theology in 1966 from Lataran University in Rome, and the Ph.D. degree from the Graduate Theological Union in Berkeley in Buddhist Studies and History of Religions in 1977. He entered the Benedictine order in 1955, was ordained in 1960, and resigned with permission in 1968.

FRITZ BURI was born in 1907 in Kerenried (Bern) and studied in Basel, Bern, Marburg, and Berlin. In 1934 he received his doctoral degree from the University of Berne in Systematic Theology. He served as pastor in two Bernese parishes, and in 1948 as minister of St. Alban in Basel and in 1957 at Basel Cathedral. During these years he also served as an army chaplain. His teaching career began in 1935 as a lecturer in Systematic Theology, and he joined the faculty at the University of Basel in 1934 as Professor of Systematic Theology and Philosophy of Religion, where both Karl Barth and Karl Jaspers were his colleagues. In 1953 he initiated the now-famous debate between Jaspers and Rudolf Bultmann. A world traveler and lecturer, he has served with distinction as visiting professor at Drew University (1966-67) and Syracuse University (1971). During the academic year 1968-69 he was Danforth Professor at the International Christian University in Mitaka (Tokyo). He has also lectured in Korea and Australia, and during the academic year 1979-80 he was visiting professor at the Roman Catholic Theological

Faculty at Lucerne. Since his "retirement" in 1977 from the University of Basel he has continued to lecture there on Buddhism and Christianity. His published work includes: *Dogmatik in Dialog,* with his colleagues M. Lochman and Heinrich Ott; *Gott in Amerika,* 2 Vols. (1970-72); *Theology of Existence* (1965); *Christian Faith in Our Time* (1966); *How Can We Still Speak Responsibly of God?* (1968); and *A Thinking Faith* (1968), and *Der Buddha-Christus als der Herr des Wahren Selbst* [The Buddha-Christ as the Lord of the True Self] (1982).

JOHN B. COBB, JR. is Ingraham Professor of Theology at the School of Theology at Claremont, Avery Professor of Theology at the Claremont Graduate School, and Director of the Center for Process Studies at Claremont. He studied at the University of Michigan, the University of Chicago, and was Fulbright Visiting Professor at Johannes-Gutenberg University, Mainz, Germany. He has also lectured and taught throughout Japan, where he was born (Kobe). He is the author of numerous important books and essays, which include: *Varieties of Protestantism* (1960); *Living Options in Protestant Theology* (1962); *A Christian Natural Theory* (1965); *The Structure of Christian Existence* (1967); *God and the World* (1969); *Liberal Theology at the Crossroads* (1973); and *Christ in a Pluralistic Age* (1975), and *Beyond Dialogue: Toward a Mutual Transformation of Christianity and Buddhism* (1982).

ROGER J. CORLESS was born near Liverpool England in 1938. He earned his B.D. degree from King's College, University of London, in 1961 and his Ph.D. in Buddhist Studies from the University of Wisconsin at Madison in 1973. In 1966 he made profession as an Oblate of the Benedictine monastery of Mount Savior, Elmira, New York, and, without renouncing his Catholicism, took refuge as a Gelugpa Buddhist in 1980. He is currently a member of the faculty of the Department of Religion at Duke University.

MASAAKI HONDA teaches philosophy and religion at the University of Occupational and Environmental Health, Japan School of Medicine, Kitakyushu, Japan. A member of the Roman Catholic church, he has long been interested in the problems of living an authentic Christian faith within the Buddhist context of Japanese culture which can affirm the depths of both Christianity and Buddhism. For this reason he has personally and profoundly experienced and reflected upon the opportunities and the risks involved in the struggle for meaningful religious faith in a religiously plural world. His dialogue with Buddhism continues through his participation in the Consultation of Zen Buddhism and Christianity.

PAUL O. INGRAM studied at the School of Theology at Claremont and the Claremont Graduate School, where he was a Fellow of the Blaisdell Institute for Advanced Studies in Comparative Religion and World Culture, and

where he received his Ph.D. in History of Religions in 1968. He studied in
Japan during the academic year 1968-69 under the auspices of a Danforth
Foundation grant awarded to him by the Society for Religion in Higher
Education. He is currently Associate Professor of Religion at Pacific Lutheran
University, Tacoma, Washington. He has published numerous essays on Japa-
nese Buddhism, as well as on the subject of Buddhist-Christian dialogue, in
the *Journal of the American Academy of Religion*, the *Japanese Journal of Reli-
gious Studies*, *Numan*, *Theology Today*, and *Dialog*. His book, *The Dharma of
Faith: A Study of Classical Pure Land Buddhism* was published in 1977 by the
University Press of America.

WINSTON L. KING is a well-known scholar-teacher in the field of history of
religions. He was educated at Andover-Newton Theological School and Harvard University. His professional career includes service as a pastor of New
England churches, army chaplain, and professor of religion on the faculties of
Grinnel College, Vanderbilt University, Colorado State University at Fort
Collins, Oberlin College, and Nashotah House. He has studied Buddhism in
Burma, India, and Japan, where he has also lectured as visiting professor in
universities in each of these countries. He is the author of numerous articles
and seven books in the fields of history of religions and Buddhist studies,
which include: *Buddhism and Christianity: Some Bridges of Understanding*
(1962); *In the Hope of Nibbana, An Essay on Theravāda Buddhist Ethics*
(1964); and his latest book, *Theravāda Meditation: The Buddhist Transformation of Yoga* (1980).

JOHN C. MARALDO is Assistant Professor of Religion and Philosophy at the
University of North Florida, Jacksonville. He studied philosophy of religion
and phenomenology at the University of Munich under Karl Rahner, Buddhism under Heinrich Dumoulin in Tokyo, and the practice of Zen discipline
under the direction of several Japanese masters. He has also been a frequent
guest of St. Bonaventure Friary (Conventical Franciscians) in St. Louis. His
publications include a book in German on hermeneutics, *The Piety of
Thinking: Essays by Martin Heidegger, With Notes and Commentary*
(co-authored with James G. Hart), and *Buddhism in the Modern World*
(co-edited with Heinrich Dumoulin). He has also translated several books
and essays on Buddhist-Christian encounter.

FREDERICK J. STRENG is Professor of History of Religions at Southern
Methodist University, where he also serves on the undergraduate and graduate faculties in Religious Studies of the College and as a member of the
faculty at Perkins School of Theology. After spending a year as a Fulbright
Scholar at Benaras Hindu University (India) as part of his graduate studies,
he received his Ph.D. degree from the University of Chicago in 1963. He has
published three books, over two dozen articles and essays, and is the general

editor of the fourteen volume Religious Life of Man Series. Among his various professional activities, he has served as president of the Society for Asian and Comparative Philosophy, as a member of the executive boards of the American Society for the Study of Religion and the regional branches of the American Oriental Society. His special interests are Buddhist philosophy, methodology in the comparative study of religion, and Buddhist-Christian dialogue.

SEIICHI YAGI was born in 1932 in a Christian family in Yokohama. He began his studies at Tokyo University in 1950, where he received his master's degree in European Antiquity and New Testament in 1957. He continued his studies in New Testament at the University of Gottingen, West Germany, from 1957 to 1959. While studying in West Germany he also acquired his first disciplined understanding of Zen literature as translated into German by Wilhelm Gundert, whom he visited in 1958. In 1960 he became docent in New Testament Studies at Kanto Gakuin University (Baptist) in Yokohama. In 1963 he published his *Formation of New Testament Thought,* for which he received the Doctor of Literature degree from Kyushu University. In 1965 he assumed his current position as Professor of German Language and Literature at Tokyo Institute of Technology. He has published widely in New Testament theology, comparative religion, and philosophy of religion. His publications include: *Shingaku Shisō no Seiritan* (The Formation of New Testament Thought); *Kirisuto to Iesu* (Christ and Jesus); *Bukkyō to Kirisutokyō no Seiten* (The Teachings of Buddhism and Christianity); *Kaku no Shūkyō* (The Religion of Awakening); and *Jiga no Kyokō to Shūkyō* (Religion and the Fiction of the Self).

Since most readers of the present volume will be persons unacquainted with Buddhist faith and practice, the following glossary includes only those Buddhist technical terms referred to by the authors of the essays collected in the volume.

Abhidharmakośa—A philosophical treatise written by Vasubandhu (fifth century) covering most of the philosophical and psychological topics of the *Abhidharma-piṭaka.*

Amida Buddha (Skt., Amitābha; Chin., A-mi-t'o)—The "Buddha of Infinite Light" who is the object of devotion in the Pure Land tradition of Buddhism. This Buddha is not identical with the historical Siddhārtha Gautama.

anātman—The doctrine of "non-self" or "no-self," meaning the nonexistence of a permanent "self" *(Ātman)* remaining substantially self-identical through time.

arhat (Pali, *arahat*)—Either "worthy one" or "slayer of the foe," depending upon which etymology is applied. One who is free from all craving and rebirth because he has attained the highest state of enlightenment by following Theravāda teaching and practice.

ārya-satya—The "Four Noble Truths," the basic doctrinal formulation of the Buddha's teachings. This doctrine states that (1) all life is "suffering" *(duḥkha)*, (2) the cause of suffering is "desire" *(taṇhā)*, (3) the cessation of suffering *(nirodha)* is possible, and (4) there is a path to the cessation of suffering *(aṣṭāngika mārga).*

Avatamsaka-sūtra (Chin., *Hua-yen ching*; Jp., *Kegonkyō*)—The "Flower Ornament Sutra." This Mahāyāna text is noted for its extensive portrayal of the bodhisattva's search for enlightenment as well as its notion of existence as one of complete identity and mutual interdependence.

bodhi—"Enlightenment," or the complete and perfect state of awareness experienced by the Buddha, or anyone else, with the attainment of nirvana.

bodhicitta—The "thought of enlightenment," sometimes translated "aspiration to enlightenment," essentially denoting a mind dedicated to achieving enlightenment. It is with the arising of *bodhicitta* that the bodhisattva begins his path to the achievement of complete enlightenment.

Bodhidharma (Chin., P'u-t'i-ta-mo) — The first patriarch of Chinese Ch'an (Zen) Buddhism. He is said to have come to China from India around A.D. 520.

bodhisattva — "Enlightenment Being" or "Buddha-to-Be." A being destined for enlightenment, a future buddha. Before becoming a buddha, Siddhārtha Gautama is regarded as a bodhisattva, meaning a future Buddha. Whereas Theravāda teaching holds there has been only one bodhisattva for this world system, Siddhārtha, the Mahāyāna tradition expands this concept to mean the ideal model on which to pattern religious practice. A bodhisattva is one who seeks enlightenment not only for himself but for all sentient beings by holding off the complete attainment of his own enlightenment until he can lead all other sentient beings to perfect enlightenment.

Buddhaghosa — Probably the greatest of all Theravāda exegetical writers. Arriving in Sri Lanka from South India in the fourth or fifth century A.D., his classic Vissuddhi-magga (Path of Purity) is the classic description of the specific practices involved in Theravāda forms of meditation.

dasabhūmayah — the "Ten Stages" of developing the wisdom achieved by the bodhisattva: (1) pramuditā or "joy" at benefiting oneself and others, (2) vimalā or "freedom" from all defilements, (3) prabhākarī or emission of the light of wisdom, (4) arcismatī or "glowing wisdom," (5) sudurjayā or overcoming all difficulties, (6) abhimukhī or the realization of wisdom, (7) duramgama or "proceeding far," (8) acalā or the attainment of "immobility," (9) sadhūmatī or the attainment of "expedient wisdom," and (10) dharmamegha or the ability to spread the Dharma as "clouds" (megha) are spread in the sky.

Dhammapada (Skt, Dharmapada) — "Stanzas on the Teaching," the second book in the Khuddaka Nikāya of the Sutta Pitaka of the Pali Canon. The central emphasis of the Dhammapada is the ethical practice of the Buddha's Dhamma.

dharma (Pali, dhamma) — The teaching or doctrine of the Buddha. Dharma is said to include all of the Buddha's sermons, doctrinal pronouncements, and practices. It is sometimes called "the Law." Dharma also came to be used as a technical term in Buddhist philosophy to denote experiential moments, that is, the constituting element of existence. Different Buddhist schools posited differing numbers of dharmas. The term is also used in a psychological sense to signify mental and emotional states.

dharmakāya — Literally the "Body of Dharma." In early Buddhist teaching this term probably referred to the "body" of doctrine. After the Buddha's death it was given a metaphysical interpretation. When incorporated into the Mahāyāna doctrine of Three Bodies (trikāya), dharmakāya was elevated to the "body of essence" or Buddhahood itself. It is the ultimate reality which can only be perceived by a buddha.

Dōgen (1200-1253) — The founder of the Sōtō Zen school (based on the Ts'ao-tung branch of Ch'an) in Japan.

Eisai (1141-1215) — The founder of the Rinzai Zen school (based on the Lin-chi branch of Ch'an) in Japan.

Hīnayāna — Literally "Smaller (or Lesser) Vehicle"; a name given to the early and conservative schools of Buddhism by the newly emergent Mahāyāna (Great Vehicle). It designates the traditional eighteen schools that arose between the first and fourth centuries after the death of the Buddha. It was originally a pejorative term in this use.

Hōnen (1133-1212) — The Japanese Buddhist who was responsible for creating the first independent Pure Land movement in Japan called Jōdo Shū or "Pure Land School."

Hui-neng — Chinese Buddhist monk of the Southern Ch'an school who became the Sixth Patriarch after a long controversy with his rival Shên-hsiu of Northern Ch'an. *The Platform Sutra of the Sixth Patriarch* is attributed to Hui-nêng.

Jōdo shinshū — "True Pure Land School" of Buddhism in Japan, founded by Shinran (1173-1262). It emphasizes faith as total trust in the saving grace of Amida to effect human salvation, as opposed to all forms of self-effort in the practice of religious disciplines meant to achieve enlightenment.

Jōdo shū — The "Pure Land School" of Buddhism in Japan, founded by Hōnen (1133-1212). It emphasizes faith and devotion to Amida Buddha, as well as repetition of Amida's name in the formula *Namu Amida Butsu* ("I take refuge in Amida Buddha").

karma — "Action" or "deed" in Sanskrit. The moral law of causation which states that what a person does in this life will have either positive or negative effects in his later rebirths. In Buddhist teaching, karma is also interpreted to mean volition, meaning a deed produced by the action of the mind.

karuñā — The "compassion" that is the primary motivating force behind the actions of the bodhisattva. It is this compassion, essentially the ability to experience the suffering of other sentient beings as if it were his own suffering, that leads the bodhisattva to make his vows to save all beings before he himself fully enters nirvana.

kōan (Chin., kung-an) — Literally "public documents" or authenticated cases of dialogue of Zen masters. Kōan are seemingly confusing statements resembling riddles which are used as objects of meditation primarily in the Rinzai tradition of Zen Buddhism.

Kyōgyōshinshō — "Treatise on Teaching, Practice, and Faith," written by Shinran as his most systematic interpretation of Pure Land teaching and practice.

Mādhyamika — The "Middle Way" Mahāyāna school founded by Nāgārjuna. Along with Yogācāra, it constitutes one of the two main philosophical schools of Mahāyāna tradition.

Mahāyāna—Literally "Great Vehicle," a tradition of Buddhism which arose gradually several hundred years after the Buddha's death, probably during the first century A.D. It is more liberal socially and more speculative philosophically than traditional Hīnayāna teachings. Mahāyāna doctrines emphasize the bodhisattva path, the concepts of *śūnyatā* (emptiness), *trikāya* (Three Bodies of the Buddha), and *tathatā* (suchness). Its major scriptures have been written in Sanskrit, Tibetan, and Chinese. Today, the Buddhists in Nepal, Sikkim, Tibet, China, Korea, and Japan are Mahāyānists.

Milindapañha—"The Questions of King Milinda," a noncanonical Pali text recording the dialogue between the Bactrian king Menander (Milinda) and the Buddhist monk Nāgasena. This text is a valuable compendium of Theravāda doctrine.

Mūlamadhyamaka-kārikās—The "Middle Stanzas" of Nāgārjuna, representing his chief work and his doctrinal position.

myōkōnin—A "superior man," refering to one who devoutly practices *nembutsu* in Pure Land teaching and practice.

Nāgārjuna—Buddhist philosopher who probably lived in the second or third century A.D. and the founder of the Mādhyamika school. He was a clever dialectician, excelled at debate, and was a mystic of high attainment. He ranks among the greatest thinkers in the history of Buddhist thought.

nembutsu—"Buddha reflection." In Japanese Buddhism, *nembutsu* refers to the practice of repeating the name of Amida Buddha in the formula *Namu Amida Butsu* (I take refuge in Amida Buddha). This practice is followed by both Pure Land schools (Jōdo Shū and Jōdo Shinshū).

nibbāna—The Pali equivalent of nirvana. For the definition, see the entry for nirvana.

nirmaṇakāya—Literally "Magical (or Apparational) Body." This term refers to the second "body" *(kāya)* of the Mahāyāna Trikāya doctrine to signify any historical buddha.

nirvāṇa—Literally "blowing out" or "extinction," and as such is the goal of Buddhist religious practice. Buddhist texts tend to be very enigmatic on the subject of nirvana, the model for which is the Buddha himself, who it is said refused to answer speculative questions about its nature. It is that which must be experienced before one can "know" its nature. According to Theravāda interpretations it is essentially release from the suffering of samsaric existence. For the Mahāyāna tradition it is the experience that saṃsāra and nirvana are not different.

nyorai—See Tathāgata.

pāramitā—"Perfection." The traditional six (sometimes ten) practices achieved by the bodhisattva on his path to complete, perfect enlightenment. They include *dāna* (giving), *śīla* (morality), *kṣānti* (patience), *vīrya* (vigor), *samādhi* (meditation), and *prajñā* (wisdom).

prajñā—Literally "wisdom." It is the sixth of the "perfections" *(pāramitās)* and is applied to the first two steps on the Eightfold Path (right understanding and right thought). The bodhisattva who attains wisdom experientially knows the nature of ultimate reality.

Prajñāpāramitā-sūtras—The "Perfection of Wisdom Sutras." This collection of sūtras often features the Buddha's famous disciples as interlocutors (such as Śāriputra). These texts frequently contrast mundane and ultimate reality, using the concept of *śūnyatā* (emptiness) as the starting point of its epistemology. These texts also form the scriptural foundation of the Zen interpretation of the Buddha's Dharma.

pratītya-samutpāda—Literally "dependent co-origination"; the Buddhist chain of causation emphasizing the interrelational and interdependent nature of all the elements which constitute existence. It is symbolized in Buddhist art as a twelve-spoked wheel, operating on the formula "because of this, that becomes; because of that, something else becomes." Since all phenomena come into existence in an interdependent way because of *pratītya-samutpāda,* they lack self-nature and are therefore impermanent.

Pure Land Sūtras—That body of literature dealing with discourses on the Pure Land of the Buddha Amitābha and consisting of three texts: (1) the *Larger Sukhavatī-vyūha-sūtra* (The Larger Sutra in the Happy Land), (2) the Smaller *Sukhavatī-vyūha-sūtra,* and (3) the *Kuan wu-liang-shou ching* (the Meditation on the Buddha of Infinite Life Sūtra).

Rinzai (Chin., Lin-chi) Zen—Japanese branch of Zen Buddhism derived from the Lin-chi branch of Chinese Buddhism and brought to Japan by Eisai (1141-1215). It emphasizes the practice of kōan meditation.

Saddharma-puṇḍarīka-sūtra (Jp., *Myōhōrengekyō)*—"Sutra on the Lotus Law of the True Dharma," a Mahāyāna sutra which teaches that even the followers of the Hīnayāna are able to attain perfect enlightenment. It is also known for its teaching that the Buddha is an eternal and absolute reality.

samādhi—Literally "concentration," meaning the concentration on a single object with a one-pointed mind. It also refers to steps six through eight of the Eightfold Path (right effort, right concentration, right mindfulness).

sambhogakāya—According to Mahāyāna teaching, the second of the three bodies *(kāya)* of a Buddha. This body, literally meaning "Enjoyment Body" or

"Reward Body," is the preacher of the Mahāyāna sutras and is perceived by those on the bodhisattva path. It is a sort of quasi-material body mediating between *nirmāṇakāya* and *dharmakāya*.

saṃsāra—The cycle of perpetual change, literally meaning "to wander through (or pass through) intensely." It is also used to designate the cycle of transmigration and is thus frequently contrasted to nirvāṇa.

saṅgha—Literally "group," and generally designates the monastic order in Theravāda countries and the lay and monastic community of devotees in Mahāyāna countries.

satori—Japanese for "enlightenment."

Senjaku-hongan-nembutsu-shū—"Treatise on the Necessity of Selecting the Original Vow of Nembutsu," a two fascicle work written by Hōnen in 1198. It is the most systematic and complete statement of Hōnen's Pure Land teachings. Better known by its shortened title *Senjakushū*.

Shinjō—The Korean monk who first introduced the Kegon (Skt., Avatamsaka; Chin., Hua-yen) school of Japan in 740.

Shinran (1173-1262)—Japanese Buddhist who was a disciple of Hōnen, but who broke from traditional Jōdo Shū and founded his own Pure Land movement called Jōdo Shinshū (True Pure Land School).

Shōbōgenzō—"The Eye and Treasure of the True Dharma," a ninety-five fascicle work written by Dōgen. The full title of the work is *Eihei Shōbōgenzō*.

skandha—Literally "heap" or "bundle." There are, according to Theravāda teaching, five interdependent *skandhas,* also translated as "aggregates," which constitute the individual. This notion is developed primarily in the Abhidharma literature.

Sōtō Zen—Japanese school of Zen Buddhism that is derived from Chinese Ts'ao-tung Ch'an. It was introduced to Japan by Dōgen (1200-1253), and emphasizes *shikantaza* (just sitting).

śraddhā—(Chin., *hsin*; Jp., *shin*)—Literally "faith" or "trust," emphasizing faith or trust in the Buddha, his Dharma, and the Saṅgha.

śūnyatā—The doctrine of "emptiness" or "voidness," although "relativity" is probably a better translation. The doctrine of *śūnyatā* does not deny that things "exist," but that all existence and the constituent elements of existence are dependent upon causation. Since the causal factors of existence are changing at every moment, there can be no static existence, and therefore no permanency of any sort. All phenomena are relative and dependent upon all other phenomena at any given moment of space-time. In Theravāda teaching this concept primarily indicates the teaching of "non-self" *(anatta).* Mahāyāna teaching goes further by denying the possibility of a self-existing nature within the *dharmas* which constitute the phenomenal world. All that can be said of all things *(dharmas)* is that they are "empty," that is, "relative," and hence interdependent. *śūnyatā* must not be confused with nihilism or a denial of the existence of phenomena in any form.

sūtra (Pali, *sutta*) — Literally "thread" and is applied to forms of literature purported to be the Buddha's sermons. In Theravāda tradition the sūtras are gathered together in the *Sūtra Piṭaka* (Basket of Sūtras). In the Mahāyāna tradition they are more random and classified according to type.

tathāgata — Literally the "Thus-come," an epithet describing Siddhārtha Gautama after he achieved complete, perfect enlightenment. It is also used to describe other Buddhas in the Mahāyāna tradition (Jp., *nyorai*).

tathatā — Literally "suchness" in the sense of things being what they really are as opposed to how unenlightened persons think, hope, or desire them to be. Sometimes translated in Mahāyāna teachings as "is-ness" and it functions as a synonym for enlightenment.

Theravāda — "Those who hold the Doctrine of the Elders." One of the eighteen schools of the Hīnayāna (Smaller Vehicle). This form of Buddhism emerged out of Mahinda's mission to Sri Lanka during the reign of King Aśoka (around 260 B.C.). They are closely related to the orthodox *vibhajjavāda* (distinctionist) doctrine of Asoka's time. Today Southeast Asian Buddhism is identified as Theravāda and it represents the sole remaining Hīnayāna tradition. Its scriptures are written in Pali.

trikāya — The doctrine of the Three Bodies of Buddha. They include the *nirmāṇakāya*, or "Apparational Body," the *sambhogakāya*, or "Enjoyment Body," and the *dharmakāya*, or "Body of Dharma."

tripiṭaka — The "Three Baskets" of the Pali Buddhist Canon, consisting of the sūtras (discourses) which contain the Buddha's teachings, the *vinaya* (ethical teachings), and the *abhidharma* (systematic commentaries on the meaning of the Buddha's teachings).

Vasubandhu — A great Buddhist commentator who as a Sarvāstivādin wrote the *Abhidharmakośa*. He was later converted to Yogācāra by his brother Asaṅga, after which he wrote numerous books expounding Yogācāra doctrine and practices.

Yogācāra — Literally "Practice of Yoga." Yogācāra is a major Mahāyāna philosophical school founded by Asaṅga and which established several new concepts in Buddhist thought, among them the "eight consciousnesses." Sometimes referred to as the "Mind only" school because of its teachings that all existing things are constituted by "mind only." Along with Mādhyamika, it represents one of the two major philosophical traditions of Mahāyāna Buddhism.

zazen—Literally "sitting in meditation," and denotes the specific meditational practice and techniques of the Zen school of Buddhism.

Zen (Skt., *dhyāna*; Pali, *jhāna*; Chin., *ch'an*) — Literally "meditation" and generally refers to the Zen schools of Japanese Buddhism established by Eisai and Dōgen in the thirteenth century.